T0303156

MICHAEL H. FRANCIS AND BOBBY REYNOLDS

Yellowstone Collectibles

An illustrated introduction to the park's historic souvenirs, books, art, and memorabilia

With contributions by (in alphabetical order):
Bob Berry, Jack and Susan Davis, Robert Goss, Tamsen Emerson Hert,
Larry and Thea Lancaster, Jay Lyndes, Leslie Quinn, Paul Rubinstein,
Elizabeth Watry, and Lee H. Whittlesey

RIVERBEND
PUBLISHING

Yellowstone Collectibles

Published by Riverbend Publishing, Helena, Montana

ISBN: 978-1-60639-136-5

Printed in the USA

1 2 3 4 5 6 7 8 VP 27 26 25 24 23 22

Cover and text design by Sarah Cauble, sarahcauble.com

Riverbend Publishing
P.O. Box 5833
Helena, MT 59604
riverbendpublishing.com

Dedication by Michael H. Francis

To my grandchildren, Davidson Joseph Tunning and Juliette Rose Tunning, who visit the park every year on Father's Day!

Dedication by Bobby Reynolds

To my wife Nhung, my daughter Jennifer Sagucio, and my cousin Patricia Richardson for all the love and support they provide.

Yellowstone Collectibles in old Haynes's glass display case, various items from Bob Reynolds Collection, Jay C. Lyndes Family Collection, and Francis Historic Collections

Contents

Foreword by Jay Lyndes 7
Preface by Michael H. Francis 9
Preface by Bobby Reynolds 11
Introduction by Jack and Susan Davis 13
Early Souvenirs 17
Transportation 33
Accomodations 57
Artwork 93
Books 109
Photography 123
Store Memorabilia 143
Anniversaries and Celebrations 183
Park Employees 187
National Park Service Collectibles 195
Paper Collectibles 203
Yellowstone Branded Products 207

Cup from old Fort Yellowstone, left by the U.S. Army when the post was turned over to the Dept. of the Interior. 1916. Old buffalo china, five by two and one quarter inch cup, makers mark on bottom.
Jay C. Lyndes Family Collection

Foreword

Jay Lyndes

After reaching Livingston, Montana Territory, in 1883, the Northern Pacific Railroad immediately produced one of the most striking advertising brochures for Yellowstone, the world's first national park. It was loosely based on Lewis Carroll's novel *Alice in Wonderland* and was subtitled "Alice's Adventures in the NEW Wonderland." It was exceptionally well done and arguably helped to start the tourist-stampede to Yellowstone that continues today.

That 1883 brochure is also greatly sought after by collectors of Yellowstone memorabilia, which is what this book is all about—the myriad of Yellowstone collectibles and souvenirs. I think the authors have done a masterful job of amassing thousands of photos of these items and merging them with their salient stories and histories.

When someone mentions "the Park" to anyone from Montana, Wyoming, or Idaho, we immediately know that nickname refers to Yellowstone. (If we refer to somewhere we take our kids to play two blocks away from our house, that place would require two names, such as Pioneer Park.) We are generally very protective of our status as the guardians of the Yellowstone even though four million people a year invade our personal space. We think we own the place.

To collect Yellowstone, one must have a genuine love for the Park and its history. My love affair with the Park began when I was five years old. My first memory of the Park started with me catching a nice cutthroat trout for our dinner at the Crazy Creek Campground. We ate it and retired to our tent for the night. Sometime later in the night I was awakened by something (a bear) sniffing the top of my head and cheek. I took a swat at it because I thought it was our dog (wrong). The dog started barking from the safety of the other corner of the tent, which woke my mother. I told her there was a bear with his head in the tent and her unearthly screams vanquished the traumatized bruin and woke the entire campground. I spent the rest of the night with my mother and little brother in our "hard-sided camper" (the car). Once I discovered that you could see bears everywhere in Yellowstone, I was hooked on the Park for life. I had found my Wonderland.

Our summer vacation nearly every year involved us going from our home in Hysham, Montana, to Cooke

City, Montana, and renting a cabin for two weeks. We fished everything we could walk to from the roads around Cooke and the northern half of the Park. We didn't have much money, so we caught our dinners, and I loved every minute of doing it. One of our rare treats was staying at the Old Faithful Inn. My grandfather also loved the Park and took my dad over the Beartooth Pass in their 1927 Overland car to stay in the Inn in about 1929 or 1930.

So, it was in my genes to collect Yellowstone. It was in this sorry condition that Mike Francis found me and suggested that we should combine our collections as it was possible someone else might be interested in the items we had accumulated during the past forty years.

Once Mike and Bob discovered where I had hidden my treasures and combined them with their collections (which are substantial), an interesting dynamic led to this book. It includes some of the earliest and most rare of the Park souvenirs and collectibles from the most dedicated and knowledgeable collectors in the genre. It has also unearthed reams of forgotten history and events, which have daily enriched our knowledge of the Park. Thanks to Mike and Bob, I have learned more about the Wonderland that is Yellowstone in the last two years than in the previous sixty-five years since I first went there. I am sure this book will do the same for your enjoyment of the wonders of Yellowstone.

Jay Lyndes's Autobiography

Family lore has it that my great grandfather on my father's side was shot in the back by Black Jack Ketcham. This event motivated a quick relocation from the Nebraska sandhills, first to Kansas and then to Montana. Thus, I became the fourth generation of a Montana ranch family. The first recorded family brand in Montana was in 1893. My grandfather and his six brothers rounded up wild horses in the Missouri Breaks in north-central Montana. My grandfather was the bronc rider as they broke the horses and sold them to the U.S. Army Cavalry in Miles City, Montana. After World War I the cavalry quit using horses and the brothers drifted apart. My grandfather married the school teacher in Hysham. He started an implement dealership and a drugstore and soda fountain. My mother's family homesteaded near Hysham, and I now own that family ranch.

I have collected something since I was six years old. When about that age, our family went to one of the first Bucking Horse Sales in Miles City. The rest of the family was watching the parade while I sneaked off and was trying out fancy saddles in the Miles City saddlery showroom. A life-long love affair was started. After college and a moderately successful career, I started buying cowboy memorabilia, Montana historical collectibles, and ranches. These became my passion for the next 30 years. Along the way we raised four children who have worked with the ranches, businesses, and collections. I still actively collect, and we raise black Angus cattle, good horses, Labrador retrievers, and grandchildren.

Preface and Acknowledgements

Michael H. Francis

The book you are holding in your hands has been a long time in coming. I purchased my first souvenir in Yellowstone Park during the summer of 1971, shortly after graduating from high school in Great Falls, Montana. After observing workers in the Park, I knew I would be coming back as an employee someday. In 1974, I did come back as a "Savage" and worked in the laundry at Lake Lodge. That summer I splurged and bought one hundred Haynes postcards at Fishing Bridge for $1.00. That was the start of my Yellowstone Park memorabilia collection. Like many employees, I kept coming back, in my case for fifteen seasons, eventually meeting my wife, Tori, at Lake Lodge.

Call them what you will, collectibles, souvenirs, mementos, keepsakes, memorabilia, curios, or knickknacks, most folks visiting the park bring home an object that was acquired and then transported home as a reminder of their park visit. As you will see in this book, these memories brought home were not always purchased, i.e., room keys, and ephemera such as brochures, maps, napkins, and luggage tags. But most items were purchased from the general stores in the park, and they could be anything from playing cards, spoons, or paperweights, to shot glasses.

There were so many items produced and sold that it would be impossible to find, catalogue, and photograph all of them, let alone learn the history of when each was made and when/where it was sold in the Park. In this book we will attempt to show the extremely rare pieces as well as some of the most common. We will also show older historic items as well as up-to-date products that can still be collected today at a reasonable price. Bob Reynolds and I do not claim to be experts because there are just too many categories of Yellowstone Park collectibles, so please let us know when you find a mistake we have made, so we can change it for the next edition.

Many people have been involved in this project, so Bob Reynolds and I wish to especially thank those willing to share with us their expertise including Jay C. Lyndes, Jack and Susan Davis, Paul Rubinstein, Bob Berry, Bob Goss, Larry and Thea Lancaster, Tamsen Emerson Hert, Leslie Quinn, and Lee Whittlesey.

My co-author Bob Reynolds has worked tirelessly on this project, and together we have been able to whittle down more than 15,000 images into what you are seeing here. The bulk of the items in this book came from the collections of Jay C. Lyndes Family Collection, the Bob Reynolds Collection, and the Francis Historic Collections.

There are many other people who have graciously allowed me to photograph items in their collections or they have sent images to us. I hope I don't miss too many of you. Thanks especially to Rick and Karen Hoeninghausen, John Alley, Tom Murphy, John Weiler, Mary Heller, Addie Wickham, and my sister Karelle Potts.

Jessica Moody was very helpful in identifying spoon-hallmarks as well as K&O Company items.

A special thanks to my friend Lee Whittlesey who looked over and edited the text for this project.

Also, thanks to Chris Cauble of Riverbend Publishing. It was his idea to make this collectibles book. We were working on another Yellowstone project when I showed him photos of some park curios and he said this would make a great book. He was right.

If you have comments, or you have something in your collection that you think Bob and I might be interested in seeing, please contact Mike at: michael@michaelfrancisphoto.com.

About Michael H. Francis

Michael H. Francis is a recently retired wildlife photographer based out of Billings, Montana. He has thirty-six books to his credit, including *Found Photos of Yellowstone: Yellowstone's History in Tourist and Employee Photos, Yellowstone Memories: 30 Years of Photographs & Stories, Watching Yellowstone & Grand Teton Wildlife*, and *Yellowstone Bears In The Wild*, all published by Riverbend Publishing. Mike worked in Yellowstone Park for fifteen seasons and during that time became interested in park history and collectibles such as the many souvenirs found in the general stores and gift shops. Since 1974 he has collected thousands of images and souvenirs of the park, most of which have never been seen by the public. He is anxious to share these items with the world.

Preface

Bobby Reynolds

After 30-plus years of digging around in pawn shops, antique shows, searching the internet, and various other means, I have found some very unique and wonderful Yellowstone National Park souvenirs and related collectible items. And I've made a lot of lifelong friends along the way.

My Yellowstone Park collecting began in the late 1980s with searching for anything related to F. Jay Haynes as I was, and still am, an avid amateur photographer. After running into my future co-author at various antique shows over the years and saying the casual, "hi, how are you," several times, around 1990 we finally talked and found out a little about each other. When Mike found out I liked photography, he suggested we get together and go to the Park and "do some photography." We have since traveled the world together, to Africa, Madagascar, and Patagonia, to name just a few beautiful destinations. But going back to the Park to do photography with Mike always feels like we are truly home.

It is because I met Michael H. Francis and came to appreciate his love for and association with the Park that I broadened my search beyond Haynes and started collecting anything related to Yellowstone.

Collecting and preserving Yellowstone items for future generations has become a lifelong passion. My hope in collaborating on this book is that you will develop a love for America's first national park and that you will enjoy the souvenirs and collectibles, that were and continue to be produced for the Park, that we are presenting here.

About Bobby Reynolds

Bobby Reynolds was born in Texas but grew up in the beautiful state of Montana. He is an avid amateur photographer and a huge fan of and collector of all things Yellowstone. Married and living in Billings, Montana, this is the second book he has co-authored. The first was *Saddleries of Montana – Montana's Makers from Territorial Times to 1940.*

150th 1872 - 2022, Yellowstone Park, 32 x 12 inch felt pennant, handmade in limited edition by Sue Davis for the park birthday celebration. *Jack & Sue Davis Collection.*

Yellowstone National Park, 150th Anniversary 1871 - 2022, made by Susan Davis, August 2021, twenty-two by eighteen and one quarter inch color poster. *Francis Historic Collections*

Introduction

Jack and Susan Davis

Souvenirs are objects that remind us of where we have traveled and what we have seen and experienced. They kindle an emotional connection to our past.

Souvenirs and Yellowstone are practically synonymous. Yellowstone National Park was established March 1, 1872, and was America's first national park. Frank Jay (F. Jay) Haynes was awarded one of the first concessionaire-licenses in Yellowstone in 1883 and established a series of fifteen Haynes Picture Shops throughout the park at popular tourist-locations. The Haynes family was the largest producer and vendor of Yellowstone souvenirs, publishing as many as fifty-five million postcards between 1899 and 1966.

Yellowstone produced its own unique souvenirs, and perhaps the most unusual was its coated specimens. These were objects coated with minerals from the hot springs, then sold to tourists. Yellowstone souvenirs before 1890 also included a wide variety of paper ephemera, stereo views, photographs, guidebooks, brochures, chromolithographs, illustrations and other materials.

Private mailing-cards were introduced in 1898. These small 3.5 x 5.5-inch pieces of cardboard morphed into penny-postcards in 1901 and quickly became the most popular and widespread souvenirs in the world, with Yellowstone leading the way in the number of different views produced.

Yellowstone Collectibles examines the widespread and diverse Yellowstone souvenirs, although it is beyond the scope of any single publication to record and review all the Yellowstone souvenirs that have been produced. This book focuses on certain categories of souvenirs that are highly prized by collectors and has been written by authorities in their respective collecting interests.

Souvenirs offer valuable clues to the social and economic environments of their time. Penny-postcards were the main form of communication before World War I, and they remained in widespread use after the war. Postcards were arguably the quintessential Yellowstone souvenir; more than 150 different publishers produced postcards of the park in the first half of the 20th century.

Railroads began constructing tracks across America after the Civil War. Jay Cooke, president of the Northern Pacific Railroad (NPRR), saw Yellowstone's location halfway between St. Paul, Minnesota, and Tacoma, Washington, as a potential tourist destination for rail-passengers. He offered financial support for Thomas Moran and William Henry Jackson to accompany the 1871 Hayden Expedition, and it was Moran's artwork and Jackson's photographs that convinced Congress to establish Yellowstone as the world's first national park.

In 1883, the NPRR was the first railroad to provide service to the park via the northern entrance at Cinnabar, Montana, and later Gardiner. The NPRR also was the first, and most prolific, publisher of materials promoting travel to the park (often referred to as "Wonderland") such as travel brochures, maps, guidebooks, stereo views, photographs, prints, posters, postcards, menus, and advertisements.

The Union Pacific Railroad (UPRR) was next to provide passenger-service to Yellowstone via the western entrance, arriving in late 1907 and beginning its service in 1908. The railroad's promotional campaign of the 1915 Panama Pacific International Exposition (PPIE) in San Francisco and the Panama-California Exposition in San Diego resulted in a record of 52,000 visitors to Yellowstone. PPIE memorabilia relating to Yellowstone remains very collectible.

The Burlington Route, the Chicago and Northwestern, and the Chicago, Milwaukee, St. Paul, and Pacific railroads also serviced Yellowstone Park and produced souvenirs. These earlier items are often hard to find and are considered by many to be highly collectible. Railroad-related items published in the Art Deco period of the mid-1920s through the 1930s are also very desirable. All these railroads produced the most souvenirs and collectibles from circa 1883 through 1916.

Motorized transportation was authorized in the national parks on July 31, 1915, and visitation increased. The National Park Service was established on August 25, 1916. Attendance in Yellowstone went from 98,000 in 1922 to more than 200,000 in 1927, increasing every year since then except during the Great Depression and World War II. Yellowstone could approach five million visitors in 2022. Setting new monthly visitation records is becoming the norm.

Many of the most collectible souvenirs—china, jewelry, figurines, to name a few—were produced in Europe and imported to the United States before WWI. The finest printed postcards were published in Germany during the Golden Age of Postcards, circa 1898 to 1915. With the onset of WWI, souvenir imports ceased for the most part. German factories were damaged or destroyed, tariffs were raised, and the economy was in decline. Souvenir production shifted from Europe to America, but the quality was inferior to what it had been during the Golden Age.

American postcard-publishers used cheaper inks and paper to reduce costs, resulting in lower-quality printing. The one exception was the Detroit Publishing Company (DPC). It was American's finest and most prolific publishing company and competed in quality with the German printers. DPC's labor-intensive chromolithographic printing-process contained an estimated 15 to 25 colors, but the cost of producing these high-quality postcards was high. The DPC could not or did not compete with the less expensive printing-processes used by other American companies and was forced into bankruptcy in 1932. Many of these DPC chromos and postcards were offered for sale in the Haynes Picture Shops in Yellowstone.

WWII dramatically changed the souvenir industry. Post WWII saw large increases in visitation to national parks and a stronger economy. In the 1950s and 1960s, View-Masters with 3-D images became popular, followed in the 1970s by coffee mugs and T-shirts. With increased visitation, souvenir sales boomed.

A few notable years for Yellowstone souvenirs included 1966, the Golden Jubilee, or 50th anniversary, of the National Park Service. This was followed by the centennial of Yellowstone National Park in 1972. The

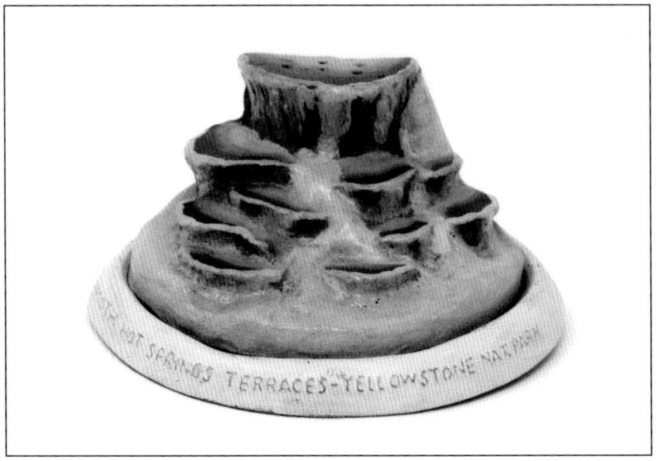

Mammoth Hot Springs Terraces, Yellowstone Nat. Park, Copyright Sept. 20th, 1921, U.S. Pat. Off., By W. C. Stuve, incense burner. *Jack & Sue Davis Collection*

Metal bear on skis, K&O metal banner, Kronheimer & Oldenbusch Co., New York, four by one and fourteen sixteenth inch. *Jack & Sue Davis Collection*

Pine Cone, Jonroth England, Bone China Imported For Yellowstone Park Co., Wyoming, 337B, Made In England, cup: four and one half by two- and three-quarter inch, saucer: five- and three-quarter inch, hand painted. *Jack & Sue Davis Collection*

Great Falls of Yellowstone. 350 ft high, handwritten on front, Copelin & Son, Photographers, 131 Lake Street, Chicago, Views In The Yellow Stone Valley, Montana, Wyoming, Thomas J. Hine photographer (not shown on mount), 1871, from Barlow Military Expedition, one of 16 stereoview images known to exist from this trip, *Jack & Sue Davis Collection*

centennial of Mammoth Hotel occurred in 1983, Lake Hotel in 1991, and Old Faithful Inn in 2004. Souvenirs and collectibles were also produced for the fires of 1988. The 125th anniversary of Yellowstone National Park was celebrated in 1997. The largest visitation to Yellowstone, and to the national parks as a whole, was in 2016 for the celebration of the NPS Centennial. One reason souvenirs from these events are collectible is that they are dated.

The Internet has affected how antiques and collectibles are bought and sold, especially with the launch of eBay in 1995. In addition, the Internet has created "virtual souvenirs" such as postcards with attached messages and images that are sent around the world instantaneously. The problem is that you cannot set a virtual souvenir on your mantel as part of your decor. Old-school souvenirs that you hold in your hands cannot be replaced with digital images.

Collecting non-virtual objects is coming back into favor. How this trend will progress is unknown. Our fifty years of experience in collecting Yellowstone souvenirs has taught Sue and me that education and interpretation are the keys to understanding and appreciating the past. It is necessary to view souvenirs in their historical context. Long after one's visit, the souvenirs acquired along the way are reminders of that special trip to Yellowstone. Whether a Moran original painting, a Jackson photograph, a penny postcard, a plastic sneaky snake, a snow globe, or a bumper sticker, they give us a connection to our emotions. It is up to each generation to share its knowledge and experience. Otherwise, the stories they have to tell will be lost for future generations.

About Jack and Susan Davis

Susan Delin was born and raised in Bozeman, Montana. Her family visited Yellowstone often when she was a young girl and it became her favorite place. Susan loved everything Yellowstone and purchased her first Yellowstone collectible in 1967, a box of Haynes postcards. This was the beginning of what would become the world's largest private Yellowstone collection, numbering more than 20,000 items. Susan married Jack Davis, and together they worked to increase and upgrade the collection. The Davis Collection now resides in the Heritage and Research Center in Gardiner, Montana, where it is available to those wishing to learn more about the park's history.

The Davises are authorities on Yellowstone antiques and collectibles and work with the park as consultants. The Fall 2001 issue of *Yellowstone Science* stated, "Susan and Jack Davis have devoted their lives to acquiring, organizing, researching, and upgrading the most complete privately held collection of park memorabilia known to exist."

Early Souvenirs

Post Exchange, Not Transferable, A.M. Graham, Fort Yellowstone Wyo., Good for 50 cents In Trade, one and one eight-inch metal token, both sides scanned, used by park soldiers. *Francis Historic Collections*

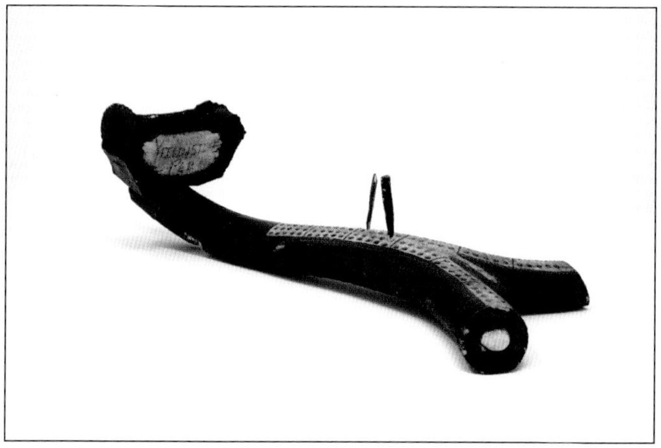

Yellowstone Park, 15-inch elk antler and ivory cribbage board, no maker. *Jay C. Lyndes Family Collection*

Yellowstone Park, 4-inch bark covered ink well with opening top, no maker. *Francis Historic Collections*

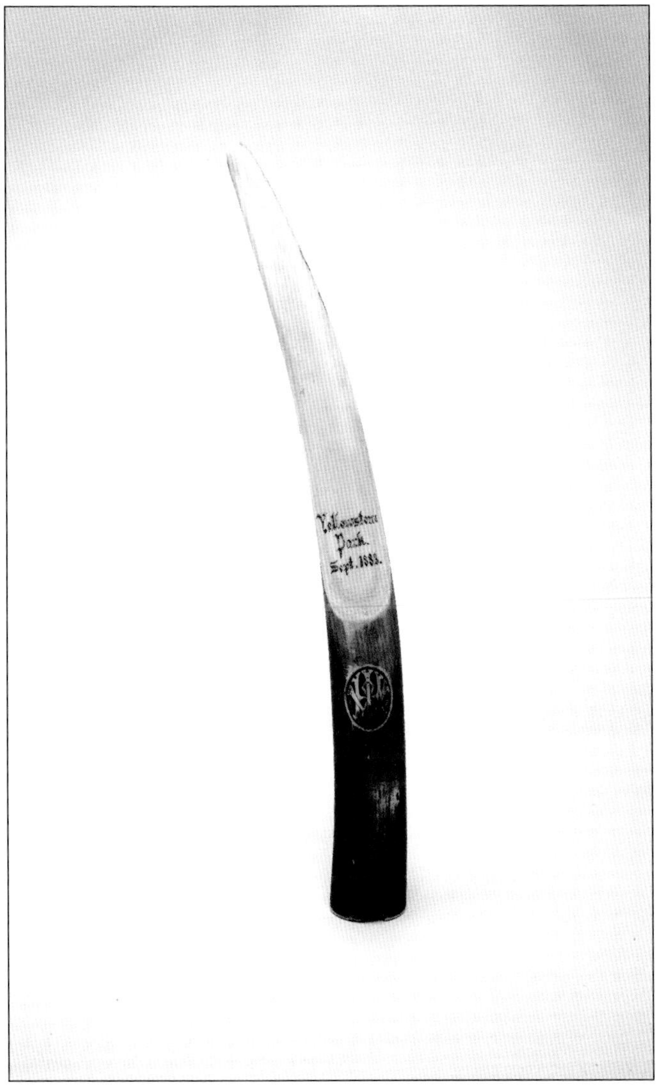

Yellowstone Park, Sept 1883, 14.5-inch carved bone souvenir, no maker. *Jay C. Lyndes Family Collection*

Yellowstone Park, 8.25 by 5-inch primitive tree orwood mug or stein with lid, no maker. *Francis Historic Collections*

"Specimen Bill" at Pulpit Terrace Coating Springs, with horseshoes and tomahawk being coated, Yellowstone National Park Series, blue letter. Photographed By T. W. Ingersoll, St. Paul, seven by four-inch stereoview card. *Jay C Lyndes Family Collection*

Coating Specimens, Mammoth Hot Springs, W. H. Jackson & Co. Photographers, black and white stereoview. Jack & *Sue Davis Collection*. Color transparency photographed by Tom Murphy, 3910 ©Tom Murphy

Coating rack at Mammoth Hot Spring Terraces, looking north. L. A. Huffman, Publisher, Miles City, Montana, seven by three and fourteen sixteenth inch stereoview card, plain verso. *Jay C. Lyndes Family Collection*

COATED SPECIMENS
A Yellowstone Creation

Robert V. Goss

Amongst the most beloved—and rare—of Yellowstone's curios are those known as "Coated Specimens." These were natural or man-made articles that were soaked in the mineral-laden waters of the Mammoth Hot Springs terraces. The objects became coated with a lustrous white, crystalline veneer composed of calcium carbonates and other trace minerals that precipitated from the hot mineral waters.

Geologist Walter Weed briefly described the process in 1890: "The escape of carbonic acid and the evaporation of the water are very rapid on the overflow slopes, below the Main Springs. In consequence of this, a coating of pure white crystalline carbonate of lime is rapidly deposited upon objects of any kind placed in the spray of the hot water, a thickness of 1/20 to 1/16 of an inch being formed in three days under favorable circumstances ... The deposit so formed is pure white and marble-like, and the little crystals sparkle in the light. If, however, the objects be permitted to remain in the spray several days longer, the deposit loses its intense whiteness and assumes a dull yellowish tint."

With proper care, many of these precious artifacts have retained their beauty for well over a century.

The person most associated with their production was Olof Adolph Andersson, or simply Ole Anderson. Born 1857 in Osstergotland, Sweden, Ole struck out and immigrated to America in February 1880. Four months later he was working as laborer in Cannon Falls, Minnesota. Ole may have worked his way across country to Montana during construction of the Northern Pacific rail line that passed through Livingston in 1883 enroute to the Pacific Coast. Or perhaps he made his way to Wonderland after hearing of its marvels and potential opportunities.

Ole Anderson apparently began his fledgling Yellowstone enterprise in 1883, as several accounts from later years mention Ole as being in business by that time. Creating coated specimens did not originate with him, but he was the person who successfully commercialized the process. Early visitors to the area readily noticed that objects such as pinecones, leaves, and sticks were heavily coated with minerals from lying in the waters at the terraces. Calvin Clawson, member of a tourist party in 1871, observed the coating process and remarked, "Twigs, small stones, and other objects placed in such situations eventually become covered with thick deposits of this nature, and the preparation artificially of ornaments of various kinds has already been successfully accomplished with little difficulty." Even in this time of little visitation, excursionists were already producing coated specimens as novelties or keepsakes.

Author Edwin James Stanley professed on a trip in 1873 that, "Beautiful specimens are also obtained by placing little baskets, frames, and other objects of mechanical genius in the water, where in a short time they become incased in a snow-white crust of rare beauty." It did not take long for people to begin monetizing the procedure for a small profit. The Earl of Dunraven, who traversed the Yellowstone in 1874, noted, "hunters, trappers, and idlers who hung around waiting for the chance to provide guide service to travelers ... also carried on a small business of selling various trinkets and coated specimens that they had prepared for the tourists." The peddling of the curios continued for the next decade by a variety of men on an informal basis. These included Frank Phiscator, "Geyser Jim" Nelson, William Davis, David Dobson, Wm. F. Ramsdell, and "Specimen Bill" Lindstrom. "Bill" was made famous in a stereoview published by photographer T.W. Ingersoll that depicted him at work on the Terraces. He is believed to have operated from around 1883-1889, apparently under the radar of park officials, or with some verbal affirmation.

To facilitate the process of coating specimens, wooden racks were constructed beneath the falling waters of the overflowing hot pools. These were generally built by commercial crafters, rather than individual curio seekers. The most productive (mineral laden) waters were those of Cleopatra, Minerva, and Jupiter Terraces, located above and to the left of Liberty Cap. These were oft-times simply termed "Coating Springs" in old photographs and stereoviews, but coating areas such as Pearl Pools, Specimen Falls, the Pulpit, and Crater Hill were also noted. Even Orange Geyser/Mound at the upper end of the terraces, has been mentioned in the literature as being a coating site. At least a half-dozen or more stereoviews published between 1871 to 1882, and produced by such luminaries as photographers Wm. H. Jackson, H.B. Calfee, and L.A. Huffman, depict complete or portions of coating racks.

Ole Anderson built his own wooden racks at some point in time, and in 1883 erected tents for himself and his new sales venture on the flats near Liberty Cap, where the Commissioner's House now stands. Although no physical records exist sanctioning his operation, it is believed Ole received verbal approval from Superintendent Patrick Conger (4/1882-9/1884) for his enterprise. Six years later, Army administrators granted Ole a written permit to conduct business. He was allowed to craft and sell various objects coated with minerals from the hot springs, bottles of colored sand from the Grand Canyon, and other curiosities. However, the sale of general wares was not permitted, as that concession was reserved for the Cottage Hotel museum store.

One of the justifications for Ole's permit was to discourage tourists from engaging in the coating process. According to historian Newell F. Joyner, visitors had, "previously been promiscuously attempting such a practice, with the resultant injury to the hot springs formations." Assigning this concession to Anderson and prohibiting the public from coating articles would hopefully control the damage while still allowing visitors to obtain natural keepsakes. This same edict likely spelled the end of Specimen Bill's coating operations.

By 1885, John Fossum, former soldier and hotel winterkeeper in the park, had joined Ole in his growing business. The nearby Cottage Hotel, run by the G.L. Henderson family, maintained a small museum/curio store on the premises, managed by daughter Jennie Henderson. They sold Ole's specimens and an advertisement from the museum in 1885 touted, "Anderson & Fossum's Famous Coated Goods." A separate ad lauded various specimens in "Every Style, Plain and Lettered. Also, Masonic and other Symbols, Crosses, Anchors, [and] Hearts."

A tourist that same year observed, "Quite a business is carried on by two men who coat all sorts of things and sell them to the tourist. They have coated horseshoes, mugs, demijohns, hats, thimbles, knives and forks, scissors—in fact almost every conceivable small object the visitors may bring . . . [and] sell for from twenty-five cents to several dollars." Curio display racks exhibited coated pinecones, silverware, toy cannons, bear and antlered elk figurines, coffee cups, flower vases, glass bottles, picture frames, toy pistols, candle sticks, and probably the most popular—horseshoes. The variety of coated objects available seemed almost limitless.

Wm. W. Wylie, founder of the Wylie Camping Co., remarked in his 1882 guidebook that the current rage was coating horseshoes. One visitor in 1886, particularly enamored of coated horseshoes, waxed poetically, "The amuletic horseshoe is in great demand. A horseshoe that is sown in corruption, ragged, rusty, dusty and with the nails still twisted in it is raised in incorruption, a thing of beauty and a joy forever. It is in very truth the materialized ghost of a horseshoe." This was an obscure Biblical reference to the raising of the dead, found in I Corinthians. Coated horseshoes displaying emblems of the various fraternal organizations, such as Masons, Knights of Pythias, and Woodmen of the World, were much in demand by those groups. Most popular with the general public were the horseshoes with "Yellowstone Park" emblazoned across the center with a bear above it.

Custom orders were also popular. Folks beginning the 4-to-5-day journey through Wonderland could drop off items with Ole to be coated and pick up their one-of-a-kind mementos upon return. One gentleman from Missouri claimed, "You can send him your favorite horse's old shoe and tell him to put your wife's initials across it; this he does with a fine wire and then places the shoe in the mineral springs and the deposits will cause the whole shoe, wire and all, to become a beautiful cream white, making a nice ornament for your house, a token of remembrance of your favorite horse, your wife and Yellowstone Park. They are very pretty and cost $1 and postage." His 'wife' may not have appreciated second billing after a horse, but nonetheless, it was still a good deal for travelers.

In the early 1890s, John Fossum moved on to other ventures, and Anderson, tired of life in tents, began pestering the Army and Department of Interior for permission to construct permanent facilities. Ultimately a lease was approved in 1895 for a plot of land between the Commissioner's house and the Cottage Hotel. Construction began the following year and the new "Specimen House" opened to the public in spring 1897. At long last Ole Anderson had an inviting and warm emporium with a cozy upstairs apartment to accommodate his growing family.

Business at the new store was increasing, but Ole was limited to selling curiosities, such as the coated specimens and the sand art creations that both he and Andrew Wald were creating. Jennie Henderson Ash opened a nearby general store to sell general wares, clothing, and other common items needed by the traveling public. To limit excessive competition, Ole's lease prohibited him from vending the same items that the general store sold. He was also a photographer and planned to add his photos to his line of merchandise. But park photographer Frank J. Haynes held that concession, and again Anderson was thwarted from diversification, a serious blow to his business plans according to family records. He was permitted to sell postcards in his 1906 lease, but not much else.

In 1908, Ole Anderson retired from Yellowstone, perchance the competition and government regulations limiting the expansion of his wares frustrated him. And a decade of living year-around in cold drafty tents may have taken a toll on his health and energy. It is not exactly known when coating specimens became completely prohibited—possibly with the termination of Ole's lease in 1908. Anna Trischman Pryor, daughter of Army post carpenter George Trischman, and husband George Pryor purchased the store and began enlarging the store soon after. A few years later sister Elizabeth Trischman became Anna's partner, and the pair went on to create an organization that dominated the general store, curio, and deli operations at Mammoth and Canyon until the early 1950s.

Ole Anderson and his family returned to their house in Great Falls, Montana, and a mere seven years later Ole passed away at age 58. Andrew Wald, consummate Sand Artist, went to work for Pryor & Trischman "pounding sand" until the early 1920s. "Sandy" breathed his last in 1933 at age 80. It has of course, been many a year since park artifacts and materials could be used for commercial purposes. But for fifty years the coated specimens and sand art produced in Yellowstone thrilled many a visitor during that era, and today continue to be prized by collectors.

About Robert V. Goss

Robert Goss lived and worked in Yellowstone and surrounding areas for more than thirty-five years, twenty of those for the Yellowstone Park Co. and its descendants. He is an avocational historian of Yellowstone and the gateway communities with a primary interest in the various concession operations in the park. He has self-published seven books and is fortunate to have authored or co-authored twenty published articles. His articles include those in Yellowstone History Journal, Yellowstone Science, Annals of Wyoming, Motor Coach Age, Points West, Montana Pioneer, and other local publications. He now lives in the Southwest, pursuing photographic interests and studying ancient cultures, while maintaining a lively interest in Yellowstone history.

Coated specimens now in Yellowstone National Park collection: 1893 Yellowstone National Park horseshoe, 1897 Yellowstone Park horseshoe, and 1889 inkwell, Yellowstone Park. *Jack & Sue Davis collection.* Color transparency photographed by Tom Murphy © Tom Murphy

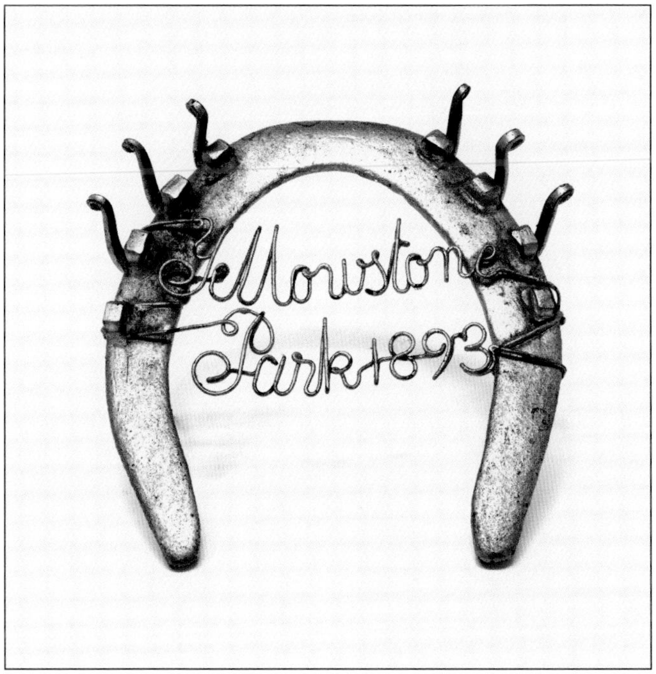

Metal horseshoe with Yellowstone Park 1893 in wire, never put on coating rack, O. A. Anderson, five and one eighth by four- and one-half inches. *Jay C. Lyndes Family Collection*

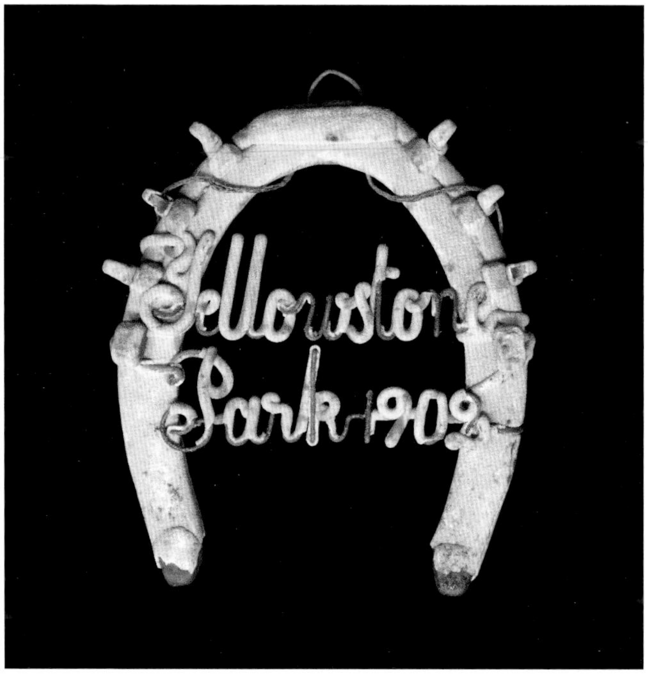

1909 coated horseshoe specimen from Mammoth Hot Springs thermal water, may have been made by Olie Anderson, five- and one-half inches by five inches. *Bob Reynolds Collection*

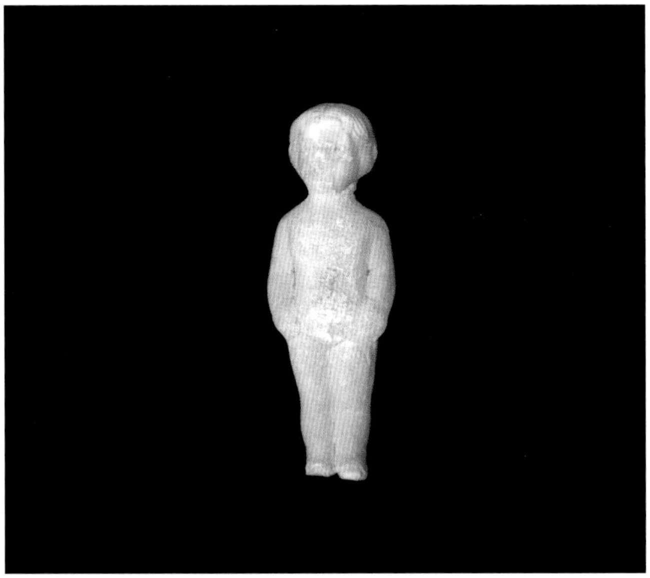

3-inch doll coated specimen, circa 1901. *Jay C. Lyndes Family Collection*

Coated wicker basket, eight and one quarter by four- and three-quarter inches. *Jay C. Lyndes Family Collection*

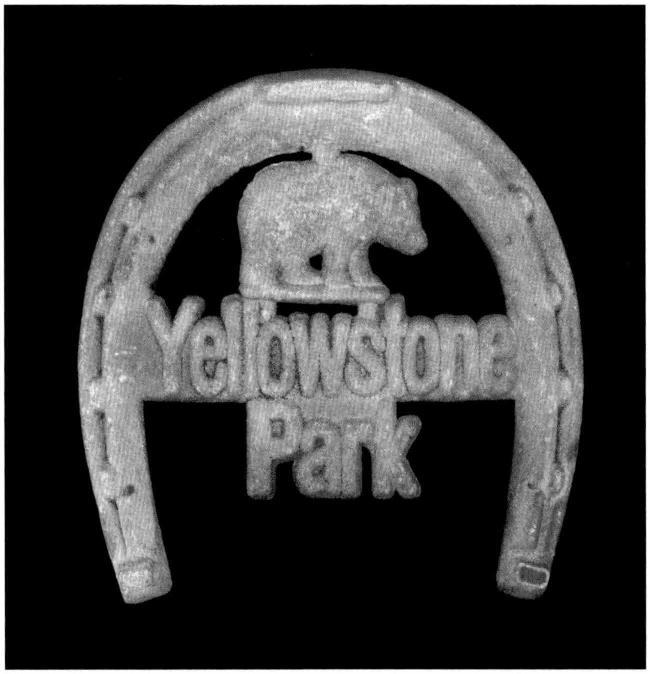

Metal horseshoe with bear coated specimen, six by six- and one-half inches. *Jay C. Lyndes Family Collection*

COLORED SANDS
A Curio Chronicle

Robert V. Goss

One of the more unique Yellowstone curiosities—and certainly the most intricate and time-consuming to create—were the bottles of sand art fabricated by both Andrew Wald and Ole Anderson. These were fashioned from variegated colored sands procured from the Grand Canyon of the Yellowstone during the mid-1880s through the early 1920s. Anderson, generally well-known for the sparkling coated specimens he created from the mineral-impregnated waters of the Mammoth Terraces, may have been the first to craft bottles of colored sands for sale to the traveling public. But it was Wald who would take artistic predominance over those unique and now valuable works of art.

From the earliest days, with limited park management, visitors no doubt collected the glistening multi-colored sands in whatever containers they had handy as souvenirs of their vacation in Wonderland. Many of our parents and grandparents did much the same on vacations through the Painted Desert and other unprotected colorful western sites. But with increased regulation and enforcement in Yellowstone by 1883, Anderson and Wald would have recognized the potential sales value of creating one-of-a-kind sand art souvenirs for park excursionists who were being prohibited from removing natural and geologic artifacts from Yellowstone. By that time Anderson was believed to have received oral permission from Superintendent Patrick Conger to establish a tent store to utilize these same elements to create curios for public purchase.

The earliest bottles of colored sand created by the men were usually abstract waves of variegated colored sands, meticulously packed in bottles and sealed tightly. Anderson's bottles generally followed this simpler pattern through his years in the park, although he did eventually create more complicated designs. Andy Wald, sometimes called "Sandy," became the expert 'Sand Artist' in Yellowstone. Establishing himself in temporary quarters at the Grand Canyon, Wald collected sand for his creations and peddled them to visitors. By the late 1880s he was creating pieces that featured bears, eagles, elk, buffalo, and other wildlife found in Yellowstone, along with waterfalls, geysers, mountains with clouds in the sky, and even lettering, in addition to the simpler designs.

The process he devised was quite complicated, requiring intense concentration and devotion. Primarily utilizing bullet-shaped bottles purchased in the East, Wald carefully arranged the grains with specially devised instruments to achieve the desired artistic effect. One tourist claimed he used seventy-two different colored shades of sand to create his work. Complicating the process was that the containers he used were open at the bottom, apparently requiring him to fabricate his designs upside-down. The bottles were then packed and tightly sealed so that the sand would not become loose and spoil the pattern. There are also examples of cylinder-shaped bottles with screw tops, round-top cylinders, short cone-top with wide base, inverted shot glass, and other shapes.

A pre-printed label was applied to the bottom identifying the bottle as being the work of Anderson or Wald. Wald's bottles most commonly read, "From the Grand Canyon of the Yellowstone. Put Up by Andrew Wald." Ole's labels usually stated, "Colors of the Grand Canon. Yellowstone National Park. Put up by O.A. Anderson, Mammoth Hot Springs, Wyoming. The Contents of this Bottle Guaranteed to Contain no Artificial Coloring."

Wald was collecting and selling his goods under the auspices of Ole Anderson's lease until 1893, when he was granted permission from the Acting Secretary of Interior to conduct his business from a tent. Ensuring his collecting practices did not permanently mar the landscape, he was under supervision of the park superintendent, and his permission could be revoked at any time. The 1900 US Census showed Wald as a boarder with the Anderson family, and he may have joined Ole at his new store, the Specimen House, which opened in 1896.

Andy Wald was not always provident is his personal habits, much to his detriment and financial well-being. He was known to be a mite fond of the drink, and the card-playing or craps that often accompanied it. He would sometimes get on a jag for a week or so, then sober up, realize he was broke, and resumed endeavors with his other "bottles."

An amusing story about him was related by the *Livingston Enterprise* in May 1908. A beer baseball game was played in Gardiner by the "Fats" and the "Leans." A single merited a glass of beer at first base and reaching third base earned three beers. Famed stagecoach driver Geyser Bob, a teetotaler, was the umpire, and Andy Wald was the bartender at first base. The game was called after two innings due to rain; probably a good thing, as twenty runs scored equaled a lot of beer quaffed. The "Leans" triumphed 14-6, perchance celebrating in the nearest saloon.

In 1908, Ole Anderson retired and sold his enterprise to sisters Anna Pryor and Elizabeth Trischman, who renamed the business Park Curio Shop. Wald worked for the sisters as "Sand Artist" until the mid-1920s, as financial reports indicate Wald was retained by the Park Curio Shop until at least 1922. He was 70 years old at that time, and his hands and nerves were probably not as steady as in the past. His bottle labels were similar to Ole Anderson's, reading, "Put up at Park Curio Shop, Guaranteed to contain the natural sands. Selected by Andrew Wald, Sand Artist."

After being debilitated for some five years, Sandy, the "Sand Man," who was once described as "the famous old-timer who lives any old place where he hangs up his hat, and is noted for his ability for pounding sand in bottles in the Yellowstone Park," passed away September 22, 1933, in Livingston, Montana, at age 82. After a brief service, Andrew Wald, "the friend of all park residents," was laid to rest the following day at Tinker's Hill cemetery in Gardiner. Charles Huntley, a resident of Gardiner, former seaman on Old Ironsides, and who rode and fought with Custer during the Indian Wars, honored this unique artist by sprinkling colored sands from Andy's beloved Grand Canyon over his casket.

Mixed collection of Glass Sand Art from sand artists A. O. Anderson and Andrew Wald. *Bob Reynolds Collection, Francis Historic Collections, and Jay C. Lyndes Family Collection*

Sands From The Grand Canyon Of The Yellowstone, label, Put Up At Park Curio Shop, Yellowstone Park, Wyoming, Guaranteed to contain the natural sands. Selected by Andrew Wald, Sand Artist. *Bob Reynolds Collection*

Grand Canyon of the Yellowstone, Put up by Andrew Wald, one- and three-quarter inch label on bottom of sand art glass paperweight. *Jay C. Lyndes Family Collection*

Colors Of The Grand Canyon, Put Up By O. A. Anderson, Mammoth Hot Springs, Wyoming, The Contents Of This Bottle Guaranteed To Contain No Artificial Coloring, Yellowstone National Park, label on bottom of sand art. *Jay C. Lyndes Family Collection*

Glass Sand Art Paperweight, three- and three-quarter inches tall, Colors Of The Grand Canon, Put Up By O. A. Anderson, Mammoth Hot Springs, Wyoming, The Contents of this bottle guaranteed to contain no artificial coloring. *Francis Historic Collections*

Glass Sand Sculpture Paperweight, 3 inches tall, Sands From The Grand Canyon Of the Yellowstone, most likely Put Up At Park Curio Shop, Yellowstone Park, Wyoming, Guaranteed to contain the natural sands, Selected by Andrew Wald Sand Artist. Handwritten on bottom: From Yellowstone Park, 1919. *Francis Historic Collections*

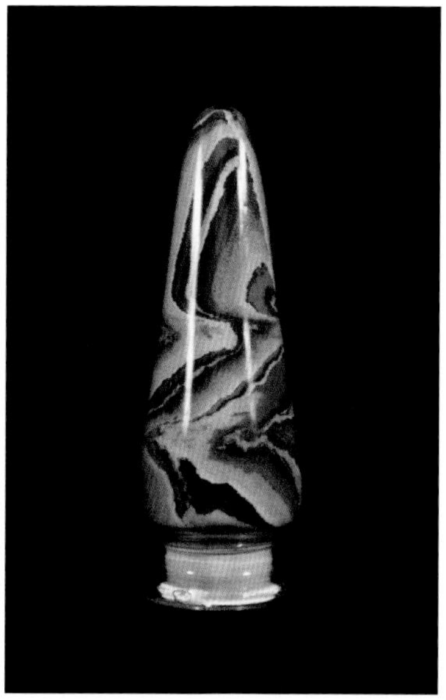

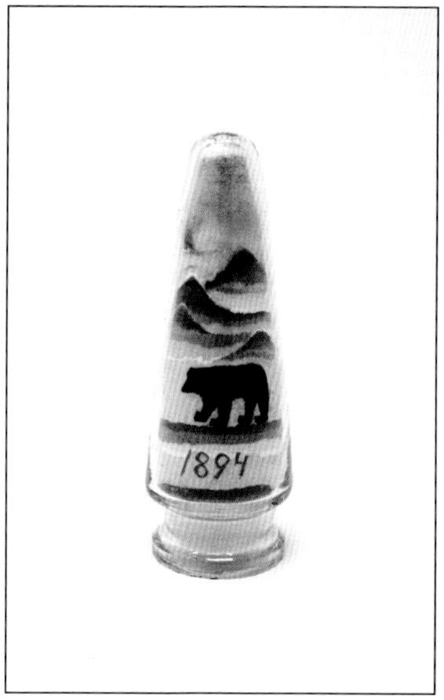

Figure 1. Sand art glass sculpture or paperweight, Park Curio Shop, Yellowstone Park, Wyoming, Selected by Andrew Wald, Sand Artist, 6 inches. *Bob Reynolds Collection.* **Figure 2.** Glass Sand Art, 6 inches, Colors Of The Grand Canyon Put Up By O. A. Anderson, Mammoth Hot Springs, Wyoming, The Contents Of This Bottle Guaranteed To Contain No Artificial Coloring, Yellowstone National Park, label on bottom of sand art. *Bob Reynolds Collection.* **Figure 3.** Made by Andrew Wald, 6-inch glass sand sculpture paperweight with label on bottom, bear. *Jay C. Lyndes Family Collection.* **Figure 4.** Made by Andrew Wald, 6-inch glass sand sculpture paperweight with label on bottom, Yellowstone and 7/ 26/ 1894 in sand. *Jay C. Lyndes Family Collection.* **Figure 5.** Made by Andrew Wald, 1894, 6-inch glass sand sculpture paperweight no label on bottom, bear. *Jay C. Lyndes Family Collection.* **Figure 6.** O. A. Anderson, 1902, 6-inch glass sand sculpture paperweight with label on bottom, Old Faithful Geyser. *Jay C. Lyndes Family Collection*

Glass Sand Art collection of mixed A. O. Anderson and Andrew Wald artist creations. *Francis Historic Collections and Jay C. Lyndes Family Collection*

Made by Andrew Wald, 4-inch glass sand sculpture with label on bottom, Yellowstone National Park, Wyoming. *Jay C. Lyndes Family Collection*

Glass Sand Sculpture Paperweight, 3 inches tall, Sands From The Grand Canyon Of the Yellowstone, Put Up At Park Curio Shop, Yellowstone Park Wyoming, Guaranteed to contain the natural sands, Selected by Andrew Wald Sand Artist, 1919. *Francis Historic Collections*

Glass Sand Sculpture Paperweight, 3 inches tall, Sands From The Grand Canyon Of the Yellowstone, Put Up At Park Curio Shop, Yellowstone Park Wyoming, Guaranteed to contain the natural sands, Selected by Andrew Wald Sand Artist. *Francis Historic Collections*

Glass screw top sand container, two and six sixteenth inch, and screw top wood container, three and one half by one inch, with Park Curio Shop Andrew Wald label, Sands From The Grand Canyon Of The Yellowstone, Put Up At Park Curio Shop, Yellowstone Park, Wyoming, Guaranteed to contain the natural sands, Selected by Andrew Wald, Sand Artist. *Tom Murphy Collection*

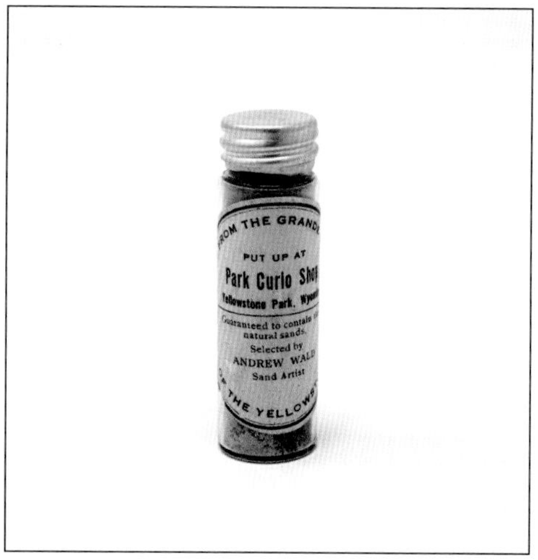

Made by Andrew Wald, two and one quarter inch glass vial sand art with label and metal screw top, Put Up At Park Curio Shop. *Jay C. Lyndes Family Collection*

Glass Sand Sculpture Paperweight, three-and three-quarter inches tall, Colored Sands of the Grand Canyon, Yellowstone National Park, Put Up By O. A. Anderson, Mammoth Hot Springs Wyoming, The Contents of this bottle guaranteed to contain no artificial coloring. *Francis Historic Collections*

Transportation:

Stagecoaches, Railroads, and Automobiles

Y.P.T. Busses Leaving U.P. Station, West Yellowstone, Montana, Yellowstone Park Company #372, I-L-10, Smith And Chandler, West Yellowstone, Montana, five and six sixteenth by three and seven sixteenth inch black and white postcard. *Francis Historic Collections*

Mammoth Hot Springs, Y.N.P., G 504 American Import Co., Publishers, Minneapolis, USA, Printed In Germany, five and six sixteenth by three and six sixteenth inch post card, dated on verso July 22, 1909. *Francis Historic Collections*

Coach in Gardiner Canon, Y.N.P., G 505 American Import Co., Publishers, Minneapolis, USA, Printed In Germany, five and six sixteenth by three and six sixteenth inch post card, postmarked on verso July 16, 1909. *Francis Historic Collections*

Four-horse coach at 4th Norris Hotel with park visitors, 1906, color magic lantern glass slide. *Francis Historic Collections*

EVOLUTION AND OPERATIONS OF
Stagecoaching in Yellowstone, 1880-1916

Lee H. Whittlesey

When Congress established Yellowstone National Park in 1872, there was no effective way to reach the place. For eight years, the few visitors who traversed the location reached it on horseback or else traveled overland by wagon and then rode horseback for the last one hundred miles or so, because there were no roads to speak of in the new Park.

In 1878, Superintendent P.W. Norris built the first road connecting Mammoth Hot Springs with Old Faithful, and the third Hayden USGS survey traveled over that road and mapped it. A crude bridle path from the west entrance had been scratched out through Madison Canyon during the previous year and Norris soon connected his new road with it. But there were still very few travelers to use these routes because real civilization remained physically located too far away.

In late 1879, owners and builders of an upstart, narrow-gauge railroad surveyed, graded, railed, and spike-pounded their way northward from Utah through Idaho and Montana territories and shakily arrived in mid-September at a tiny spot they had already designated Beaver Canyon. The railhead was now only about sixty-five air miles from Yellowstone but still nearly two hundred road-miles away. That road-distance would be reduced to around one hundred miles, as locals improved area roads, but in 1879, it was too late in the season for stagecoaching operations to evolve from nothing to full operations.

Actual stagecoaching to Yellowstone began in 1880 from Beaver Canyon. While the rail-men continued to labor northward toward Butte, Montana, the Gilmer & Salisbury Stage Line began making plans to operate from whatever terminuses the moving railroad established. But before G&S could get going, six brothers from Salt Lake City moved into Beaver Canyon and established their own stagecoaching line. Known first as the Yellowstone National Park Stage Line and later as the Bassett Brothers, Beaver Canyon, this company operated for at least seventeen years (1881-1897) in bringing tourists to the west entrance of Yellowstone National Park and ultimately to Marshall's Hotel at the Lower Geyser Basin.

Nearly simultaneously, George Marshall and his partner started the Marshall & Goff Stage Line running first from Red Rock, Montana to the park's west entrance, and then from Virginia City, Montana to the park's west entrance, planning to move with the railroad's railhead wherever it would be located. Their first known passenger was pioneer newspaperman William F. Wheeler of Deer Lodge, to whom George Marshall apparently offered a free ticket because he had no other passengers on his advertised opening day of August 9, 1880. Whether offering the ticket to Wheeler in hoping to get free newspaper publicity or in merely having someone to ride with him, or both, Marshall and Wheeler set out from Red Rock, Montana and drove through Centennial Valley to Henry's Lake and on to Yellowstone's Marshall's Hotel. If Marshall had other stage-passengers before October 1, they have gone unmentioned in the known literature, but on October 1, Marshall picked up his second passengers—Carrie and Robert Strahorn—at Virginia City, to which they had probably been driven by the Gilmer & Salisbury Company.

George Marshall's small transportation company soon folded, as he concentrated instead on running his hotel in Yellowstone, but the Bassett Brothers found success and continued operating for at least seventeen years from Beaver Canyon and later from nearby Spencer, Idaho. Meanwhile, the Gilmer & Salisbury Stage Line continued its stagecoaching in most of Montana, even operating for a couple of years past the arrival of the new Northern Pacific Railroad.

The NPRR took longer to arrive in Montana Territory than did the Utah & Northern, but it was much larger and had greater capitalization. Its owners built westward through North Dakota in the 1870s, eventually splitting near Glendive and sending one branch west into Washington and another branch southwesterly up the Yellowstone River. As they laid rails in Montana, towns sprang up: Glendive (1881), Forsyth, Billings, Park City, Big Timber, and Livingston (all 1882).

In January of 1883, the NPRR began building its Yellowstone Branch south through Paradise Valley to Yellowstone National Park. Travel to the national park began in earnest that year as passengers flocked to wherever the railhead was located, and the Wakefield and Hoffman Stage Lines picked them up at those moving termini and took those early visitors to the Park. Because of a land dispute, the Park terminus settled at Cinnabar, Montana (three miles west of present Gardiner), and the town of Gardiner (established 1880) did not become the railhead for Yellowstone until 1902-1903.

Headquartered at Mammoth Hot Springs, George Wakefield, operating his stage line under the auspices of the Yellowstone National Park Improvement Company (later the Yellowstone Park Association), partnered with Charles Hoffman and later F. Jay Haynes to offer the national park's largest stagecoaching operation to visitors, 1883-1892. In that year, the U.S. Department of Interior granted a new lease to Silas Huntley and Harry W. Child, who took over Wakefield's fleet and operations and ran them as the Yellowstone National Park Transportation Company, which became the YPT Company in 1898. Notwithstanding the admission of the first automobiles into Yellowstone in the summer of 1915, this company continued operating stagecoaches through the summer of 1916, and in 1917, it sold all its stagecoaches and purchased over one hundred motor-busses (seven and eleven-passenger). Thus, motorization of Yellowstone began in earnest.

During this period (1883-1916), three other in-park transportation companies operated stagecoaches in Yellowstone: the Wylie Camping Company (1881-1916), the Monida & Yellowstone Stage Line (1898-1916), and the Shaw & Powell Camping Company (1897-1916), along with dozens of independent stagecoaching and camping companies headquartered outside the Park in the towns of Cinnabar, Gardiner,

Livingston, Bozeman, Dillon, and Monida, Montana, along with Beaver Canyon, Idaho, and even St. Anthony, Idaho.

Thus, the stagecoaching era in Yellowstone lasted for 36 years (1880-1916), and following that time the Yellowstone Park Transportation Company continued operating with busses that met trains until the railroads abandoned passenger-service in the 1960s. The NPRR continued bringing freight to Yellowstone until the mid-1970s, and the rails were removed between Gardiner and Livingston in 1976. The Yellowstone Park Transportation Company still operates bus tours and snowcoach tours within the Park today, having been continuously in existence for 138 years—1883-2021.

About Lee H. Whittlesey

Lee Whittlesey's forty-five-year studies in the history of the Yellowstone region have made him an expert on Yellowstone's vast literature and have resulted in numerous publications. He is the author, co-author, or editor of sixteen books and more than fifty journal articles. Coming in 2021 is his *This Modern Saratoga of the Wilderness: A History of Mammoth Hot Springs* (National Park Service). He and NPS Interpreter Sarah Bone have completed their two-volume, thirty-year book *The History of Mammals in the Greater Yellowstone Ecosystem, 1796-1881: An Interdisciplinary Analysis of Thousands of Historical Observations*, and it was published in late 2020 by Kindle Direct Publishing of Seattle. In 2015, Lee published a new edition of Truman Everts's *Lost in the Yellowstone*, a new edition of his well-known book *Death in Yellowstone*, and his book *Gateway to Yellowstone: The Raucous Town of Cinnabar on the Montana Frontier* (Rowman and Littlefield with Two Dot Books).

Whittlesey served as Park Historian for the National Park Service at Yellowstone National Park for 25 years, and previously served in that park as Archivist, Ranger Naturalist/Interpreter, Law Enforcement Ranger, and in numerous other positions. He has a master's degree in history from Montana State University and a law degree (Juris Doctor) from the University of Oklahoma. On May 19, 2001, because of his extensive writings and long contributions to Yellowstone National Park, Idaho State University conferred upon him an Honorary Doctorate of Science and Humane Letters. On May 3, 2014, Montana State University awarded him an honorary Ph.D. in history. From 2006 through 2011, he served as an adjunct professor of history at Montana State University.

Whittlesey retired as Park Historian for the National Park Service at Yellowstone National Park on April 30, 2018. He now lives in the Livingston, Montana area, where he has just finished his latest book, which is volume one of a two-volume history of stagecoaching in Montana, Idaho, and the Yellowstone region. It is entitled *"Off with the Crack of a Whip!": Stagecoaching Through Yellowstone*. He continues to write whenever he can. For example, his article that appeared in *Montana the Magazine of Western History* in the Spring, 2020 issue entitled "Abundance, Slaughter, and Resilience of the Greater Yellowstone Ecosystem's Mammal Population: A View of the Historical Record, 1871-1885," has just won (June, 2021) the Forest History Society's (FHS) Theodore C. Blegen Award, which annually recognizes the best scholarship in forest and conservation history published in a journal other than Environmental History (https://foresthistory.org/awards-fellowships/blegen-award/).

Whittlesey also published *The Guide to Yellowstone Waterfalls and Their Discovery* (2000, Westcliffe Publishers) in which he and two co-authors revealed to the world for the first time the existence of more than 300 previously unknown waterfalls in Yellowstone National Park. For this accomplishment, he was featured on ABC News, NBC News, the Discovery Channel, the Travel Channel, and *People* magazine. He appeared in Ken Burns's five-part special on national parks, the Arun Chaudhary film shot for President Obama's White House, the British Broadcasting Corporation's hour-long program entitled "Unnatural Histories—Yellowstone," and most recently on Montana PBS's history of Yellowstone. He is often seen on regional and local television talking about Yellowstone's history.

STAGECOACH COLLECTIBLES

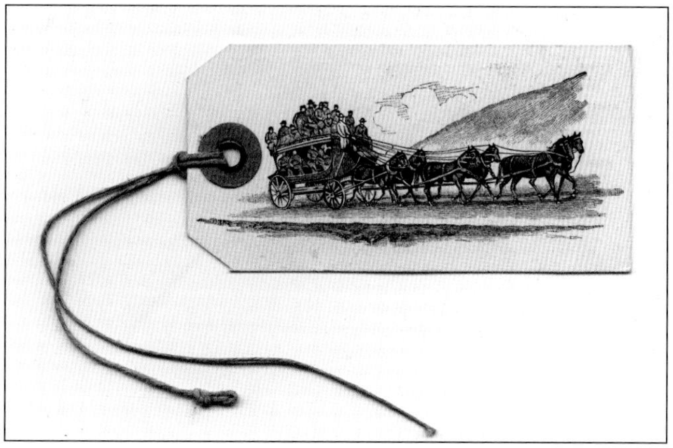

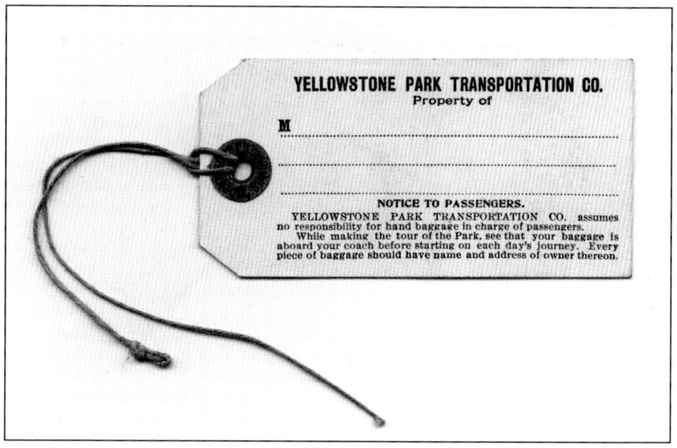

Figures 1 and 2. Yellowstone Park Transportation Co., paper luggage or baggage tag, three and thirteen sixteenth by one and fourteen sixteenth inch, tallyho stagecoach. *Tom Murphy Collection*

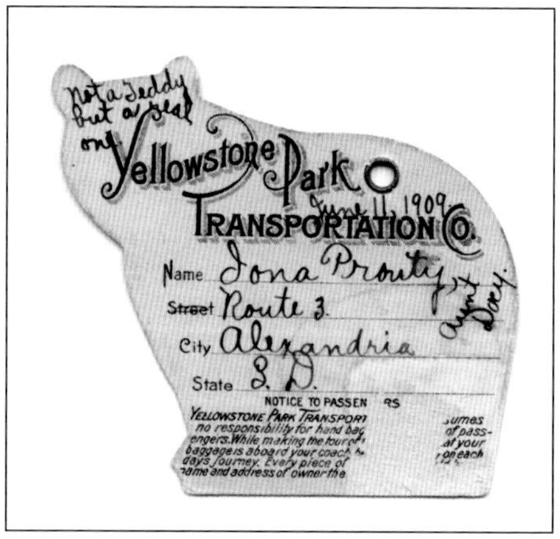

Black Bear two-sided luggage tag, Yellowstone Park Transportation Co., two and three quarter by three-inch paper baggage tag, circa 1909. *Francis Historic Collections*

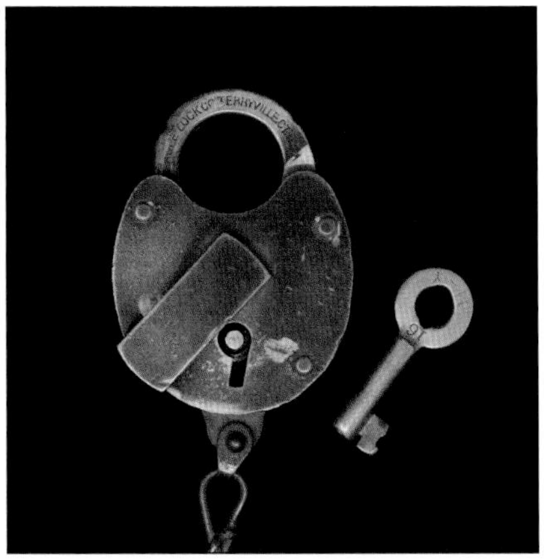

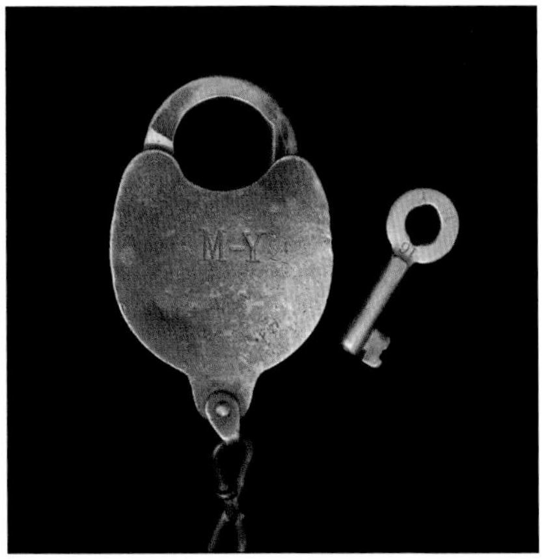

Figures 1 and 2. M-Y, Monida - Yellowstone Stage Co., metal lock with key, Eagle Lock Co., Terryville, CT, USA, views of front and reverse. *Bob Reynolds Collection.* **Figure 3.** Y.P.T.Co. 344, Gardiner, MT., W.W. Wilcox Co., Chicago, one and five sixteenth by one and six sixteenth inch brass fob luggage tag. *Jay C. Lyndes Family Collection.* **Figure 4.** Y.N.P. 20 Transportation Co., three and one quarter by one and five sixteenth inch metal hat band, slight curve to fit on hat, Northwestern Stamp Works, St Paul, Minn. *Jay C. Lyndes Family Collection.* **Figure 5.** National Park Transportation Co., 208, N. W. Stamps Works, St Paul, one and three quarter by one- and three-quarter inch copper luggage fob. *Jay C. Lyndes Family Collection.* **Figure 6.** Yellowstone Park Transportation Co., with bear logo, 2-inch plastic luggage tag, Made by Whitehead & Hoag Co., Newark, N.J. *Jay C. Lyndes Family Collection*

Yellowstone Park Via M-Y The Monida Line, From The Oregon Short Line R.R., An Ideal Coaching Tour On The Crest Of The Rocky Mountains, Monida & Yellowstone Stage Co., St. Paul, Minn., Monida, Mont., Pioneer Press Co., St. Paul, Minn., Season 1902, June 1st To Sept. 15th, eight and one quarter by three and three quarter inch brochure, 1 page folded, W.W. Humphrey, Genl. Mgr., Monida, Mont., F. Jay Haynes, President, St Paul, Minn. *Bob Reynolds Collection*

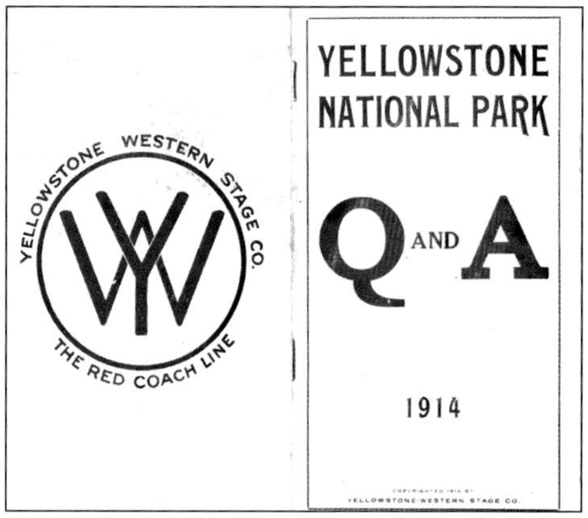

Yellowstone National Park, Q And A, 1914, Copyrighted 1914 By Yellowstone - Western Stage Co., six by three and seven sixteenth inch soft cover booklet, 20 pages including covers, Yellowstone Western Stage Co., The Red Coach Line, The Pioneer Press Company, St. Paul. *Bob Reynolds Collection*

Twenty by nine and one eighth inch wood and metal stagecoach model with luggage, Yellowstone Park Transportation Co., #138, Abbot - Downing, plans for this coach were drawn from a coach found by Ivan Collins at Rancho El Provindencia in Los Angeles, California. The model was completed on Dec. 27, 1946. Built in 1999 by Howard Cagley. *Jay C. Lyndes Family Collection*

Yellowstone Park, Tally-ho Stagecoach curtains made especially for Y.P.Co, used at Canyon Village & Lake Lodge Deluxe Cabins, each panel forty-six- and one-half inches. *Francis Historic Collections*

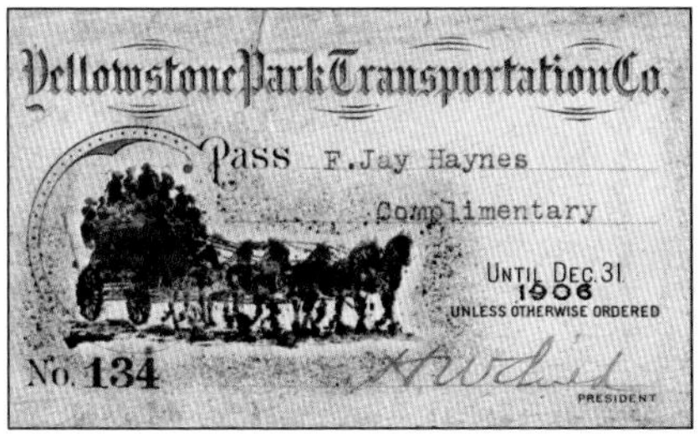

Yellowstone Park Transportation Co. Pass, F. Jay Haynes, Complimentary, Until Dec. 31, 1906, No. 134, signed by H. W. Child, four and one eighth by two- and one-half inch paper card stagecoach pass. *Jay C. Lyndes Family Collection*

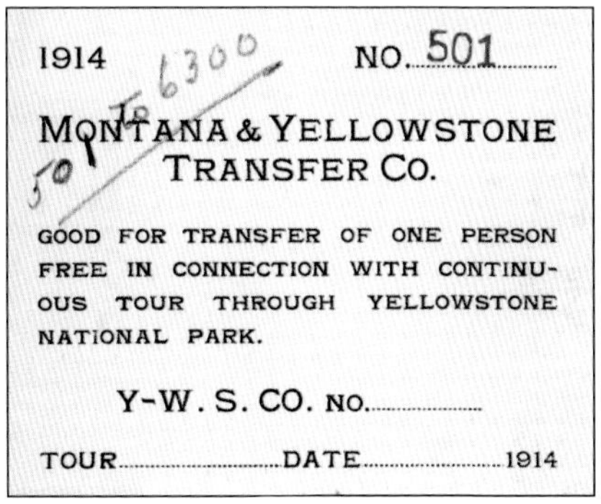

Montana & Yellowstone Transfer Co, Good for transfer of one person free in connection with continuous tour through Yellowstone National Park, Y-W S Co, 1914, No 501, three by two- and one-half inch paper ticket for stagecoach use. *Jay C. Lyndes Family Collection*

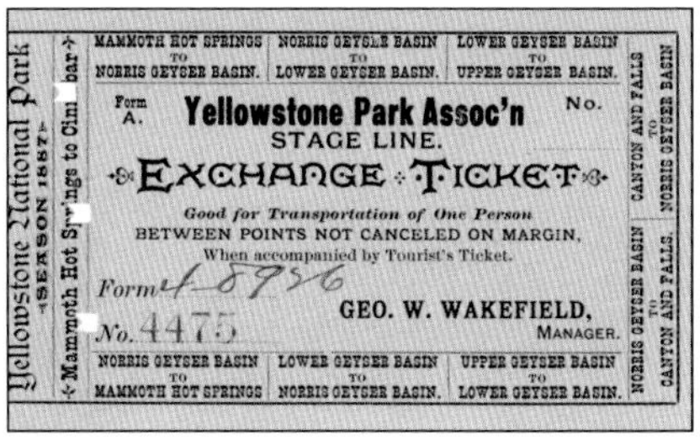

Yellowstone Park Assoc'n Stage Line, Exchange Ticket, No 4474, Geo. W. Wakefield, Manager, August 1, 1890, four and one quarter by two- and one-half inch paper ticket, Form A. *Jay C. Lyndes Family Collection*

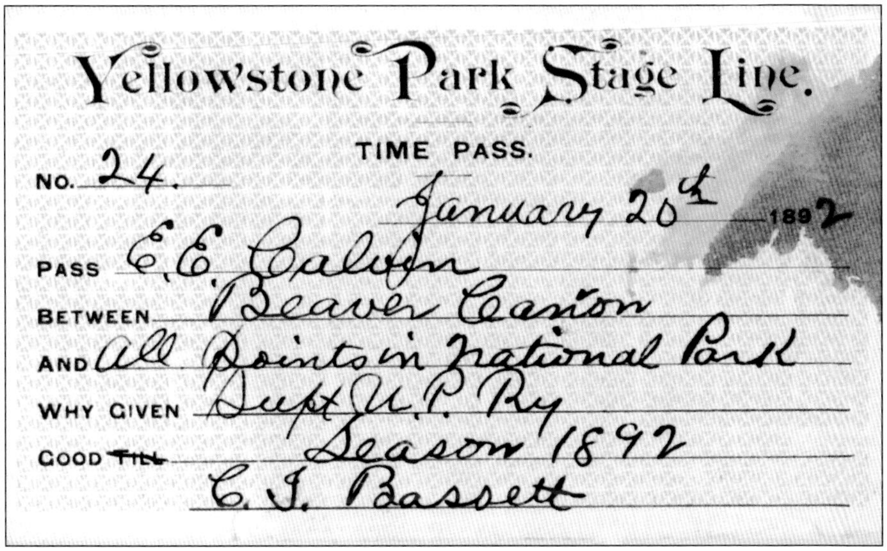

Yellowstone Park Stage Line, Time Pass, No. 24, January 20th 1892, Pass - E.E. Calvin, Beaver Canon, All Points in National Park, Supt. U.P. RY, Season 1892, signed by E. J. Bassett, three and fourteen sixteenth by two and one quarter inch card. *Jay C. Lyndes Family Collection*

Yellowstone National Park, Via The M - Y Stage Line, July 4th 1912 with button pin having no clasp and red, white and blue ribbon, total length five and six sixteenth by two inches. *Bob Reynolds Collection*

Yellowstone Western Stage Co., 1915, one and one quarter inch metal button pin. *Jay C. Lyndes Family Collection*

Yellowstone Western Stage Co., 1916, one and one quarter inch metal button pin. *Jay C. Lyndes Family Collection*

M - Y, Monida & Yellowstone Stage Co., one and one quarter inch button pin, Western Badge & Nov. Co., John A. Lethert, Prop., Badges, Banners, Buttons, Saint Paul, Minn. *Jay C. Lyndes Family Collection*

M - Y, Monida & Yellowstone Stage Co., one and one quarter inch button pin, most likely made by Western Badge & Nov. Co., John A. Lethert, Prop, Badges, Banners, Buttons, Saint Paul, Minn. *Jay C. Lyndes Family Collection*

Yellowstone National Park, Via the M - Y Stage Line, one and one quarter inch button pin. *Francis Historic Collections*

Yellowstone National Park, Via The YW Stage Line, one and one quarter inch metal button pin. *Jay C. Lyndes Family Collection*

Yellowstone Park Via M - Y Stage Line, Union Pacific & Oregon Short Line, 3 inch gummed sticker with bison or buffalo head. *Bob Reynolds Collection*

Yellowstone - Western Stage Co., Yellowstone Park, From The Oregon Short Line & Union Pacific Railroad, 3 inch gummed sticker with coach. *Bob Reynolds Collection*

The Railroads

Michael H. Francis

Railroads were integral to the early days of Yellowstone National Park. Starting in 1886, railroad companies helped finance the construction of a series of hotels near park attractions. The railroads understood that promoting the park produced more passengers on their trains. Thus began many years of numerous guidebooks and brochures produced by the railroads. Many of these publications are some of the most highly sought collectibles, not only by Yellowstone aficionados but also by railroad collectors.

The "Wonderland" Northern Pacific RR guidebooks were published yearly, and most are very rare. The earliest Wonderland guidebook was published twice in 1883; the first printing had thirty pages, the second forty pages. Neither edition had the word "Wonderland" on the cover. Another collectible version of this series is the Wonderland Junior, a smaller book sized to fit in a pocket; these may be harder to find than the larger versions.

Another favorite Northern Pacific publication was printed two years in a row with slight differences. This brochure is titled Alice's Adventures in the New Wonderland, The Yellowstone National Park. It was printed in 1885 and 1886. If the brochure has "Poole Bros. Chicago." on the front cover near the base of Alice's dress, it is the 1885 version; if not, it is 1886.

Other railroads which promoted the park were Union Pacific, Oregon Short Line, Chicago, Burlington & Quincy, Chicago, Milwaukee & St. Paul, and Rock Island Line.

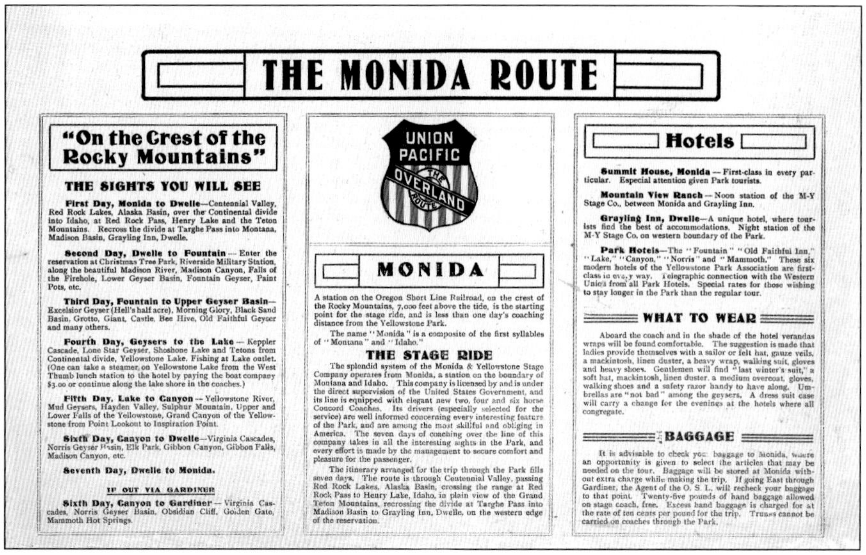

THE MONIDA ROUTE

"On the Crest of the Rocky Mountains"

THE SIGHTS YOU WILL SEE

First Day, Monida to Dwelle—Centennial Valley, Red Rock Lakes, Alaska Basin, over the Continental divide into Idaho, at Red Rock Pass, Henry Lake and the Teton Mountains. Recross the divide at Targhe Pass into Montana, Madison Basin, Grayling Inn, Dwelle.

Second Day, Dwelle to Fountain — Enter the reservation at Christmas Tree Park, Riverside Military Station, along the beautiful Madison River, Madison Canyon, Falls of the Firehole, Lower Geyser Basin, Fountain Geyser, Paint Pots, etc.

Third Day, Fountain to Upper Geyser Basin—Excelsior Geyser (Hell's half acre), Morning Glory, Black Sand Basin, Grotto, Giant, Castle, Bee Hive, Old Faithful Geyser and many others.

Fourth Day, Geysers to the Lake — Keppler Cascade, Lone Star Geyser, Shoshone Lake and Tetons from Continental divide, Yellowstone Lake. Fishing at Lake outlet. (One can take a steamer on Yellowstone Lake from the West Thumb lunch station to the hotel by paying the boat company $3.00 or continue along the lake shore in the coaches.)

Fifth Day, Lake to Canyon — Yellowstone River, Mud Geysers, Hayden Valley, Sulphur Mountain, Upper and Lower Falls of the Yellowstone, Grand Canyon of the Yellowstone from Point Lookout to Inspiration Point.

Sixth Day, Canyon to Dwelle—Virginia Cascades, Norris Geyser Basin, Elk Park, Gibbon Canyon, Gibbon Falls, Madison Canyon, etc.

Seventh Day, Dwelle to Monida.

IF OUT VIA GARDINER

Sixth Day, Canyon to Gardiner — Virginia Cascades, Norris Geyser Basin, Obsidian Cliff, Golden Gate, Mammoth Hot Springs.

UNION PACIFIC THE OVERLAND ROUTE

MONIDA

A station on the Oregon Short Line Railroad, on the crest of the Rocky Mountains, 7,000 feet above the tide, is the starting point for the stage ride, and is less than one day's coaching distance from the Yellowstone Park.

The name "Monida" is a composite of the first syllables of "Montana" and "Idaho."

THE STAGE RIDE

The splendid system of the Monida & Yellowstone Stage Company operates from Monida, a station on the boundary of Montana and Idaho. This company is licensed by and is under the direct supervision of the United States Government, and its line is equipped with elegant new two, four and six horse Concord Coaches. Its drivers (especially selected for the service) are well informed concerning every interesting feature of the Park, and are among the most skillful and obliging in America. The seven days of coaching over the line of this company takes in all the interesting sights in the Park, and every effort is made by the management to secure comfort and pleasure for the passenger.

The itinerary arranged for the trip through the Park fills seven days. The route is through Centennial Valley, passing Red Rock Lakes, Alaska Basin, crossing the range at Red Rock Pass to Henry Lake, Idaho, in plain view of the Grand Teton Mountains, recrossing the divide at Targhe Pass into Madison Basin to Grayling Inn, Dwelle, on the western edge of the reservation.

Hotels

Summit House, Monida — First-class in every particular. Especial attention given Park tourists.

Mountain View Ranch — Noon station of the M-Y Stage Co., between Monida and Grayling Inn.

Grayling Inn, Dwelle—A unique hotel, where tourists find the best of accommodations. Night station of the M-Y Stage Co. on western boundary of the Park.

Park Hotels—The "Fountain" "Old Faithful Inn," "Lake," "Canyon," "Norris" and "Mammoth." These six modern hotels of the Yellowstone Park Association are first-class in every way. Telegraphic connection with the Western Union from all Park Hotels. Special rates for those wishing to stay longer in the Park than the regular tour.

WHAT TO WEAR

Aboard the coach and in the shade of the hotel verandas wraps will be found comfortable. The suggestion is made that ladies provide themselves with a sailor or felt hat, gauze veils, a mackintosh, linen duster, a heavy wrap, walking suit, gloves and heavy shoes. Gentlemen will find "last winter's suit," a soft hat, mackintosh, linen duster, a medium overcoat, gloves, walking shoes and a safety razor handy to have along. Umbrellas are "not bad" among the geysers. A dress suit case will carry a change for the evenings at the hotels where all congregate.

BAGGAGE

It is advisable to check your baggage to Monida, where an opportunity is given to select the articles that may be needed on the tour. Baggage will be stored at Monida without extra charge while making the trip. If going East through Gardiner, the Agent of the O. S. L. will recheck your baggage to that point. Twenty-five pounds of hand baggage allowed on stage coach, free. Excess hand baggage is charged for at the rate of ten cents per pound for the trip. Truns cannot be carried on coaches through the Park.

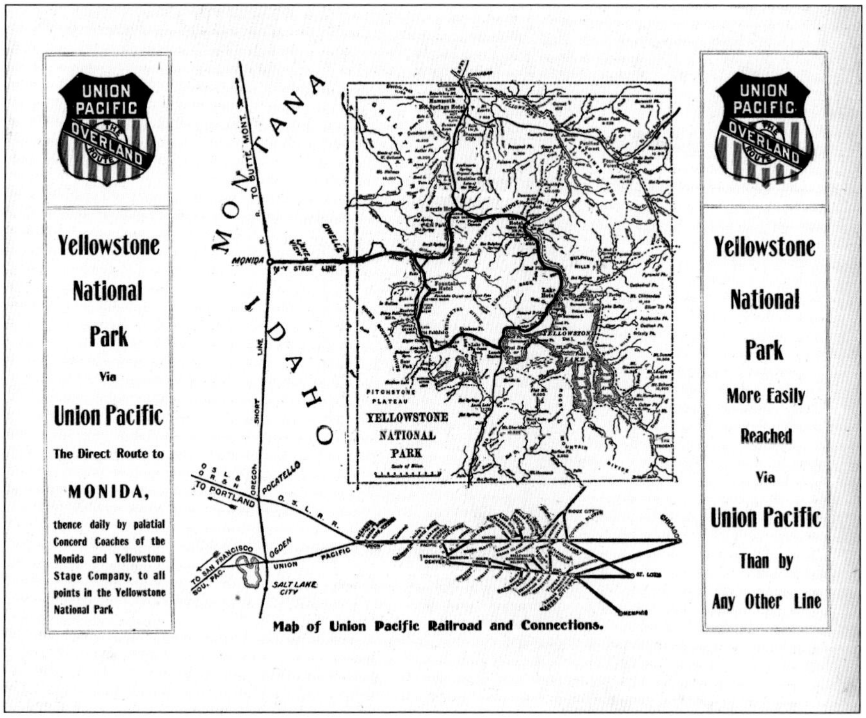

The Monida Route, Union Pacific, The Overland Route, "On the Crest of the Rocky Mountains", twelve and one quarter by ten and one quarter inch manila paper folder with map, 12 color prints by F. Jay Haynes. *Bob Reynolds Collection*

Figure 1. Wonderland or The Pacific Northwest and Alaska, By John Hyde, Copyrighted, 1888, by Chas S. Fee, General Passenger and Ticket Agent, Northern Pacific Railroad, St Paul, nine and one half by six- and three-quarter inch soft cover book or magazine, 96 pages with map. *Jay C. Lyndes Family Collection.* **Figure 2.** Wonderland or The Pacific Northwest and Alaska, By John Hyde, Copyrighted, 1889, by Chas S. Fee, General Passenger and Ticket Agent, Northern Pacific Railroad, St Paul, nine and one half by six- and three-quarter inch soft cover book or magazine, 96 pages with map. *Jay C. Lyndes Family Collection.* **Figure 3.** The Wonderland of the World, Minnesota, Dakota, Montana, Idaho, Oregon, Washington, British Columbia, Alaska, nine and one half by six- and three-quarter inch booklet or magazine, Rand, McNally & Co., Printers and Engravers, Chicago, Copyright 1884, by Chas. S. Fee, General Passenger Agent, Northern Pacific Railroad, St. Paul, 64 pages. *Jay C. Lyndes Family Collection.* **Figure 4.** A Ramble in Wonderland, By Albert B. Guptill, Illustrated from Photos By Haynes, Copyright, 1891, By Chas S. Fee, General Passenger and Ticket Agent, Northern Pacific Railroad, St Paul, nine and one half by six- and three-quarter inch soft cover book, 107 pages with map. *Jay C. Lyndes Family Collection.* **Figure 5.** A Ramble through Wonderland, By Albert B. Guptill, Copyrighted, 1892, by Chas S. Fee, General Passenger and Ticket Agent, Northern Pacific Railroad, St Paul, nine and six sixteenth by six- and three-quarter inch soft cover book or magazine, 105 pages with map. *Jay C. Lyndes Family Collection.*

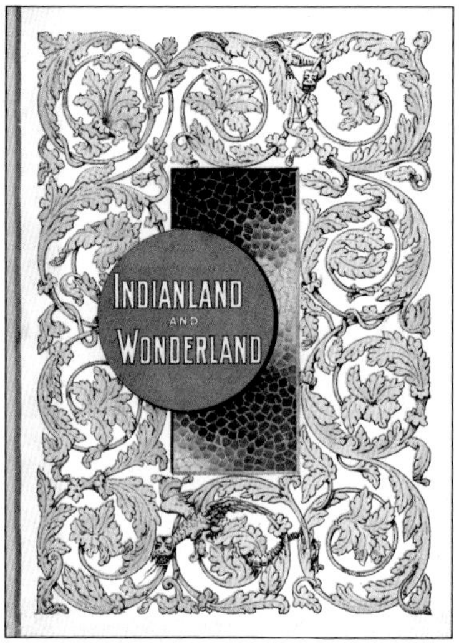

Figure 1. The Yellowstone National Park, Rand, McNally & Co., Printers, Engravers and Electrotypers, Chicago, ILL., eight and five sixteenth by six- and three-quarter inch booklet, 30 pages, Issued By The General Passenger Department, Northern Pacific Railroad, 1883, this is the first of the WONDERLAND Series. *Jay C. Lyndes Family Collection.* **Figure 2.** 6000 Miles Through Wonderland, By Olin D. Wheeler, Illustrated from Photos By Haynes, Copyright, 1893, By Chas S. Fee, General Passenger and Ticket Agent, Northern Pacific Railroad, St. Paul, nine and one half by six- and three-quarter inch soft cover book, 107 pages with map. *Jay C. Lyndes Family Collection.* **Figure 3.** Indianland and Wonderland, By Olin D. Wheeler, Illustrated, Copyright, 1894, by Chas S. Fee, General Passenger and Ticket Agent, Northern Pacific Railroad, St Paul, nine and one half by six and fourteen sixteenth inch soft cover book or magazine, 109 pages with map. *Jay C. Lyndes Family Collection.* **Figure 4.** Wonderland '98, By Olin D. Wheeler, Illustrated, Copyright, 1898, by Chas S. Fee, General Passenger and Ticket Agent, Northern Pacific Railway, St Paul, nine and one half by six and fourteen sixteenth inch soft cover book or magazine, 106 pages with map. *Jay C. Lyndes Family Collection.* **Figure 5.** Wonderland '99, By Olin D. Wheeler, Northern Pacific Railway, Copyright 1899, By Chas S. Fee, General Passenger and Ticket Agent, nine and three quarter by six and fourteen sixteenth inch magazine, 108 pages, Rand McNally & Co., Printers, Chicago. *Francis Historic Collections*

Figure 1. Wonderland Junior, Yellowstone Park Route, Chas S. Fee, General Pass and Ticket Agt., St Paul, Minn., five and one quarter by three- and three-quarter inch booklet, 40 pages with map, circa 1891. *Jay C. Lyndes Family Collection.* **Figure 2.** Wonderland Junior, The Dining Car Line, Northern Pacific, 1893, Chas S. Fee, Gen'l Pass'r and Ticket Agt, St Paul, Minn, five and one quarter by three- and three-quarter inch booklet, 48 pages with map. *Jay C. Lyndes Family Collection.* **Figure 3.** Wonderland Junior, The Northern Pacific Railroad, 1895, Chas S. Fee, Gen'l Pass'r and Ticket Agt, St Paul, Minn, five and one quarter by three- and three-quarter inch booklet, 64 pages with map. *Jay C. Lyndes Family Collection.* **Figure 4.** Wonderland Junior, Pioneer Press Co., St. Paul, Minn., five and five sixteenth by three and six sixteenth inch booklet, 32 pages, 1889. *Tom Murphy Collection.* **Figure 5.** Wonderland Junior, The Northern Pacific Railroad, 1896, Chas S. Fee, Gen'l Pass'r and Tkt. Agt, St Paul, Minn, five and fourteen sixteenth by three- and three-quarter inch booklet, 64 pages with map. *Jay C. Lyndes Family Collection.* **Figure 6.** Wonderland Junior, The Dining Car Line, 45 pages, five and one quarter inch by three and six sixteenth inch booklet, 1892, Northern Pacific, Chas S. Fee, Gen. Pass'r and Ticket Agt, St Paul, Minn. *Bob Reynolds Collection*

Figure 1. Thro Wonderland with Lieut. Schwatka, Wonderland or Alaska and the Inland Passage by Lieut. Frederick Schwatka with John Hyde, Copyrighted 1886, by Chas S. Fee, General Passenger Agent, Northern Pacific Railroad, St Paul, nine and ten sixteenth by six and twelve sixteenth inch soft cover book or magazine, 96 pages with map. *Jay C. Lyndes Family Collection.*

Figure 2. Sketches of Wonderland, By Olin D. Wheeler, Illustrated, Copyright, 1895, By Chas S. Fee, General Passenger and Ticket Agent, Northern Pacific Railroad, St Paul, nine and one quarter by six- and three-quarter inch soft cover book, 109 pages with map. *Jay C. Lyndes Family Collection.*

Figure 3. A Journey Thro Wonderland or The Pacific Northwest and Alaska, By Elia W Peattie, Copyrighted, 1890, by Chas S. Fee, General Passenger and Ticket Agent, Northern Pacific Railroad, St Paul, nine and one half by six- and three-quarter inch soft cover book or magazine, 94 pages with map. *Jay C. Lyndes Family Collection.*

Figure 4. Alice's Adventures In The New Wonderland, The Yellowstone National Park, Northern Pacific RR, The Wonderland Route, to the Pacific Coast, Chas S. Fee, Gen'l Pass Agent, St Paul, eight and one quarter by seven and one half inch brochure, 1885, with 1882 map by Carl J. Hals and A. Rydstrom, Civil Engineers, 1 page folded, this printing with Poole Bros Printing and Engravers, Chicago on front cover twice and back cover, Alice letter dated Sep 2d 1884. *Jay C. Lyndes Family Collection*

Figure 1 . Yellowstone National Park, Union Pacific, Standard Road of the West, New And Direct Route, See Picturesque Colorado, nine and one eighth by eight-inch brochure, 1 page folded, 1912, Copyrighted for Union Pacific Railroad Company and Oregon Short Line Railroad Company by Gerrit Fort, P.T. M., Omaha, Neb., 1912. *Jay C. Lyndes Family Collection.* **Figure 2.** Burlington Escorted Tours, Burlington Route, Vacations Without a Care, Glacier, Yellowstone, Rocky Mountain National and Colorado, J G Delaplaine, Manager, five and one half by three-inch booklet. *Jay C. Lyndes Family Collection.* **Figure 3.** The Yellowstone National Park, Northern Pacific Railroad, The Yellowstone Park Route, To Puget Sound and Alaska, seven and one half by eight and one quarter inch brochure, Poole Bros., Chicago, Copyrighted 1895 By Chas. S. Fee, 1895 map on verso. *Bob Reynolds Collection.* **Figure 4.** Where Gush The Geysers, Oregon Short Line, All Rail Route to the Yellowstone, ten and one quarter by eight-inch booklet, back cover plain, 1910, Text By Edward F. Colborn, Photos By F. J. Haynes, 40 pages, Poole Bros. Chicago, double page map 4-9-1910. *Jay C. Lyndes Family Collection.* **Figure 5.** Where Gush The Geysers, Oregon Short Line, All Rail Route To The Yellowstone, 9 x 8-inch brochure, Text By Edward F. Colborn, Photography By F. J. Haynes, Engraved And Printed By The Williamson - Haffner Co., Denver, 40 pages including covers, D.E Burley, General Passenger Agent, Oregon Short Line R.R., Salt Lake City, Utah, 1909 Season, interior map 9-1-08. *Jay C. Lyndes Family Collection.* **Figure 6.** Wonderland, 1905, Northern Pacific Railway, St. Paul Minn., by Olin D. Wheeler, A. M. Cleland General Passenger Agent, nine and three quarter by seven-inch book, 127 pages. *Francis Historic Collections*

Figure 1. Wonderland, 1903, By Olin D. Wheeler, Illustrated, Copyright, 1903, By Chas S. Fee, General Passenger and Ticket Agent, Northern Pacific Railroad, St Paul, nine and one half by six- and three-quarter inch soft cover book, 112 pages with map. *Jay C. Lyndes Family Collection.* **Figure 2.** Wonderland 1900, By Olin D. Wheeler, Illustrated, Copyright, 1900, by Chas S. Fee, General Passenger and Ticket Agent, Northern Pacific Railway, St Paul, Minn, nine and three quarter by six and fourteen sixteenth inch soft cover book or magazine, 132 pages with map. *Jay C. Lyndes Family Collection.* **Figure 3.** Wonderland, 1902, By Olin D. Wheeler, Illustrated, Copyright, 1902, By Chas S. Fee, General Passenger and Ticket Agent, Northern Pacific Railroad, St Paul, nine and ten sixteenth by six and fourteen sixteenth inch soft cover book, 112 pages. *Jay C. Lyndes Family Collection.* **Figure 4**. Wonderland, 1901, The History of a Trademark, Rand McNally & Co., Engravers and Printers, Chicago, By Olin D. Wheeler, Northern Pacific, Copyrighted 1901, by Chas S. Fee, General Passenger and Ticket Agent, Northern Pacific Railway, St Paul, six by three- and one-half inch booklet, 32 pages, makes this a "Wonderland Junior." *Bob Reynolds Collection.* **Figure 5.** A Trip To Yellowstone National Park, Over The Union Pacific By Richard Henry Little, seven by five and one eighth inch soft cover book, 76 pages, Copyrighted for Union Pacific Railroad Company by E. L. Lomax, G.P.A., Omaha, Neb., 1909. *Bob Reynolds Collection.* **Figure 6.** Wonderland, 1906, By Olin D. Wheeler, Illustrated, Copyrighted 1906, by Chas S. Fee, General Passenger Agent, Northern Pacific Railway, St Paul, nine and ten sixteenth by six and twelve sixteenth inch soft cover book or magazine, 75 pages with map. *Jay C. Lyndes Family Collection.*

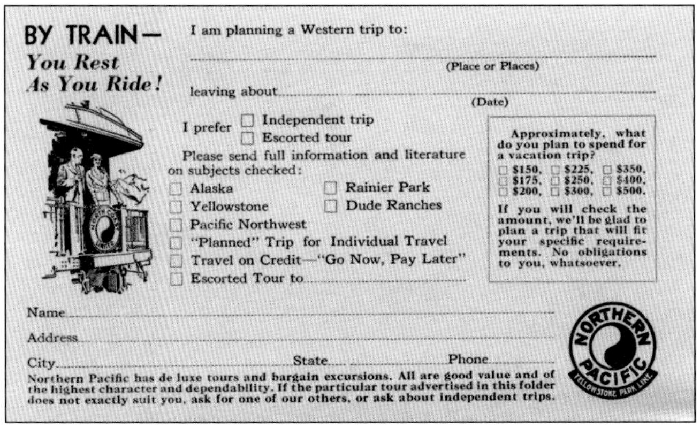

POST CARD, Mr. F. G. Scott, General Agent, Northern Pacific Railway, 73 E. Jackson Blvd., Chicago, Ill., advertising card for ordering western trip information, five and seven sixteenth by three and one quarter inch. *Francis Historic Collections*

Friends of Yours in Yellowstone Park Wake up long enough to say - Merry Christmas, Northern Pacific, Yellowstone Park Line, envelope, six and one half by three- and three-quarter inch. *Francis Historic Collections*

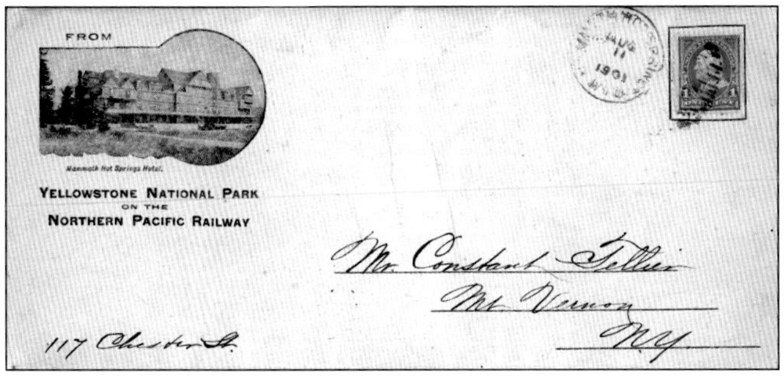

Yellowstone National Park, Northern Pacific Railway, 1901, nine and one eighth by four and one quarter inch brochure, 1 page folded includes 1898 map by Poole Bros Chicago, Chas S Fee Genl Passr and Ticket Agent, St. Paul Minn cover, original folding mailer with brochure glued in for viewing, sent August 11, 1901. *Jay C Lyndes Family Collection*

The Gallatin Gateway into Yellowstone, Chicago Milwaukee & St. Paul Railway, 5991, six and three sixteenth by three and three sixteenth inch ink blotter. *Francis Historic Collections*

Constant Geyser - Norris Basin, Magic Lantern Glass Haynes Slide Lecture, Yellowstone Park, Northern Pacific, Yellowstone Park Line, To accompany the exhibit of Northern Pacific Lantern slides of Yellowstone Park, collection of 109 images, from post 1916 (automobile era), collections are not numbered with standard Haynes numbering. *Jay C. Lyndes Family Collection*

2430. Sylvan Lake on Cody Road to Yellowstone Park, Published By J. L. Robbins Co., Spokane, Wash., Made in USA, R-87975, five and five sixteenth by three and six sixteenth inch color postcard. *Francis Historic Collections*

592 Tires in use two seasons. Average mileage so far 8000. Blowouts to date 6. No wonder they use Goodyear's only on Yellowstone Park busses., verso: What do you think of this for a fleet of busses? All on Goodyear Cords, too., W.M. Nichols out there at Yellowstone Park says, "Only six blowouts in 4,856,855 tire miles." Not bad, is it?, postmarked Aug. 28, 1923, five and one half by three and seven sixteenth inch postcard. *Francis Historic Collections*

Yellowstone Trail, eleven sixteenth inch round metal cuff links, no maker. *Bob Reynolds Collection*

Yellowstone Trail, Montana, So. Dakota, No. Dakota, Minnesota, 1914, one and nine sixteenth inch metal fob. *Bob Reynolds Collection*

Yellowstone Trail Sign on building with vehicles, route to Yellowstone National Park. *Francis Historic Collections*

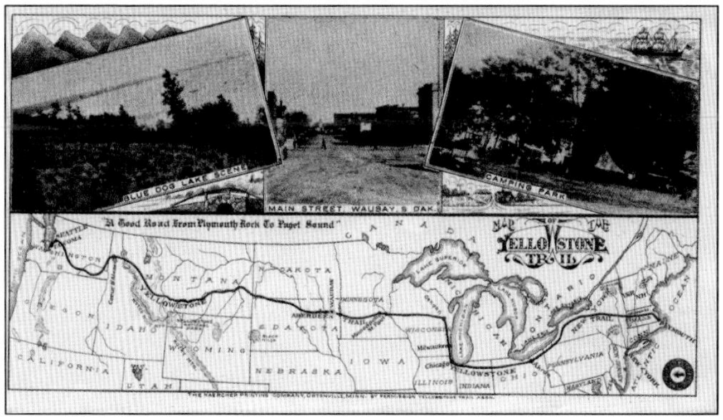

Yellowstone Trail, A Good Road From Plymouth Rock to Puget Sound, The Kaercher Printing Company, Ortonville, Minn, six and one half by three and ten sixteenth inch envelope, Railside Cafe, Wm. L. Nelson, Prop., Waubay, S. Dak., On The Yellowstone Trail. *Francis Historic Collections*

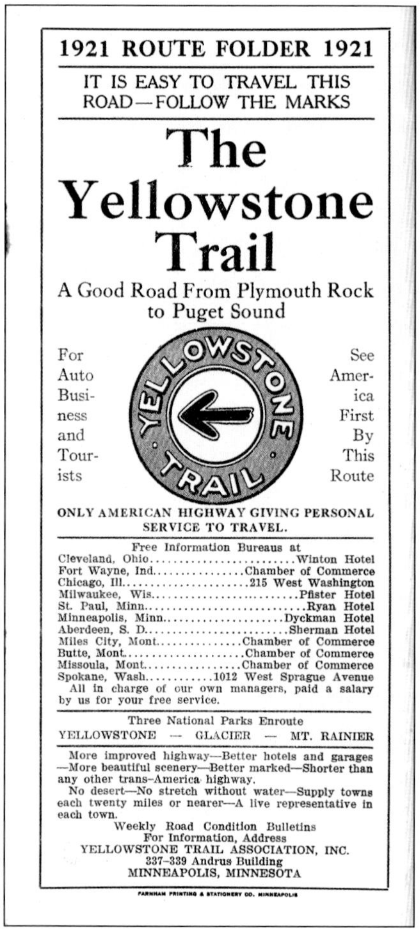

1921 ROUTE FOLDER 1921

IT IS EASY TO TRAVEL THIS ROAD—FOLLOW THE MARKS

The Yellowstone Trail

A Good Road From Plymouth Rock to Puget Sound

For Auto Business and Tourists

YELLOWSTONE TRAIL

See America First By This Route

ONLY AMERICAN HIGHWAY GIVING PERSONAL SERVICE TO TRAVEL.

Free Information Bureaus at

Cleveland, Ohio.........................Winton Hotel
Fort Wayne, Ind................Chamber of Commerce
Chicago, Ill......................215 West Washington
Milwaukee, Wis..........................Pfister Hotel
St. Paul, Minn............................Ryan Hotel
Minneapolis, Minn.....................Dyckman Hotel
Aberdeen, S. D.........................Sherman Hotel
Miles City, Mont..............Chamber of Commerce
Butte, Mont....................Chamber of Commerce
Missoula, Mont.................Chamber of Commerce
Spokane, Wash...........1012 West Sprague Avenue

All in charge of our own managers, paid a salary by us for your free service.

Three National Parks Enroute

YELLOWSTONE — GLACIER — MT. RAINIER

More improved highway—Better hotels and garages—More beautiful scenery—Better marked—Shorter than any other trans-America highway.

No desert—No stretch without water—Supply towns each twenty miles or nearer—A live representative in each town.

Weekly Road Condition Bulletins
For Information, Address
YELLOWSTONE TRAIL ASSOCIATION, INC.
337–339 Andrus Building
MINNEAPOLIS, MINNESOTA

FARNHAM PRINTING & STATIONERY CO. MINNEAPOLIS

1921 Route Folder, It Is Easy To Travel This Road - Follow The Marks, The Yellowstone Trail, Yellowstone Trail Association, Inc., 337 - 339 Andrus Building, Minneapolis, Minnesota, Farnham Printing & Stationary Co., Minneapolis, nine by four and one quarter inch folding brochure, 32 pages. *Bob Reynolds Collection*

Yellowstone Trail, one and ten sixteenth by one and seven sixteenth inch metal fob, Whitehead & Hoag, Newark, N.J., reverse has Entrance Arch, "We Want In", Aug. 5-6 1913, Livingston. *Jay C. Lyndes Family Collection*

Yellowstone Trail, Brevas, United States Internal Revenue stamp, Cigars Class C, 50 cents, Act of 1917, Series of 1917, Union Made Cigars, Factory No. 63, N.F. Nelson, Maker, Milbank, So. Dak, Yellowstone Trail From Coast To Coast, eight and three quarter by five and one quarter by two- and three-quarter inch box. *Bob Reynolds Collection*

Yellowstone Park, five inch by three and one quarter inch metal bear license plate topper. *Jay C. Lyndes Family Collection*

Twelve by four- and one-half inch metal license plate topper, Yellowstone Park, America's Scenic Wonderland. *Jay C. Lyndes Family Collection*

Yellowstone Park, America's Scenic Wonderland, eleven and one half by four and five sixteenth inch colored metal license plate topper, no maker. *Bob Reynolds Collection*

Yellowstone, 805, TWA Services, license plate, 12 x 6 inch. *Bob Reynolds Collection*

Yellowstone Park Company, No 22, 12 x 6-inch metal license plate. *Francis Historic Collections*

America's 1st, Yellowstone National Park, Established 1872, Copyright RPG Designed in the USA, metal license plate, $9.47, eleven and fourteen sixteenth by five and fourteenth sixteenth inch. *Francis Historic Collections*

Yellowstone, The Land Of Wonders, ten and one half by two and twelve sixteenth inch metal license plate topper, no maker, Yellowstone Park. *Bob Reynolds Collection*

Yellowstone National Park, Old Faithful, metal license plate topper, no maker, six and one quarter by five and ten sixteenth inch. *Bob Reynolds Collection*

Yellowstone Park Camps, Yellowstone National Park, Old Faithful Geyser & Bear, 2-sided, three and one half by two-inch luggage or baggage tag. *Jay C. Lyndes Family Collection*

Yellowstone Park Transportation Co., three and one eighth inch baggage or luggage tag with leather strap, Whitehead & Hoag Co., Newark, NJ. *Bob Reynolds Collection*

WHAT TO DO
AT
MAMMOTH

INFORMATION CONCERNING LOCAL POINTS OF INTEREST

Published by
YELLOWSTONE PARK TRANSPORTATION CO.
YELLOWSTONE PARK
WYOMING

What To Do At Mammoth, Information Concerning Local Points Of Interest, Published by Yellowstone Park Transportation Co., Yellowstone Park, Wyoming, 1 page folded, five and three quarter by three- and three-quarter inch. *Francis Historic Collections*

1936 White Model 706 Tour Bus, 7-inch Die cast metal body in box, The Open Top Bus Company, Price $ 19.95, 2002, Made in China. *Francis Historic Collections*

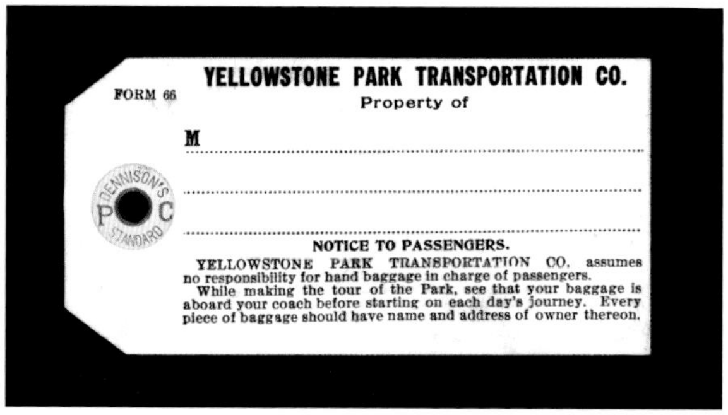
FORM 66 **YELLOWSTONE PARK TRANSPORTATION CO.**
Property of
M ....
DENNISON'S P C STANDARD
NOTICE TO PASSENGERS.
YELLOWSTONE PARK TRANSPORTATION CO. assumes no responsibility for hand baggage in charge of passengers.
While making the tour of the Park, see that your baggage is aboard your coach before starting on each day's journey. Every piece of baggage should have name and address of owner thereon.

Yellowstone Park Transportation Co., Form 66, Dennison's Standard PC, three and three quarter by one and fourteen sixteenth inch paper luggage or baggage tag. *Bob Reynolds Collection*

Accomodations:

Hotels and Camps

See Yellowstone Right! 1913 Season, June 15 - Sept. 10, For Your Pocket or Hand Bag, The Wylie Company operates eight permanent summer camps - E.A. Shilton: District Tourist Agent: 17th and Tremont Sts. : Denver, Colo, two sided five and one half by three and six sixteenth inch card, Yellowstone Park, "Wylie Way", 1883 - Thirty Years Successful Service – 1913. *Francis Historic Collections*

Cottage Hotel, Logs, Ingersoll View Company, St. Paul Minn., USA, High Grade Original Views, Sold only by Subscription, seven by three and one half inch black and white stereoview card. *John Alley Collection*

No. 116 Hotel, Upper Basin, Yellowstone National Park, 7 x 4 inch black and white stereoview, no publisher or photographer, circa 1885 to 1894, also known as Shack Hotel. *John Alley Collection*

McCartneys 1st Hotel in Yellowstone Park, European and American Views, plain verso, seven by three and one half inch stereoview. *Francis Historic Collections*

Rustic Retreats, Cozy Camps, and Grand Hotels

Tamsen Emerson Hert

A Congressional act in 1872 set aside a "tract of land in the Territories of Montana and Wyoming" as a pleasuring ground for the people. The act also authorized the granting of leases for small parcels of ground for the erection of buildings to accommodate visitors in the new reservation. The location of such leases as well as any construction plans, however, required approval by the Secretary of the Interior. Thus, began Yellowstone's long and complex lodging-concession history with numerous individuals and companies contributing to the development of hotels, camps, and lodges throughout Yellowstone's history.

Among the first lodging establishments were three rustic log structures. James McCartney settled at Mammoth Hot Springs in mid-1871 and built bathhouses and a primitive, rough-hewn cabin to handle the few tourists and invalids that sought to "take the waters." McCartney's Hotel (1871-1912) was the first national park hotel. Though McCartney was eventually declared a squatter and dismissed from the park, his hotel on Clematis Gulch remained in operation as a hotel until 1883 when the new National Hotel opened. The old building remained in service as housing for assistant park superintendents and later as a Chinese laundry until it was lost to a fire on the evening of December 4, 1912.

In 1880, George Marshall built the park's second hotel, a two-story structure at the "Forks of the Firehole River" in the Lower Geyser Basin. The first known tourists to stay at Marshall's that October were newspaperman and railroad promoter, Robert Strahorn, accompanied by his wife Carrie. Robert's impression of the new hotel was fairly positive, but Carrie recalled that the log house was "far from being finished, and the part we occupied was partitioned off with a canvas wagon cover...while the unfilled chinks between the logs allowed the rigorous October breezes to fan us at will." In 1884, Marshall and new partner George Graham Henderson erected a second hotel near Marshall's original structure. For unknown reasons, Marshall sold out to Henderson at the end of the year. Henderson then partnered with Henry E. Klamer in 1885 and renamed the establishment the Firehole Hotel. They in turn sold out to the Yellowstone Park Association (YPA) in 1886, which operated the hotel until 1891. This hotel was abandoned in 1891 as that company opened the Fountain Hotel, and the old buildings were burned down in September of 1891.

The third of the "pioneer" hotels was Yancey's Pleasant Valley Hotel located in the northern section of the park, near Tower Fall. "Uncle" John Yancey operated a mail station beginning in 1882 and in 1884 added a two-story log cabin to be used as a hotel. Yancey played host to many notable visitors including Owen Wister, Ernest Seton Thompson and Senator George Graham Vest. Yancey attended President Theodore Roosevelt's laying of the cornerstone for the new arch at the North Entrance on April 24, 1903 and shortly afterward succumbed to pneumonia, passing away on May 6, 1903. His nephew, Dan Yancey inherited the property, which he operated for a few years. On April 16, 1906, a fire destroyed the hotel.

With the advance of the Northern Pacific Railroad (NPRR) across Montana in the early 1880s coupled with the construction of the Yellowstone branch line to the north entrance in 1883, it became necessary to provide more refined accommodations for the increasing number of tourists. In the fall of 1882, speculators established the Yellowstone National Park Improvement Company to build hotels in the park. Construction of the "National" Hotel began late that year, with the intention of the hostelry being completed and opened for the 1883 season. L.S. Buffington, St. Paul architect, designed the Queen Anne structure. Four stories tall and narrow with a veranda stretching across its entire south elevation, it was a mammoth structure with all the modern amenities. Originally a structure of dark red and green, it was repainted yellow for a brief time in the late 1880s before being returned to a reddish-brown ("terra cotta"). The hotel opened on August 1, 1883. Early renovations of the building included the addition of a North Wing and the partial removal of the fourth floor, both in 1913. The original structure was razed in 1936 to make way for a restaurant and cafeteria. Cottages, designed by Robert C. Reamer, were added in 1938. Today only the 1913 wing remains. The Mammoth Hot Springs Hotel was renovated again in 2018.

The Cottage Hotel, built in 1885, by members of the G. L. Henderson family, provided a lower-cost alternative to the National Hotel. A delightful three-story log structure, it sported a veranda which wrapped around the front and east sides with a balcony above to match. It operated as a hotel until 1912, and then served as a dormitory for employees until it was closed and razed in 1964.

Superintendents and visitors were interested in having more luxurious accommodations located near the major scenic locales around the park. The hotel company erected temporary "hotels" near Old Faithful Geyser, the Grand Canyon of the Yellowstone, Yellowstone Lake, and Norris Geyser Basin in the early 1880s. The Yellowstone Park Association built the first hotel at the Norris Geyser Basin late in 1886. Unfortunately, this two-story frame structure was lost to fire before it opened. A fire lit in an unfinished chimney resulted in total destruction on July 14, 1887. It was succeeded by tent hotels and shacks until another substantial hotel was built in 1901. The second "real" hotel at Norris, also known as a lunch station, stood on the hill immediately north of Porcelain Basin. It was abandoned in 1917 and razed in 1927.

Park superintendents continually commented on the need for additional facilities and the unmet expectations that the hotel company would provide them. The YPA finally made good on their obligation and from 1889-1891 three new hotels were built. The first of these, regarded as the "second" Canyon Hotel opened in 1890. Earlier, a temporary, prefabricated structure served the needs of the visitors from 1886 to 1890. The new hotel, a plain frame structure was constructed on the hillside overlooking the Grand Canyon

34 N.P. Park, Fountain Hotel, Magic Lantern Glass Haynes Slide Lecture, Northern Pacific, Yellowstone Park Line, To accompany the exhibit of Northern Pacific Lantern slides of Yellowstone Park. *Jay C. Lyndes Family Collection*

Uncle John Yancey. He established a mail station in Pleasant Valley in 1882 and built his rustic hotel in 1884 to cater to fishermen and to travelers to and from Cooke City, black and white photo postcard, six and one half by four and three quarter inch, Copyright The Yellowstone Foundation, Pomegranate, Box 6099, Rohnert Park, CA 94927. *Francis Historic Collections*

Park visitors camping with Aron "Tex" Holm along with staff and A. Holm Camp No.19 Cody, WY chuck wagon and tents. *Francis Historic Collections*

The Loop Sylvan Pass Cody Road, Yellowstone Park, 2, Tex Holm black and white photo collection, eight and one half by six and one half inch print. *Francis Historic Collections*

of the Yellowstone. Architect Robert Reamer worked his magic on this edifice in 1910-1911, creating a grand hotel. The "New Canyon Hotel" considered the third Canyon Hotel, was an example of Reamer's skill in creating a variety of styles. While structural issues plagued the building beginning in 1890, this magnificent hostelry stood on that hillside until it was deemed unsafe and closed following the 1958 season. Sold to the Carlos Construction Company for demolition, the Canyon Hotel suffered a fire of mysterious origin that destroyed the shell of the hotel on August 8, 1960.

The Fountain Hotel replaced the Firehole Hotel at the Lower Geyser Basin. Construction started in 1889, but the new building did not open until 1891. Visitors made day trips to the Upper Geyser Basin from this location. A three-story frame building, it faced south toward the Fountain Geyser. Two elements made this place special, piped-in hot water from Leather Pool for hot baths and calcimined walls from the nearby Fountain Paint Pot. The opening of Old Faithful Inn in 1904, coupled with the introduction of motorized vehicles in 1915, led to its demise. With the introduction of automobile transportation in 1915, greater distances could be traveled and the need for two large hotels so close together was unnecessary. Closed and abandoned in 1917, it was demolished ten years later.

The Lake Hotel at Yellowstone Lake was the third of the facilities constructed from 1889-1891. The simple three-story frame-structure, painted a soft yellow, also opened in 1891. Robert Reamer refashioned its plain design in 1903-1904 by adding Ionic columns to the front, which gave the hotel's façade a classical, Colonial appearance. The building underwent a succession of renovations from 1903 until the 1940s, including the addition of a porte-cochere in 1919, which was enclosed in 1926 to enlarge the lobby, and a new lounge and porte-cochere constructed. Additions and renovations returned this grand dame of national park hotels to its turn-of-the century appearance in time for its centennial celebration in 1991, and listing on the National Register of Historic Places on May 16, 1991. On February 27, 2015, the Lake Hotel was recognized as a National Historic Landmark and in May 2016, celebrated its 125th anniversary.

It took time for an adequate structure to rise in the Upper Geyser Basin. From 1883 to 1903, tent hotels and ramshackle wooden structures filled the need. In 1885, approximately on the same site where the Old Faithful Inn stands today, the first hotel, aptly named the "Shack" Hotel was built. It burned in 1894 and was soon replaced by another rickety structure. The world owes a debt of gratitude to Harry W. Child, who with partner Silas S. Huntley, took over the YPA in 1898. Child assumed full control of the hotel company upon Huntley's death in 1901. He took to heart the need for a suitable hotel at such a significant location. Through contacts at the Hotel Del Coronado, in San Diego, California, he learned of a promising young architect, Robert C. Reamer. Impressed by Reamer's work, Child hired him as the YPA company architect.

Reamer's first responsibility was to oversee the construction of the new hotel at the Upper Geyser Basin. His masterpiece, the Old Faithful Inn, opened on June 1, 1904, and ever since has inspired log homes and resort hotels across the country. The Inn underwent a series of expansions with an East Wing added in 1913, a West Wing and extension of the porte-cochere in 1927-28, and the Bear Pit Lounge in 1936. This icon of national park hotels was named to the National Register of Historic Places on July 23, 1973, and became a National Historic Landmark on May 28, 1987. Even though the Old Faithful Inn was threatened by the 1988 fires, it miraculously escaped destruction and thus survived to celebrate its centennial with a gala in 2004.

A Shaw & Powell Camping Wagon, Y.N.P., G 573 American Import Co., Publishers, Minneapolis, USA, Printed In Germany, five and six sixteenth by three and six sixteenth inch post card. *Francis Historic Collections*

Shaw & Powell Party Touring, Y.N.P., G No. 415. American Import Co., Publishers, Minneapolis, USA, Made In Germany, five and five sixteenth by three and six sixteenth inch post card. *Francis Historic Collections*

On Top of Mount Washburn with Holmes, black and white postcard postmarked Dec 28, 1908, five and six sixteenth by three and eleven sixteenth inch. *Francis Historic Collections*

Park visitors posing outside of Wylie tent number 23, black and white magic lantern glass slide. *Francis Historic Collections*

Harry W. Child had a vision and a passion for the hospitality business in Yellowstone. His grand hotels stationed at the most scenic locations around the park, set the standard for other national park hotels. However, not all of Yellowstone's visitors had the expendable income to patronize the park hotels. Pragmatic entrepreneurs such as W.W. Wylie, Amos Shaw and J.D. Powell, Howard H. Hays, and others crafted more informal and inexpensive, yet still charming ways to accommodate visitors.

Intrigued by Wonderland in 1880, William Wallace Wylie developed a novel experience for tourists of lesser means. In 1882, he began offering guided camping trips into the park. A little over a decade later, the popularity of his method overwhelmed his "movable" operation. He applied for and was granted a lease in 1896 to erect four permanent camps and two lunch stations. In 1905, an enterprising young man from Metropolis, Illinois took a summer position with the Wylie operation. Soon enough, Howard H. Hays would become a marketing genius promoting the "Wylie Way" across the United States. Wylie sold his operation to Arthur W. Miles of Livingston, Montana in 1906. Judiciously, Miles held on to the camp company's renown by retaining the Wylie name for his newly acquired enterprise, which he called the Wylie Camping Company.

Several smaller camping operations like Wylie's early movable camps were conducted from nearby gateway towns such as the "Bryant Way" in West Yellowstone, Montana; Aron "Tex" Holm's Yellowstone Park Camping Company; the Frost and Richard Camping Company in Cody, Wyoming; and the Shaw & Powell Camping Company in Gardiner, Montana. Eventually, Shaw & Powell grew to be Yellowstone's second largest camping company, and in 1913 became the second camping operation granted permission to erect permanent camps.

When Congress established the National Park Service in 1916, Director Stephen T. Mather announced the consolidation of the lodging concessions. While in the past monopolies had been considered evil, Mather now championed a "regulated monopoly" in Yellowstone. In addition to the merger of the transportation businesses, the various camping companies were combined to create the Yellowstone Park Camping Company (1917-1919). The permanent camps of both Wylie and Shaw & Powell were reduced to single camp-operations at Mammoth, Upper Geyser Basin, Lake Outlet and Canyon. The Wylie camp at Swan Lake Flat was the first to be relocated, and it went to the bench below the Mammoth terraces. In 1917, the first lodge-facility was built at this site. In 1923, a lobby, dining room, kitchen, offices, and recreation hall were added. In 1940, Mammoth Lodge closed and was removed in 1949.

W. W. Wylie considered Howard Hays to be the "greatest tourist expert in the tourist world" and credited Hays with developing the "Wylie Way" slogan. In 1917, H.H. Hays left Wylie to operate the tourist bureau of the Union Pacific/Chicago North Western rail-system. Successful there, he became the Manager of the Bureau of Service, National Parks and Monuments, for the United States Railroad Administration in 1918. The opportunity to return to Yellowstone came just a year later when he purchased the camping concession. With auto-tourism on the rise, Hays immediately began to convert the camps into large operations with rustic-styled lodge buildings, dining rooms, and recreation halls.

Construction of Roosevelt Lodge began in autumn 1919, and was completed in 1920. While Roosevelt was the smallest of the rustic lodge-facilities, it was considered by many to be the most idyllic with its twin stone fireplaces occupying each end of the building and its covered porch with oversized chairs offering visitors a cozy, down-to-earth ambiance. The Roosevelt Lodge

Historic District was added to the National Register of Historic Places on April 4, 1983. A centennial celebration was planned for 2020, but due to the national pandemic, it was postponed.

The Wylie Camp at the Lake was selected as the site for a rustic lodge-construction, and it was well underway by October, 1919. The lobby sported a stone fireplace on its east end. Steps leading to the dining room were adjacent. In 1929, a porte-cochere, supported by log columns was added to the front. This structure was removed in the mid-1960s. In 2019-2020, the Lake Lodge cafeteria was remodeled and renamed the Wylie canteen in honor of W.W. Wylie, whose tent-camp had earlier stood on this site.

Shaw & Powell established their Canyon Camp on the south side of the Grand Canyon of the Yellowstone River in 1913. As part of H.H. Hays's expansion of the camps, new tent cabins were erected in 1923-24. The log lodge-building was expanded in 1925 using plans drawn up by Bozeman architect, Fred F. Willson. The site was soon considered to be too close to the canyon rim, and structures were removed as part of the Mission 66 program in 1957. Many of the cabins were relocated for use at other sites around the park while others were demolished or sold. The Canyon Lodge lobby was disassembled and moved to Nevada City, Montana, where it stands today as part of that town's outdoor history museum.

In the Upper Geyser Basin, the Old Faithful Lodge was positioned on the former Shaw & Powell Camping Company location. Construction of the lodge, which would contain a dining hall and kitchen, began in 1923 under the leadership of Chief NPS Landscape Engineer Daniel R. Hull and architect Gilbert Stanley Underwood. Additions in 1927 provided a lobby, office, curio shop, and F. Jay Haynes's picture-stand. This addition was seen as one which "harmonizes splendidly with the environment of the lodge."

In 1924, Hays sold the Yellowstone Park Camps Company to Vernon Goodwin, a friend and associate of Harry W. Child. Prior to selling the concession, Hays had planned to expand Mammoth Lodge as well as construct a new facility—Sylvan Pass Lodge. This new lodge, actually a lunch station, was located near the East Entrance on the former site of the Wylie Camp. Operating as the Vernon Goodwin Company, the corporation saw these plans realized. In 1928, Harry Child bought out Goodwin and the operation was renamed the Yellowstone Park Lodge and Camps Company.

As the twentieth century progressed, tourism increased. Facilities were neglected and fell into disrepair. Some were removed, others renovated. By the late 1940s, lodging was not meeting the needs of the public. In the mid-1950s, new National Park Service Director Conrad Wirth devised his own plan to address the needs of all the nation's parks at a national level. Designed to enhance the visitor experience, his system-wide "Mission 66" program launched in 1956 was intended to improve national park facilities in time for the 50th anniversary of the National Park Service in 1966. Yellowstone National Park was selected as the first park to participate in this program and plans became extensive.

At the Canyon, the goal was to remove all the visitor services from both sides of the rim between the Upper and Lower Falls. A site north of the canyon was selected for the new Canyon Village. Ground-breaking for the new area was held May 25, 1956. The "modern" lodge, completed in July 1957, contained all visitor services including dining options while overnight accommodations consisted of separate cabins and motel units.

In the mid-1990s two new lodges, Cascade Lodge (1993) and Dunraven Lodge (1998), were built amidst the collage of 1950s "modernism." The "Canyon Lodging Redevelopment Project," 2014-2016, provided the newest accommodations in Yellowstone. Five new lodges were built to complement the "Mission 66" and rustic architectural styles found in the area. These modular buildings, with design elements reminiscent of the old Canyon Hotel, replaced nearly all of the original 1950s cabins.

Another "village" planned in the mid-1940s was Grant Village on the southern shores of Yellowstone Lake. This area was designed to accommodate visitor services that needed to be relocated from West Thumb where a Hamilton store, gas station, photo shop, and other facilities had operated since the 1920s. It would take decades for the Grant Village plan to be realized. Construction of the six lodge buildings began in 1980 and were completed and ready for visitors in 1982. Originally identified alphabetically, the lodges today are named: Antelope, Bear, Coyote, Deer, Elk and Fox. The new village was threatened and evacuated on at least two occasions during the fires of 1988.

In the 1970s, accommodations necessary for those visiting Wonderland in the winter were added. Using a building that was formerly part of the Camper's Cabin area near Old Faithful Inn, the concessioners established the first Snow Lodge in 1971-72. The old structure was razed in 1998 making way for a new, modern, Snow Lodge that opened in phases between 1998 and 1999. Dedication ceremonies were held May 14-15, 1999.

For more than 150 years, a variety of lodging concessioners constructed buildings, added amenities, and labored to meet the accommodation needs of Yellowstone's visiting public. Throughout that time, owners and operators of these enterprises endeavored to appease visitors' expectations with lodging ranging from rustic log structures to cozy camps ad majestic grand hotels. Ultimately, the distinctly unique architecture found in Yellowstone became a benchmark for national park architecture across the country.

About Tamsen Emerson Hert

Tamsen Emerson Hert is Special Collections Librarian in charge of the Emmett D. Chisum Special Collections, University of Wyoming Libraries. She holds master's degrees in library science and history from Emporia State University. The author of several articles about the cultural history of the Greater Yellowstone Ecosystem, she is currently working on several Yellowstone projects and is finalizing a manuscript on the history of the hotels, camps, and lodges of Yellowstone National Park with her co-authors Elizabeth Watry and Lee Whittlesey. Ms. Hert is past-president of the Wyoming State Historical Society and a member of the Montana Historical Society, Western History Association, National Council of Public History, and Western Writers of America. She currently serves on the editorial board for the *Yellowstone History Journal*.

Made expressly for Yellowstone Park Association, Trade Mark Registered, various pieces with bear logo, Yellowstone Park Association Hotels. *Bob Reynolds Collection*

Made expressly for Yellowstone Park Association, Trade Mark Registered, two and six tenth by five and one eighth inch coffee cup with handle and bear logo. *Bob Reynolds Collection*

Made expressly for Yellowstone Park Association, Trade Mark Registered, three and one eighth by two- and three-quarter inch egg cup with bear logo, Yellowstone Park Association Hotels. *Bob Reynolds Collection*

Made expressly for Yellowstone Park Association, Trade Mark Registered, two and ten sixteenths by two- and one-half inch small handled creamer with bear logo, Yellowstone Park Association Hotels. *Bob Reynolds Collection*

Made expressly for Yellowstone Park Association, Trade Mark Registered, five and one half by three and one quarter inch butter or fruit plate with bear logo, Yellowstone Park Association Hotels. *Bob Reynolds Collection*

Made expressly for Yellowstone Park Association, Trade Mark Registered, nine and three quarter by four- and three-quarter inch salad or fruit bowl with bear logo, Yellowstone Park Association Hotels. *Bob Reynolds Collection*

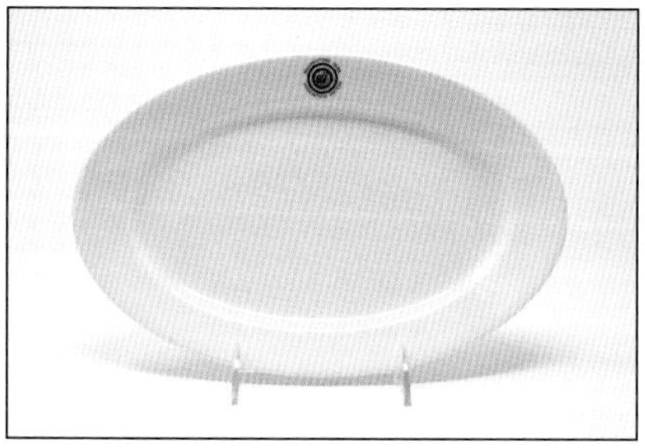

Made expressly for Yellowstone Park Association, Trade Mark Registered, eleven by seven-inch platter with bear logo, Yellowstone Park Association Hotels. *Bob Reynolds Collection*

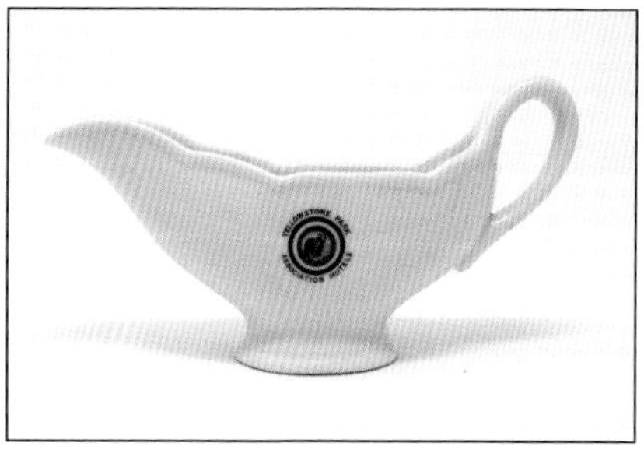

Made expressly for Yellowstone Park Association, Trade Mark Registered, seven by three- and one-half inch gravy boat with handle and bear logo, Yellowstone Park Association Hotels. *Bob Reynolds Collection*

Made expressly for Yellowstone Park Association, Trade Mark Registered, two and six tenth by five and one eighth inch coffee cup with handle and bear logo, verso. *Bob Reynolds Collection*

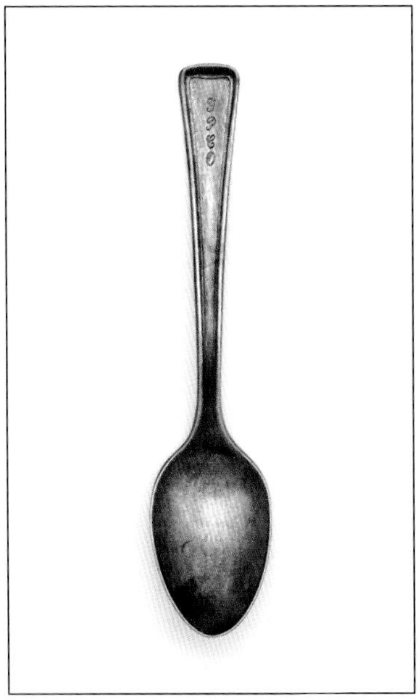

Figure 1. Oneida LTD, Sherrill, NY in business from 1877 to present, Canyon Hotel on handle, six-inch place spoon. *Bob Reynolds Collection.* **Figure 2.** Maker unknown, YPH on handle, Yellowstone Park Hotels, six- and three-quarter inch plain place spoon. *Bob Reynolds Collection.* **Figure 3.** YPCO, Yellowstone Park Company, 6-inch spoon, DOHRCO Gramercy, Dohrmann Hotel Supply Co, San Francisco. *Francis Historic Collections.* **Figure 4.** Y.P.H. MESS, Yellowstone Park Hotels employee mess hall, seven and one eighth inch dessert spoon, made by William A Rogers, Silver Nickel R. *Francis Historic Collections.* **Figure 5.** YPH or Yellowstone Park Hotels on handle, used in dining room, five- and one-half inch spoon, Durable, Reed & Barton Silversmith, circa 1907 to 1916. *Jay C Lyndes Family Collection*

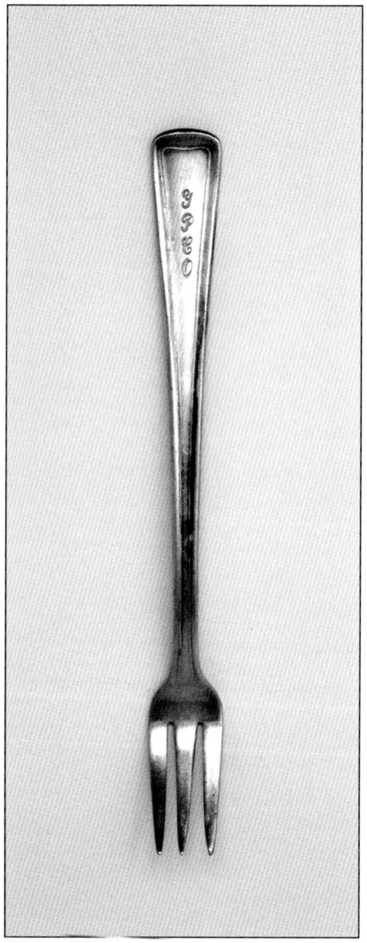

Victor Silver Company, Derby, CT, this mark used after 1922 on hotel and restaurant flatware, reverse makers marks, YPCO on handle, Yellowstone Park Co, six-inch A1 Sterling pickling fork, Norman Pattern. *Bob Reynolds Collection*

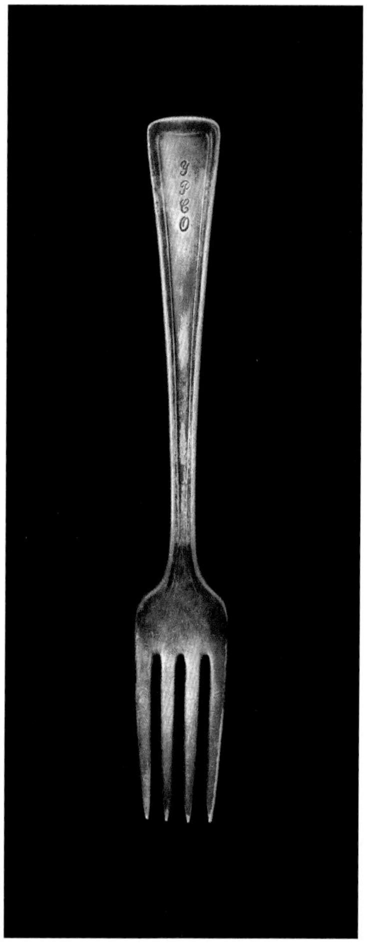

YPCO on handle, 7-inch fork, same pattern as Victor S Co, reverse shows company hallmark, DOHRCO - Dohrmann Hotel Supply, San Francisco. *Jay C Lyndes Family Collection*

Maker unknown, YPH on handle, Yellowstone Park Hotels, seven- and three-quarter inch plain place fork. *Bob Reynolds Collection*

Y.P.A., Mammoth Springs Hotel, 34, N.W. Stamp Works, St Paul, Minn., one and three quarter by one and three quarter inch copper fob. *Jay C Lyndes Family Collection*

Fountain Hotel, YPA, 103, three and one eighth inch metal vintage key fob or tag, NW Stamp WKS St. Paul Minn, Yellowstone Park Association. *Francis Historic Collections*

Mammoth Hot Springs Hotel, YPA, three- and three-quarter inch metal hotel key fob, 65, N W Stamp Works, St Paul Minn, Yellowstone Park Association. *Francis Historic Collections*

Canyon Hotel, Yellowstone Park, Wyo, 106, two and three quarter inch metal hotel room key fob with key, no maker. *Francis Historic Collections*

Lake Hotel, Yellowstone Park, Wyo, brass fob and key, with no guest room number, instead reverse has MAMM. FILE - ROOM, two- and three-quarter inch. *Jay C Lyndes Family Collection*

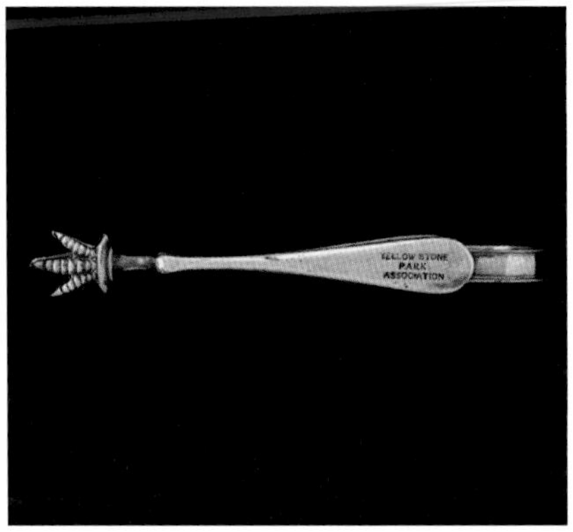

Claw metal tongs, Yellowstone Park Association, four- and three-quarter inches. *Francis Historic Collections*

Canyon Village, Yellowstone Park, Wyo., B-25, two and three quarter inch fob plus key. *Bob Reynolds Collection*

Yellowstone Park Transportation Co., luggage or baggage tag with Fountain Dispensary keys. *Jack & Sue Davis Collection*

Norris Bar 1 key and fob, three and ten sixteenth inch. *Jack & Sue Davis Collection*

Upper Basin Bar, 99, five and one half inch metal key fob or tag which includes key, N W Stamp Works, St. Paul, Minn. *Francis Historic Collections*

END DRS JUNIP, Juniper Dorm, Mammoth Hot Springs, Yellowstone National Park, two and one quarter inch metal key to dormitory door, made by Schlage. *Francis Historic Collections*

Fountain Linen Room, 2, 89, copper metal key fob with key, one and six sixteenth inch. *Francis Historic Collections*

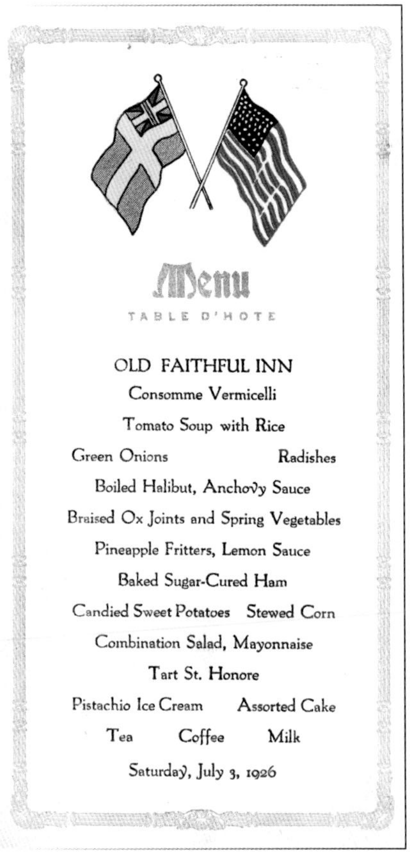

Menu
TABLE D'HOTE

OLD FAITHFUL INN
Consomme Vermicelli
Tomato Soup with Rice
Green Onions Radishes
Boiled Halibut, Anchovy Sauce
Braised Ox Joints and Spring Vegetables
Pineapple Fritters, Lemon Sauce
Baked Sugar-Cured Ham
Candied Sweet Potatoes Stewed Corn
Combination Salad, Mayonnaise
Tart St. Honore
Pistachio Ice Cream Assorted Cake
Tea Coffee Milk
Saturday, July 3, 1926

Menu, Table D'Hote, Old Faithful Inn, Saturday, July 3, 1926, six and fourteen sixteenth by three and ten sixteenth inch card. *Bob Reynolds Collection*

Lunch
Orange Juice Tomato Juice Cocktail
Consomme Celestine
Green Onions Radishes Dill Pickles
Spaghetti with Italian Meat Sauce, Parmesan
Roast Young Tom Turkey, Savory Dressing
Cranberry Sauce
Ragout of Veal, Parisienne Vegetables
Scrambled Eggs with Minced Ham & Green Peppers
Whipped Potatoes Fresh Garden Peas in Butter
Cold Boiled Ham with Potato Salad
Individual Combination Salad, Russian Dressing
Parker House Rolls
Apricot Pie
Cabinet Pudding Lime Sherbet
Spice Layer Cake
Tea Coffee Milk Iced Tea
Mammoth Hotel Sunday, August 15, 1937
YELLOWSTONE PARK, WYOMING

Lunch Menu, Sunday, August 15, 1937, Mammoth Hotel, Yellowstone Park, Wyoming, eight and one quarter by four and one eighth inch card. *Jay C Lyndes Family Collection*

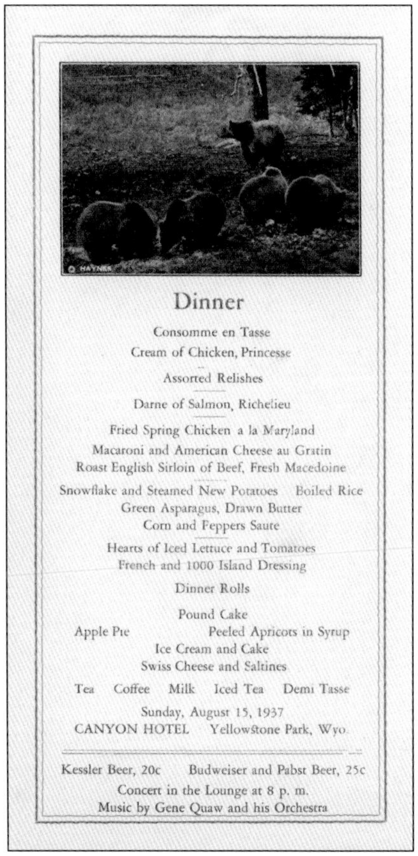

Dinner
Consomme en Tasse
Cream of Chicken, Princesse
Assorted Relishes
Darne of Salmon, Richelieu
Fried Spring Chicken a la Maryland
Macaroni and American Cheese au Gratin
Roast English Sirloin of Beef, Fresh Macedoine
Snowflake and Steamed New Potatoes Boiled Rice
Green Asparagus, Drawn Butter
Corn and Peppers Saute
Hearts of Iced Lettuce and Tomatoes
French and 1000 Island Dressing
Dinner Rolls
Pound Cake
Apple Pie Peeled Apricots in Syrup
Ice Cream and Cake
Swiss Cheese and Saltines
Tea Coffee Milk Iced Tea Demi Tasse
Sunday, August 15, 1937
CANYON HOTEL Yellowstone Park, Wyo.
Kessler Beer, 20c Budweiser and Pabst Beer, 25c
Concert in the Lounge at 8 p. m.
Music by Gene Quaw and his Orchestra

Dinner Menu, Sunday, August 15, 1937, Canyon Hotel, Yellowstone Park, Wyo, eight and one quarter by four and one eighth inch card, Concert in Lounge at 8 pm, Music by Gene Quaw and his Orchestra. *Jay C Lyndes Family Collection*

Program of Events
for July 5th

9:00 a.m. and 2:15 p.m. *FORMATION DRIVE*

Automobiles will leave for the Hot Springs, the Terraces and Buffalo Corral. Ascent during trip 550 feet. Distance 6 miles; fare $1.00. Guests desiring to make journey afoot will find guide in office to accompany them leaving at same time.

2:00 p.m. *SWIMMING AND DIVING CONTESTS*

1. 100-yard dash for men
2. 50-yard dash for girls
3. Under-water race for men
4. Fancy diving for girls
5. Fancy diving for men
6. Cigarette race for men and women

At Mammoth Camp Plunge

8:30 p.m. *GRAND COSTUME BALL EN MASQUE*

Three prizes awarded to best talent, as follows: 1st. Best costumed lady. 2nd. Best costumed gentleman. 3rd. Best sustained couple.

At Mammoth Hotel and Mammoth Camp

Menu
TABLE D'HOTE

Chicken Gumbo, 1776 Clear Consomme, 1926

Olives Celery

Tenderloin of Silver Salmon, White Plains

Fancy Sweetbreads and Chicken in Patties, Saratoga

Orange Glace, LaFayette

New Peas, Valley Forge Cream Whipped Potatoes

Broiled Filet Mignon, Paul Revere

Hearts of Lettuce, Betsy Ross Dressing

Frozen Pudding, Mon Desire

Fresh Strawberries, Mousse

Petit Mignardises

American Cheese and Saltines

Tea Coffee Milk Iced Tea

MAMMOTH HOTEL *Sunday, July 4th, 1926*

Figure 1. The Fourth Of July, 1926, Mammoth Hotel, Yellowstone Park Wyoming, 1 page folded, six and one half by four- and three-quarter inch Menu and Program of Events. *Francis Historic Collections.* **Figure 2.** The Fourth Of July, 1926, Mammoth Hotel, Yellowstone Park Wyoming, 1 page folded, six and one half by four- and three-quarter inch Menu and Program of Events interior. *Francis Historic Collections.* **Figure 3.** Coffee Shop, Yellowstone Park Company, menu, eleven by eight- and one-half inch, Rise and Shine breakfast menu. *Francis Historic Collections* **Figure 4.** Canyon Lodge Lunch Menu, Snap Shots, Yellowstone National Park 1930s, eight and one half by seven-inch laminated menu, circa 2019, CL/11L, Xanterra Parks & Resorts. *Francis Historic Collections.* **Figure 5.** Old Faithful Inn, Yellowstone National Park, Lunch Menu, 1 page folded, 2019. *Francis Historic Collections*

Y.P. Hotels, fifty-eight and one half by nineteen- and one-half inch cloth flag, grommets missing, Yellowstone Park. *Jay C Lyndes Family Collection*

Yellowstone Park Company, five inch by six- and three-quarter inch waxed butter tub, No 3 Lilly Tub, Made in USA by Lily - Tulip Cup Corporation, New York NY 73002. *Francis Historic Collections*

Yellowstone Park Hotels, one and one quarter inch button pin with bear in red, white and blue logo, The Whitehead & Hoag Co., Newark, N.J. *Jay C Lyndes Family Collection*

Yellowstone Park Association Hotels, five and one quarter inch red, white, and blue with bear sticker, 1907. *Jay C. Lyndes Family Collection*

Y P Co, 1 inch metal bear face shower token. *Francis Historic Collections*

Yellowstone Park Lodge, Shoe Cleaner cloth, fifteen by four and one eighth inch. *Francis Historic Collections*

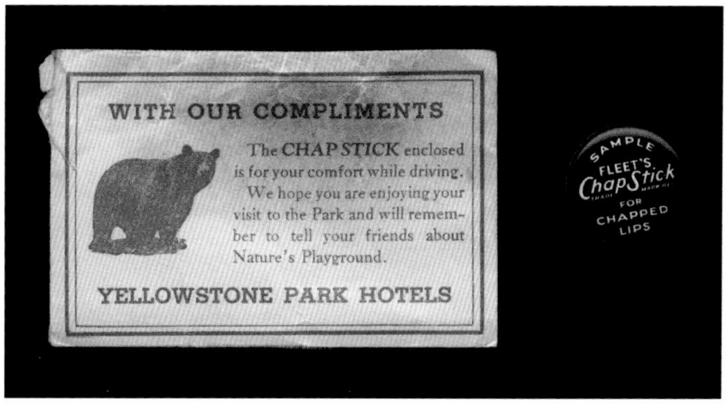

With Our Compliments, The Chapstick enclosed is for your comfort while driving. Yellowstone Park Hotels, three and three quarter by two and one quarter inch paper envelope. *Tom Murphy Collection*

Old Faithful Inn, Yellowstone, five by two- and one-half inch metal hanging ornament no maker. *Francis Historic Collections*

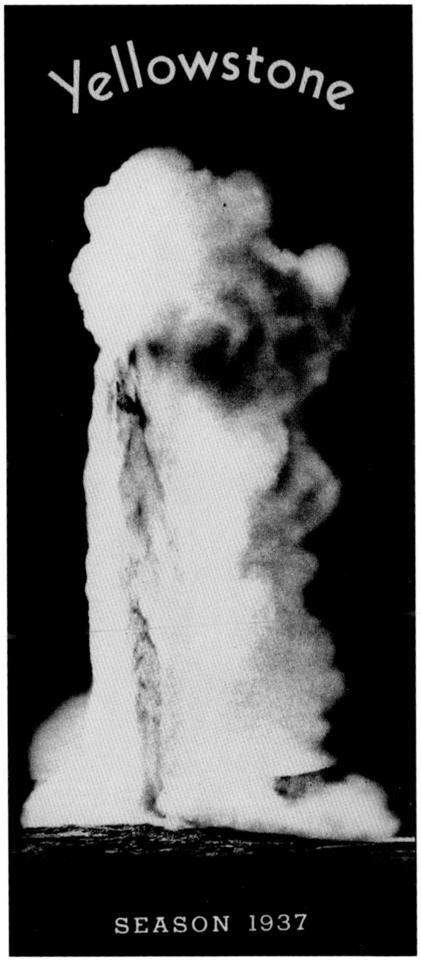

Yellowstone Park, Season 1941, Folder B, Hotels - Lodges - Tourist Cabins, Yellowstone Park Company, Y.P.Co., 9 x 4 inch brochure. *Bob Reynolds Collection*

Yellowstone, Season 1937, Yellowstone Park Company, Y.P.Co, 9 x 4 inch brochure, 11 pages. *Jay C. Lyndes Family Collection*

Yellowstone National Park, a world apart, Yellowstone Park Company, 1965, Folder prepared by Sage Advertising Service, Helena, Montana, 9 x 4 inch brochure. *Jay C. Lyndes Family Collection*

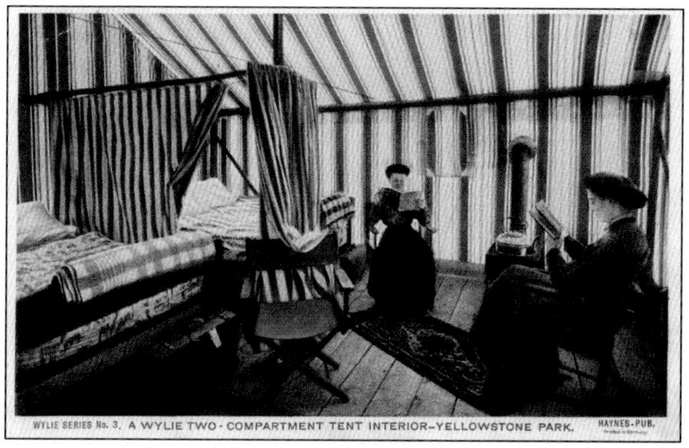

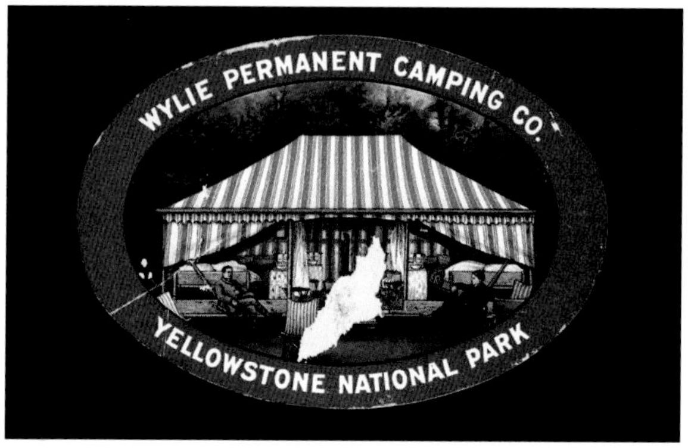

Figure 1. 9470. Ready to depart at Wylie Gibbon Lunch Camp, Yellowstone Park, Wyo., Pub. by The Acmegraph Co., Chicago, five and five sixteenth by three and six sixteenth inch post card. *Francis Historic Collections.* **Figure 2.** Wylie Series No. 3, A Wylie Two - Compartment Tent Interior - Yellowstone Park., Haynes -Pub, Printed in Germany, five and seven sixteenth by three and seven sixteenth inch post card. *Francis Historic Collections.* **Figure 3.** A Wylie Compartment Tent, Wylie's Camp Roosevelt, color postcard, Yellowstone Park - Wylie Permanent Camping Co., Series 4. *Francis Historic Collectibles.* **Figure 4.** Wylie Permanent Camping Co., Yellowstone National Park, three and fourteen sixteenth by two and ten sixteenth gummed advertising oval sticker. *Bob Reynolds Collection.* **Figure 5.** Wylie Permanent Camps., Yellowstone National Park., printed on #7 US Government Postal card, circa 1897, five and one half by three and one quarter inches. *Bob Reynolds Collection*

The Yellowstone News.

FOR FRIENDS OF THE "WYLIE WAY"

VOLUME 1—No. 1 | SPRING, 1915 | PRICE: YOUR GOOD WILL

PLAYING WITH THE GEYSERS AND BEARS

A Clever Story by One Who Was Never There

"HO, FOR YELLOWSTONE"

What Yellowstone Must Be Like

PARK GAME SHIPPED TO OTHER STATES

Col. Brett Tells About It in Annual Report

A GAME CENSUS

NOW FOUR WAYS TO YELLOWSTONE

A New Side-Trip Service from Butte, Mont.

THE LEADER OF THE "WYLIE WAY"

A Little Story About A. W. Miles

NO CHANGE IN RATES FOR 1915

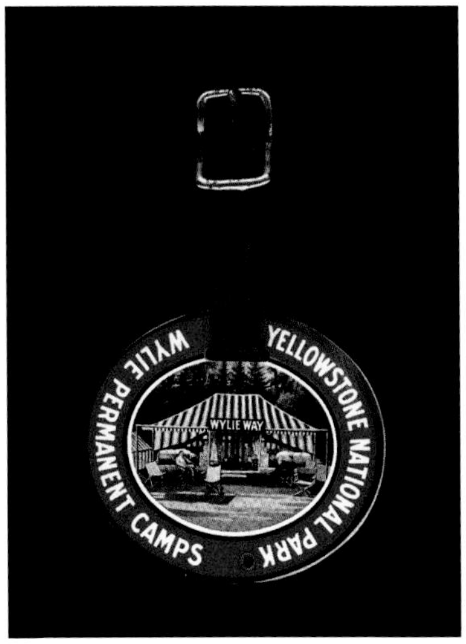

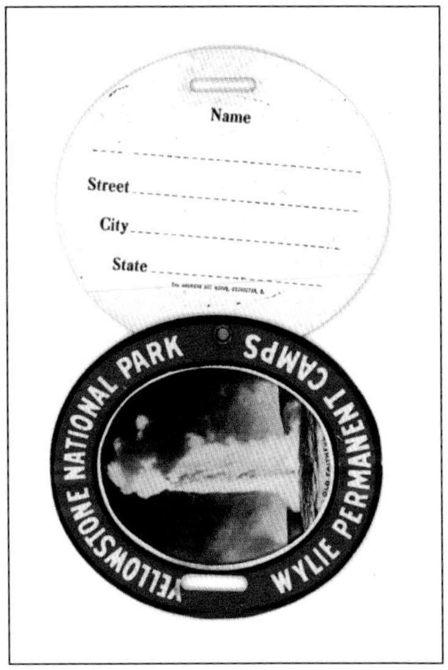

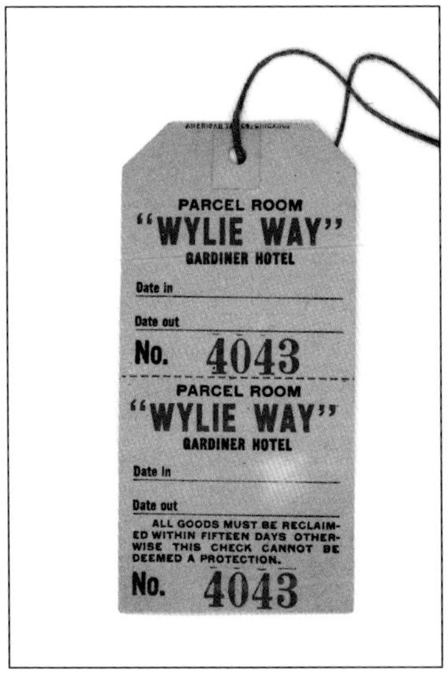

Figure 1. The Yellowstone News, For Friends of the "Wylie Way", Spring 1915, Volume 1 - No 1, 4-page newspaper, fifteen and one quarter by eleven and one quarter inch, Wylie Permanent Camping Co, Livingston, Montana, page 1. *Jay C. Lyndes Family Collection.* **Figure 2.** Wylie Permanent Camps, Yellowstone National Park, two and one quarter inch luggage or baggage celluloid tag, each two sided with various scenes, at least six different views including tent camp, Old Faithful Geyser, and mule deer. *Jay C. Lyndes Family Collection.* **Figure 3.** Wylie Permanent Camps, Yellowstone National Park, two and one quarter inch luggage or baggage celluloid tag, each two sided with various scenes, at least six different views including tent camp, Old Faithful Geyser, and mule deer. *Jay C. Lyndes Family Collection.* **Figure 4.** Wylie Permanent Camps, Yellowstone National Park, two and one quarter inch luggage or baggage celluloid tag each two sided with various scenes there are at least six different views including tent camp, Old Faithful Geyser, and mule deer, circa 1912 to 1916. *Bob Reynolds Collection.* **Figure 5.** Wylie Permanent Camps, Yellowstone National Park, two and one quarter inch luggage or baggage celluloid tag each two sided with various scenes, there are at least six different views including tent camp, Old Faithful Geyser, and mule deer, circa 1912 to 1916. *Bob Reynolds Collection.* **Figure 6.** Wylie Way, Parcel Room, Gardiner Hotel, No 4043, American Tag Co, Chicago, five and one quarter by two- and one-half inch, luggage tag. *Jay C. Lyndes Family Collection*

Yellowstone National Park, Wylie Permanent Camping Co, Park Season June 15 to Sept 15, 1908, A. W. Miles, President and Manager, eight and one half by four-inch brochure. *Jay C. Lyndes Family Collection*

Yellowstone National Park, Wylie Permanent Camping Co., thirty-page folded brochure, 1909, eight and one half by four inches. *Francis Historic Collections*

Yellowstone National Park, Wylie Permanent Camping Co., thirty-page folded brochure, 1910, eight and one half by four inches. *Francis Historic Collections*

"Wylie – Way", Yellowstone Park, A Pictorial Hand Book, Wylie Permanent Camping Co, Park Season June 15 to Sept 10, 1912, A. W. Miles, President and Manager, 9 x 4-inch brochure, 1 page folded. *Jay C. Lyndes Family Collection*

Yellowstone Park, "Wylie Way," 1916 Park Season June 15 to Sept 10. A. W. Miles, President and Manager, 9 x 4-inch brochure, Poole Bros Chicago. *Jay C. Lyndes Family Collection*

Yellowstone Park, "Wylie Way", Wylie Permanent Camping Co., one-page folded brochure, 1914, eight and one half by four inches. *Francis Historic Collections*

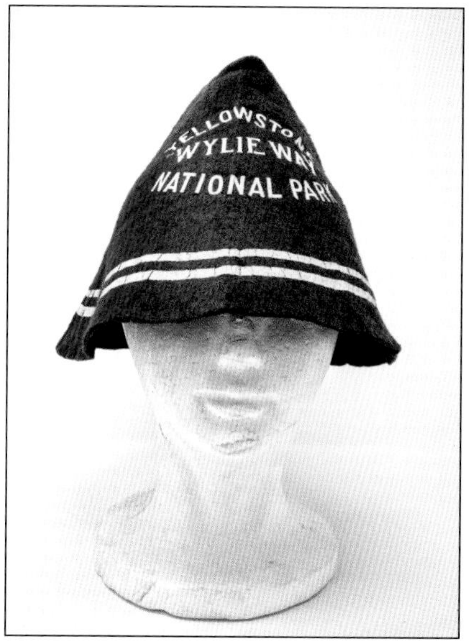

Wylie Way, Yellowstone National Park, Rittmiller, Barnes & Thompson, Chicago, Joy-Lid, Copyright 1914, blue coloration, thirteen by nine inch felt hat. *Francis Historic Collections*

Wylie Way, Yellowstone National Park, Rittmiller, Barnes & Thompson, Chicago, Joy-Lid, Copyright 1914, soft pastel red coloration, thirteen by nine inch felt hat. *Jay C. Lyndes Family Collection*

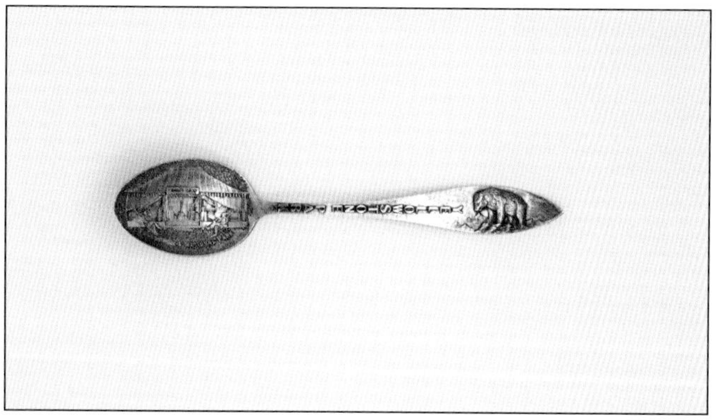

Bear with Yellowstone Park on handle, engraved Wylie Way, Yellowstone National Park in bowl, five- and one-half inch sterling spoon, Watson Company, Attleboro Mass, in business 1880 to 1955. *Jay C. Lyndes Family Collection*

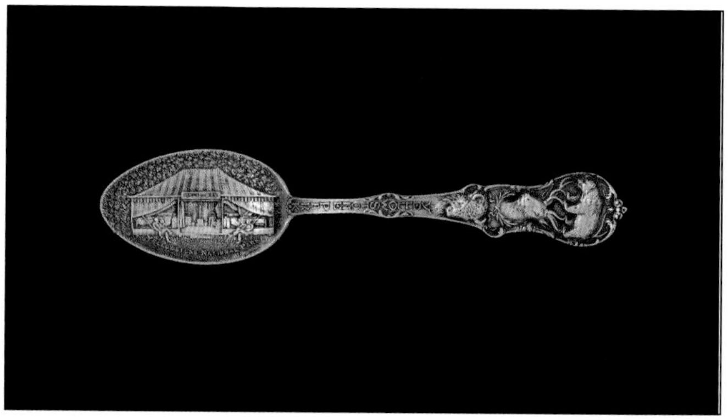

Bear, Staghorn & Bison handle, Wylie Way, Yellowstone National Park engraved in bowl, six-inch sterling spoon, Watson Company, Attleboro Mass, in business 1880 to 1955. *Jay C. Lyndes Family Collection*

Shaw & Powell Camping Co., Permanent Camps, Yellowstone National Park, Burley & Company, Hotel Dept., Chicago, P, five and three quarter by two- and one-half inch bowl. *Bob Reynolds Collection*

Shaw & Powell Camping Co, Permanent Camps, ten- and one-half inch platter. Burley & Company, Hotel Dept., Chicago P. *Jay C. Lyndes Family Collection*

Shaw & Powell Camping Co., Permanent Camps, Yellowstone National Park, three and one half by four-inch sugar bowl without lid, Burley & Company, Hotel Dept., Chicago, P makers mark on bottom. *Bob Reynolds Collection*

Shaw & Powell Camping Co., Permanent Camps, Yellowstone National Park, three and one eighth inch butter dish, Burley & Company, Hotel Dept., Chicago P. *Jack & Sue Davis Collection*

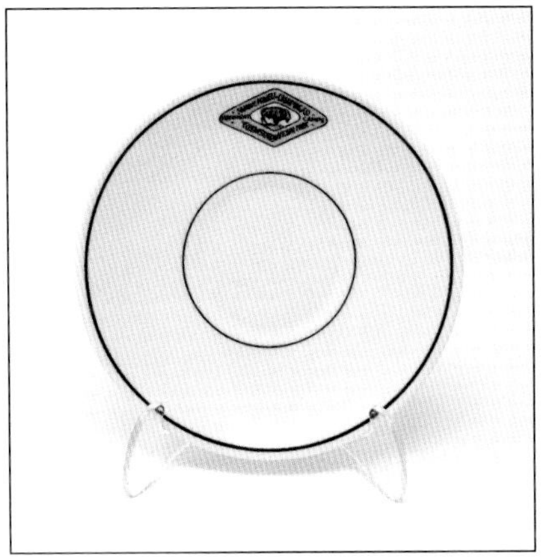

Shaw & Powell Camping Co., Permanent Camps, Yellowstone Park, 6-inch saucer, Burley & Company, Hotel Dept., Chicago P, 1862 Greenwood China Trenton NJ 1876. *Francis Historic Collection*

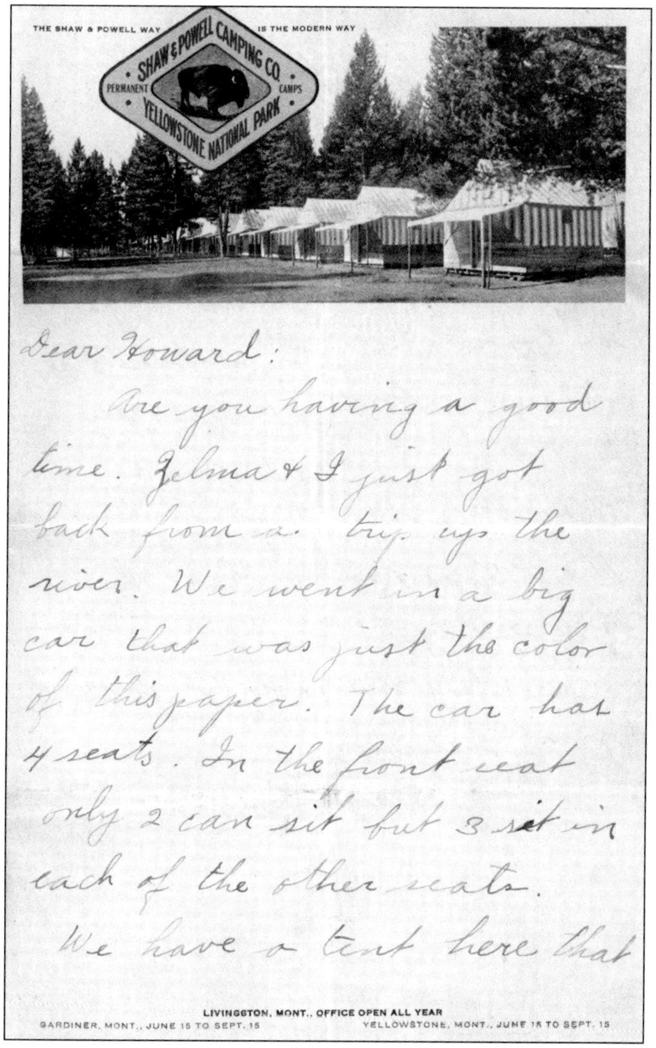

THE SHAW & POWELL WAY IS THE MODERN WAY

SHAW & POWELL CAMPING CO.
PERMANENT CAMPS
YELLOWSTONE NATIONAL PARK

Dear Howard:

Are you having a good time. Zelma & I just got back from a trip up the river. We went in a big car that was just the color of this paper. The car has 4 seats. In the front seat only 2 can sit but 3 sit in each of the other seats.

We have a tent here that

LIVINGSTON, MONT., OFFICE OPEN ALL YEAR
GARDINER, MONT., JUNE 15 TO SEPT. 15 YELLOWSTONE, MONT., JUNE 15 TO SEPT. 15

Shaw & Powell Camping Co., Permanent Camps, Yellowstone National Park, The Shaw & Powell Way Is the Modern Way, Livingston, Mont., Office Open All Year, Gardiner, Mont., June 15 to Sept 15, Yellowstone , Mont., eight and six sixteenth by five and six sixteenth inch letterhead. *Bob Reynolds Collection*

5 1-2 DAY TRIP $30.00 6 1-2 DAY TRIP $35.00

CAMPS ARE PUT UP EVERY NIGHT ON A GOOD CLEAN GRASSY CAMP GROUND ON THE BANKS OF A BEAUTIFUL STREAM AND IN SIGHT OF THE PRINCIPAL POINTS OF INTEREST.

A TRIP THRU

YELLOWSTONE NATIONAL PARK WITH

Shaw & Powell Camping Co.

A LOCAL CAMPING COMPANY THAT CANNOT BE EXCELLED FOR GIVING COMFORT AND ENJOYMENT TO THEIR TOURISTS

WE PERSONALLY CONDUCT EACH PARTY

ASK FOR GUIDE BOOKLET

Shaw & Powell Camping Co., - Livingston, Montana

A Trip Thru Yellowstone National Park with Shaw & Powell Camping Co., 5 1/2 Day Trip $30, 6 1/2 Day Trip $35, Camps Are Put Up Every Night on a Good Clean Grassy Camp Ground On The Bank Of A Beautiful Stream And In Sight Of The Principal Points Of Interest., We Personally Conduct Each Party - Ask For Guide Booklet- Shaw & Powell Camping Co., Livingston, Montana, on reverse: Table of Distances & Altitudes, four and one half by two and three quarter inch business card. *Bob Reynolds Collection*

A Trip Through the Park

Seven-Day Trip for $30.00.

An Entire New Outfit for Use in Conducting Parties Through the Park.

Other Arrangements at Reasonable Rates.

We Have Had Ten Years Experience in Handling Camping Parties

YOU SEE EVERY POINT OF INTEREST.
OUR OUTFITS ARE THE BEST.

OUR OUTFIT STARTS FROM CINNABAR.
HUNTING TRIPS A SPECIALTY.

SHAW & POWELL, Livingston, Montana.

A Trip Through the Park, Shaw & Powell, Livingston, Montana, We have had Ten Years Experience in Handling Camping Parties, four and one half by two- and three-quarter inch paper card. *Jay C. Lyndes Family Collection*

Shaw & Powell Camping Co., Permanent Camps, Yellowstone National Park, two and three quarter by two-inch gummed sticker. *Bob Reynolds Collection*

One of the Shaw & Powell Camping Cos., Permanent Camps, Yellowstone National Park, Livingston, Montana, three by two and one quarter inch double sided cellulite baggage or luggage tag, The American Art Works. *Jay C. Lyndes Family Collection*

Shaw & Powell Permanent Camps, Livingston, Montana, Yellowstone National Park, buffalo logo, fourteen sixteenth of an inch button pin. *Jay C. Lyndes Family Collection*

Shaw & Powell Camping Co., Livingston, Mont, 47, one and six sixteenth by one and five sixteenth inch luggage metal fob. *Bob Reynolds Collection*

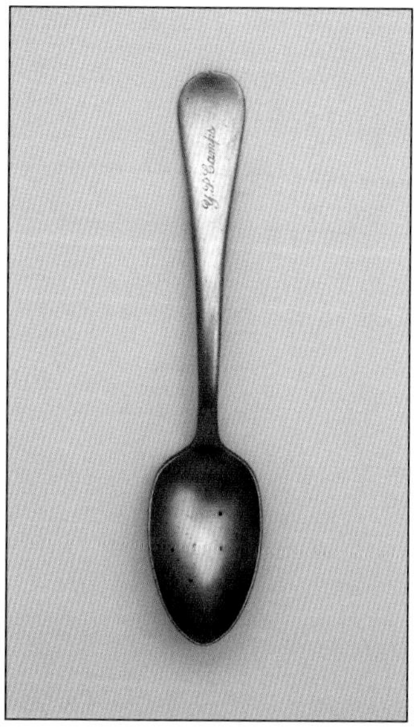

Figure 1. American Silver Co., Bristol and Waterbury, CT, 1901 to 1935, 1900 Windsor Pattern, YP Camps, seven and one half inch nickel silver fork. *Bob Reynolds Collection.* **Figure 2.** American Silver Co., Bristol & Waterbury, CT, in business 1901 to 1935. Wylie Way on handle, seven and one eighth inch nickel silver spoon. *Bob Reynolds Collection.* **Figure 3.** Y P Camps on handle, Dohrco Nickel, knife used in dining room, nine and one quarter inch. *Jay C. Lyndes Family Collection.* **Figure 4.** Y.P. Camps, eight and one quarter inch serving spoon, made by ASCO, nickel silver, American Silver Company, Bristol, Connecticut, in business from 1901 to 1935. *Francis Historic Collections.* **Figure 5.** Y.P. Camps, Yellowstone Park Camps, 6 inch spoon, made by HESCO-MEXICAN 6. *Francis Historic Collections*

Yellowstone Park, Yellowstone Park Camping Co, The Camp Way, Park Season, June 25 - September 15, 1918, 30-page booklet, 9 x 4 inches, A. W. Miles, President and Manager. *Jay C. Lyndes Family Collection*

Yellowstone Park, Yellowstone Park Camping Co, The Camp Way, Park Season, June 20 - September 15, 1919, 14-page booklet, 9 x 4 inches, A. W. Miles, President and Manager. *Jay C. Lyndes Family Collection*

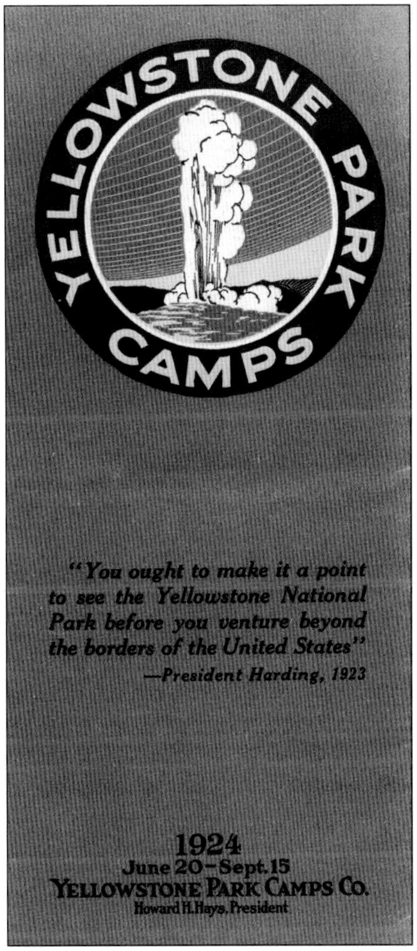

Yellowstone Park Camps, 1924, June 20 - Sept. 15, Yellowstone Park Camps Co., Howard H. Hays, President, 9 x 4-inch brochure. *Francis Historic Collection*

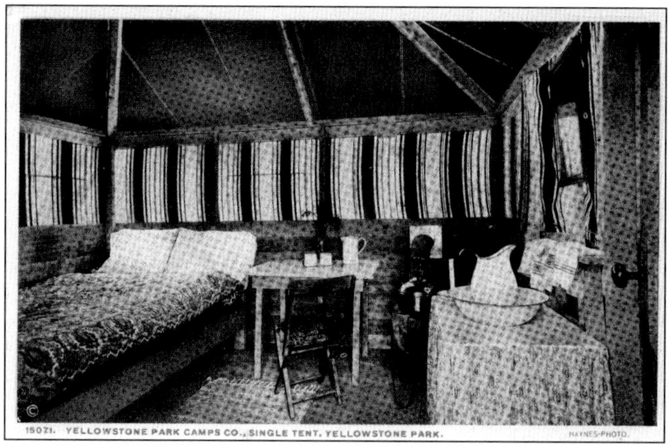

Yellowstone Park Camps Co., Single Tent, Yellowstone Park, Haynes-Photo, Published By Haynes, St. Paul, Official Photographer, Yellowstone National Park, Copyright By Haynes, St. Paul, five and six sixteenth by three- and one-half inch color post card. *Francis Historic Collection*

Yellowstone Park Camps

Automobile Tourists will find our diversified service convenient, enjoyable and economical.
Stop at our Main Camps for meals and lodgings, or live in our housekeeping tents
and take meals or lunches at our Cafeterias and Lunch Counters.

SIX MAIN CAMPS LOCATED NEAR THE MOST IMPORTANT WONDERS AND SCENIC ATTRACTIONS

MAMMOTH HOT SPRINGS—Facing the springs and with verandas affording an unsurpassed view of the gorgeously colored Terrace Mountain.

OLD FAITHFUL—In the Upper Geyser Basin, within a few rods of Old Faithful, the Giant, the Giantess, Grotto, and a dozen other world famous geysers.

YELLOWSTONE LAKE—On the beautiful Lake Shore, with lodges among the woods.

GRAND CANYON—Close to the Great Fall, amid the pines, and within a few steps of the Cayon's edge.

CAMP ROOSEVELT—On the Tower Falls road; a splendid place for saddle horse trips, to fish, rest, and see beaver, bear, buffalo, deer, elk, other Park animals.

SYLVAN PASS LODGE—The fine new lodge on the Cody road, located amid some of the most spectacular mountain scenery in America.

RATES—$4.50 per day, American plan. All meals, $1; lodging, $1.50. Children under eight, half rate; children in arms, free.

RATES AT SYLVAN PASS LODGE

Lunch, $1.50 per person; children under 8, half rate.

MAMMOTH SWIMMING POOL AT MAMMOTH CAMP

Enjoy the novelty and pleasure of a bath and swim in this new pool, with warm water from the famous Mammoth Hot Springs flowing constantly through it. Open days and evenings. Admission, suit and towel, 50c.

Barber shops at Mammoth, Old Faithful, Lake, and Grand Canyon Camps.

CAFETERIAS AND LUNCH COUNTERS

Three Cafeterias and Delicatessens located in the Public Automobile Camps at Old Faithful, West Thumb, Lake, (Fishing Bridge).

Lunch Counter and Delicatessen at Grand Canyon, near Public Automobile Camps.

Meals and lunches served at all Cafeterias and Lunch Counters. Hot cooked foods sold to be carried to your camp. Moderate prices for all service.

HOUSEKEEPING TENTS IN PUBLIC AUTOMOBILE CAMPS

Housekeeping Tents in Public Automobile Camps at Mammoth, Old Faithful, West Thumb, Lake, (Fishing Bridge), Grand Canyon.

Tent or cabin, occupied by one person, per day, 75c.

Tent or cabin, occupied by two or more persons, per day, each person, 50c.

Children under eight, half of above rates; children in arms, free.

Tents or cabins are available, furnished with the following equipment:

Single Tent or Cabin—One double bed stead, one bed spring, one stove, one wash stand, one table, one bench.

Double Tent or Cabin—Two double bed steads, two bed springs, one stove, two wash stands, two tables, two benches.

Persons using Housekeeping Tents may rent mattresses, blankets, sheets, pillows, pillow cases, towels, and ordinary kitchen articles.

GOVERNMENT FEE FOR AUTOMOBILES, $3.00

Operated by Yellowstone Park Camps Company

VERNON GOODWIN, President *Address:* Yellowstone Park, Wyoming E. H. MOORMAN, Gen. Mgr.

Camps Information including locations, rates and cafeterias and lunch counters plus housekeeping tents, verso: Map Of Yellowstone Park And Table Of Distances, Poole Bros., Chicago, 6207C, 8-12-24, 1927 guest usage, Yellowstone Park Camps Company, Vernon Goodwin, President, E. H. Moorman, Gen. Mgr., one page folded 9 x 8 inch. *Francis Historic Collections*

Yellowstone Park Camps, The Popular Service, four by two- and three-quarter inch paper sticker. *Jay C. Lyndes Family Collection*

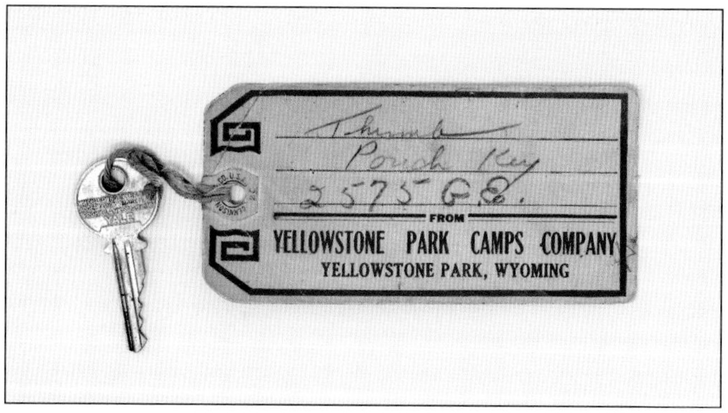

Yellowstone Park Camps Co., Yellowstone Park , Wyoming, luggage or baggage tag with Thumb Pouch key, 2575 G.E., four and three quarter by two and six sixteenth inch tag. *Jack & Sue Davis Collection*

Camping in Natures Wonderland, The Bryant Way, Bryant - Spence Tours, 457 - 459 Monadnock Block, Chicago, 1909, eight by four- and one-half inch booklet, 22 pages, cover. *Bob Reynolds Collection*

Yellowstone National Park, Safety First, The Old Faithful Camping Co., Printed by McKee PTG Co., Butte, W.N. and O.M. Hefferlin, 1915, 1 page folded, six and one half by three and one quarter inch brochure. *Francis Historic Collections*

A Trip Through The Yellowstone National Park, Marshall's Camping Transportation, Livingston, Mont, The Livingston Enterprise Print, five and three quarter by three- and one-half inch booklet, 11 pages. *Jay C. Lyndes Family Collection*

Visit Yellowstone National Park--
Nature's Wonderland

GARLAND BROS., Tourist Agents
1005 Third Avenue
NEAR MADISON
SEATTLE

SEE OTHER SIDE

$5 per Day Pays All the Cost!

For Transportation, Board and all Necessary Expenses.

If you love nature, you will prefer this to the ten dollar per day way.

$35 for the Seven Days' Tour

COACHING and CAMPING in YELLOWSTONE NATIONAL PARK

No extras of any kind required. Comfortable covered coaches, water-proof tents, good beds and everything to make the trip a lasting pleasure. The comforts of home combined with the delights of out door life.

We make reservations for camping parties entering Yellowstone Park nearly every day, FROM GARDINER on the north, via the Northern Pacific Railway, and FROM YELLOWSTONE on the west via the Oregon Short Line from Salt Lake, Ogden or Pocatello. Ask for booklet,

"CAMPING IN NATURE'S WONDERLAND"

GARLAND BROS., TOURIST AGENTS,
1005 THIRD AVE.

Camping In Yellowstone, $5.00 Per Day "The Bryant Way", Visit Yellowstone National Park -- Nature's Wonderland, Garland Bros., Tourist Agents, 1005 Third Avenue Near Madison, Seattle, 5 x 3-inch card. *Francis Historic Collections*

Northern Pacific, Yellowstone Park Line, Special Train To Yellowstone National Park, September 1913, six and ten sixteenth inch chain brooch pin with ribbon, Mrs. F. P. Copper, Western Badge & Novelty Co., John A Lethert, Prop., Manufacturers of Badges, Banners Buttons, Flags, Souvenirs, Mirrors, Etc., St Paul, Minn. *Bob Reynolds Collection*

Cody Road thru Yellowstone Park, Frost & Richard, Cody, Wyoming, Licensed Guides & Hunters, Yellowstone Park And Big Game Country, eight and fourteen sixteenth by four-inch brochure, 32 pages, McGuire Printing Co., Denver, Colo. *Jay C. Lyndes Family Collection*

Personally Escorted Tours, Yellowstone National Park, Roth Tours, Main and First Streets, Marshalltown, Iowa, 9 x 4-inch brochure, 1 page folded, circa 1920s. *Bob Reynolds Collection*

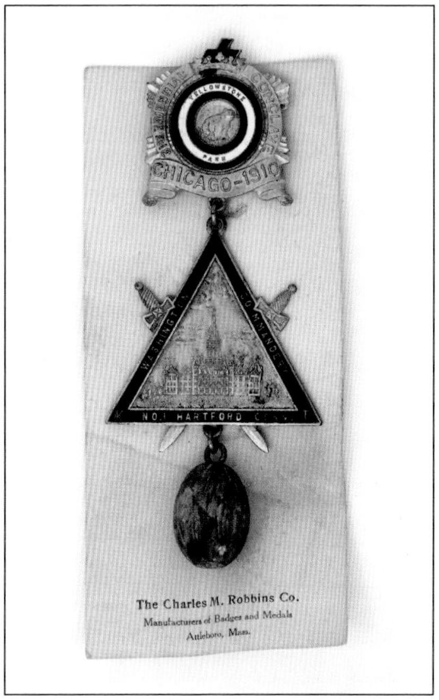

Yellowstone Park, Vacation Tours, 1916, A Magazine About Escorted Trips to and through Yellowstone under the Leadership of Competent Conductors, seven and one half by five and one quarter inch booklet, 16 pages, Poole Bros, Chicago. *Jay C. Lyndes Family Collection*

1910, 31st Triennial Conclave, Washington Commandery, No. 1 Hartford, Conn., Knights of Columbus, four and three quarter by two-inch total, brooch pins on original card, Charles M. Robbins Co., Manufacturers of Badges and Medals, Attleboro, Mass. *Bob Reynolds Collection*

Yellowstone National Park Tour, one- and one-half inch round bear pin back. *Francis Historic Collections*

Artwork

Grand Canyon, YNP, Punch Bowl and base, T&V Limoges Depose, France, hand painted, fourteen by nine- and one-half inch. *Jay C. Lyndes Family Collection*

Unsigned T&V studio painted 14.5-inch-high urn, Old Faithful Y.N.P., circa 1910. *Lancaster Yellowstone Collection*

Yellowstone Limoges by Tresseman & Vogt*

Larry and Thea Lancaster

When reflecting on their Yellowstone souvenirs, many collectors consider their hand-painted Tressemann & Vogt Limoges porcelain to be among their most cherished items. This disquisition briefly reviews the history of porcelain-painting in the United States, the history of Tressemann[1] & Vogt (T&V) and then discusses the T&V Limoges souvenir-pieces found in Yellowstone collections.

The full history of painting on porcelain[2] stretches back to ancient times, but the art form did not materially intersect with American history until the 1860's. It was in that decade that the European porcelain manufacturers found a ready market for their wares in the United States. The driving force for this market was the American woman, who had either embraced china painting as a hobby or found employment in the thriving cottage-industry that developed around the art.

Among the top manufacturers which shipped hard-paste Limoges to American shores during the golden age of china-painting (1860-1920) was the French company Tressemann & Vogt. The company, established in 1882 in the Limoges region of France, decorated white-ware blanks made by other manufacturers and exported those decorated pieces to the United States. In 1891, the company expanded into manufacturing its own white-ware for decoration and exportation.

The France-based T&V Company had a New-York-based partner, Vogt & Dose, run by Charles Vogt, the brother of Gustave Vogt, owner of the French operations. Vogt & Dose served as the Unites States imports side of the business, receiving both decorated pieces and undecorated blanks from France. The decorated pieces were marketed and sold by Vogt & Dose directly to various retail outlets around the United States. The blanks were marketed and sold "as is" to the amateur china-painting market or were decorated in the Vogt & Dose's New York studio before being marketed and sold to the retail outlets. The T&V/Vogt & Dose partnership continued until 1907, when Charles Vogt sold his side of the business. T&V remained in business in France until Gustave Vogt sold his side of the business in 1919 to Martial Raynaud.

Yellowstone T&V souvenir pieces held in collections today are classified into three categories: (1) T&V white-ware pieces decorated with amateur paintings; (2) T&V white-ware pieces decorated with T&V studio paintings; and (3) non-T&V white-ware pieces decorated with T&V studio paintings.

The earliest known Yellowstone T&V Limoges pieces are those painted by amateur painters. As a class, amateur-painted pieces bear one of the two T&V factory manufacturing-marks applied under the glaze on the bottom of the piece. Because these pieces were not decorated in a factory, this category of Limoges lacks a factory studio-decoration mark.

An excellent example of early amateur-painted Limoges is a set of five, 9.25-inch plates painted by an amateur known today only by the initials "K.D.P." This set pictorially captures the camping spots occupied by the artist's party as they traveled north to south through Yellowstone in the summer of 1894.

The popularity of painting Yellowstone scenes on T&V white-ware remained strong with amateurs throughout the golden age. As evidence of this continued interest, is a very large (11"x16.5") untitled T&V manufactured plaque painted in the latter part of the golden age. The painting, exeucted by Zula S. Rimer (1890-1941)[3], is a copy of the important Haynes Yellowstone photograph #16343. The photo was taken in 1916 by Haynes employee, Elliott W. Hunter, and copyrighted by J. E. Haynes in 1917. When it was first published, Haynes titled the photo "Babes in the Wood." In 1920, Haynes retitled the image "The Mother Bear," and then, circa-1930, he re-titled the image for a third time to "Madonna in the Wild."[4] Since the photograph was taken in 1916, the date of the untitled painting on the Limoges is post-1916, placing it in the last part of the golden age. It is interesting to note that the manufacturer's mark on the white-ware plaque is of the 1892-1907 era, making the white-ware much older than the painting. Because the piece was decorated by an amateur, it has no factory studio-mark.

Perhaps due to the success of the 1909 Seattle World's Fair, which nearly doubled attendance to Yellowstone, or for some other business reason, T&V decided to launch its own factory-decorated "Yellowstone Line" around 1910. This Line, the second category of T&V Yellowstone Limoges, is composed of 15 known different pottery shapes, each decorated with a popular Park scene. Each scene, six of which are known, graces more than one shape of pottery. The white-ware mark on the pottery is either the early 1892-1907 era mark or the later era mark of 1907-1919. Because these pieces were painted in a T&V factory studio, they also bear a T&V studio-decoration mark, applied on top of the glazing on the underside of the piece. In all cases, the decoration mark is the one used for pieces painted from 1907 to 1919. Unfortunately, there is no way to determine if the decoration was painted in the T&V French studio or in the Vogt & Dose New York studio. In general, there is also no way to determine who painted the images as only a few of the pieces are signed and there is no known corporate documentation listing company artists.

The third category of T&V souvenir-china is composed of pieces having a T&V studio-decoration applied to white-ware manufactured by a company other than T&V. These pieces bear a non-T&V manufacturer's white-ware mark paired with a T&V studio mark. A fine example belonging to this category is a signed plaque entitled "The Great Falls of the Yellowstone. Y.N.P." The back of the plaque displays the T&V studio-decoration mark and a manufacturer's mark from Latrille Freres, a French company which made white-ware from 1899 to 1913.

Theres is little or no extant documentation giving evidence as to which retailers carried and sold T&V Yellowstone Limoges. An examination of Park concessionaire inventory-records shows no listing of Limoges pottery. This search has included the Canyon Art Shop located in the Grand Canyon Hotel and the Art Shop in the Mammoth Hotel. However, based on the number of pieces collectors have discovered in the gateway communities, there is reason to believe these *objets d'art* were indeed sold in the greater Yellowstone region. In addition, still affixed to one surviving piece (12.5-inch charger) is a "Pitkin & Brooks" department store tag. ("Pitkin & Brooks" was a Chicago firm that operated from 1872 to 1938 and made a business of importing and decorating Limoges.) The tag gives solid proof that, while likely sold around the Park, Yellowstone Limoges was also retailed in at least one large metropolitan center.

Tressemann & Vogt was not the only porcelain company in this early era to leverage Yellowstone's natural beauty as a way of bolstering its financial bottom line. Other companies such as Wheelock (USA), the Limoges China Company (USA), Bauer Rosenthal & Company (Germany) and Victoria (Austria) produced porcelain products decorated with Yellowstone scenes. While these companies vied for the Yellowstone-market dollar in porcelain, they failed to capture significant market shares, due largely to the lack of the quality and breadth found in the T&V product line. Even today, Yellowstone collectors recognize this distinction and place a premium on Tressemann & Vogt porcelain.

[1] Alternate spelling "Tressemanes" exists.
[2] Porcelain is one of the three forms of pottery, earthenware and stoneware being the other two. An excellent discussion on porcelain and its characteristics as compared to the other forms of pottery can be found in Mary Frank Gaston's *Collector's Encyclopedia of Limoges Porcelain*, Third Edition, pages 9-18.
[3] Commonwealth of Pennsylvania; Department of Health; Bureau of Vital Statistics, Certificate of Death Record #24830 for Zula R. Rimer.
[4] *Haynes Product Catalogues -1876-1967*, by Laurence H. Lancaster, 2016.

About Larry and Thea Lancaster

Larry and Thea Lancaster have a life-long connection with Yellowstone that began in the early 1970s when, as college students, they both worked in the Park during summers. As a result of this connection to the Park, in the 1980s they began their "Lancaster Yellowstone Collection," an archive with an emphasis on research material. Over time, they have continued to develop their collection as well as to write and lecture on the Park. Larry is a contributor to the *Yellowstone History Journal* and the author of *Haynes Product Catalogues – 1876 to 1967*, a comprehensive guide to Haynes products. His latest work, *Yellowstone Travel Posters – The First 100 Years*, is scheduled for release in 2022.

Larry and Thea live in Tulsa, Oklahoma, where they have resided for the last thirty years. They have two daughters, Dr. Amanda Goodwin and Dr. Emily Boldrin, and four grandchildren.

Side 1: Unsigned T&V studio painted 14.5-inch-diameter punch bowl, The Great Falls of the Yellowstone, Y.N.P., circa 1910. *Lancaster Yellowstone Collection*

Side 2: Unsigned T&V studio painted 14.5-inch-diameter punch bowl, Grand Canon, Y.N.P., circa 1910. *Lancaster Yellowstone Collection*

Unsigned T&V studio painted 2.375-inch-high cup and 5.75-inch-diameter saucer. Kepler's Cascade, Y.N.P., circa 1910. *Lancaster Yellowstone Collection*

Unsigned T&V studio painted 6.25-inch-high cider pitcher, Kepler's Cascade, Y.N.P., circa 1910. *Lancaster Yellowstone Collection*

Unsigned T&V studio painted 6-inch-high tobacco jar, Old Faithful, Y.N.P., circa 1910. *Lancaster Yellowstone Collection*

Unsigned T&V studio painted 4.88-inch-wide x 2.75-inch-high powder jar with lid, Grand Canyon, Y.N.P., circa 1910. *Lancaster Yellowstone Collection*

Signed by Fesiiez, 13.5-inch x 10-inch T&V framed painting, The Great Falls of the Yellowstone. *Jay C. Lyndes Family Collection*

Jula (Zula?) S. Rimer painted 11-inch-wide x 16.5-inch-high T&V plaque, makers stamp on bottom. Image based on Haynes' photograph #16343 "Babes in the Woods," circa 1917. *Lancaster Yellowstone Collection*

Unsigned T&V studio painted 7.5-inch-wide x 5-inch-high dresser tray, The Great Falls of the Yellowstone, Y.N.P., circa 1910. *Lancaster Yellowstone Collection*

Old Faithful Geyser YNP T V Limoges twelve- and one-half inch china plate hand painted France Depose Tressman Voight with makers stamp on reverse circa 1907 to 1919 Yellowstone Park. *Jack & Sue Davis Collection*

K.D.P painted 9.25-inch-diameter T&V plate, Yanceys, Yellowstone Park August 1894. *Lancaster Yellowstone Collection*

K.D.P painted 9.25-inch-diameter T&V plate, Lower Pacific Creek Camp September 1894. *Lancaster Yellowstone Collection*

K.D.P painted 9.25-inch-diameter T&V plate, Pacific Creek Camp September 1894. *Lancaster Yellowstone Collection*

K.D.P painted 9.25-inch-diameter T&V plate, Camp on Slough Creek, Hell-roaring River, July 1894. *Lancaster Yellowstone Collection*

Unsigned T&V studio painted 10.25-inch-diameter plate, Liberty Cap, Mammoth Hot Springs, Y.N.P., circa 1910. *Lancaster Yellowstone Collection*

Unsigned T&V studio painted 8.25-inch-diameter plate, Golden Gate, Y.N.P., circa 1907 to 1919. *Lancaster Yellowstone Collection*

T&V decoration mark used between 1907 and 1919. *Lancaster Yellowstone Collection*

T&V manufacturer's underglaze mark used between 1907 and 1919. *Lancaster Yellowstone Collection*

Entrance Arch at Gardiner, Montana, original pencil art work on heavy paper, 1910, north entrance to Yellowstone National Park. *Francis Historic Collections*

Elk during winter in Lamar Valley, Yellowstone National Park, 18 x 12-inch original oil painting, J. Inman artist Billings, MT. *Francis Historic Collections*

The Falls, Jack Beauchamp (1906-1957), signed, original serigraph or silk screen print, nine and one half by eight inches. *Bob Reynolds Collection*

Lower Falls from Artist Point, Grand Canyon of the Yellowstone, original oil painting by Carl Tolpo on August 4 to 5, 1953, 10am to 2pm, 16 x 12 inch, purchased on June 25, 2019 from his son, Vincent Tolpo. *Francis Historic Collections*

Yellowstone Falls from below Point Lookout, No. 733, Aug. 18, 1885, J. E. Stuart (1852-1941), original framed sketch oil painting in color, art 14 x 22 inches, frame twenty-eight and one quarter by twenty and one quarter inches. *Jay C. Lyndes Family Collection*

Great Falls of the Yellowstone from Below, framed color oil on board original art, Herbert W. Brackmeir, 1932, frame twenty-three by eighteen and one eighth inch, painting nineteen by fourteen- and one-half inch. *Jay C. Lyndes Family Collection*

Old Faithful Geyser during eruption, Upper Geyser Basin, hand painted original art, by M. J. Bauer, frame 35 x 29 inches, art twenty-three and one half by twenty-nine- and one-half inches. *Francis Historic Collections*

The Grand Canyon of the Yellowstone, framed original oil on canvas, by F. H. Cutting, 1938, frame thirty-five by twenty-nine- and three-quarter inches, artwork 25 x 30 inches. *Jay C. Lyndes Family Collection*

Elk along river with thermal background, Yellowstone Park, framed color original oil painting by Julie Jeppsen, frame forty-two and one half by nineteen- and one-half inch, painting thirty-seven and one half by fifteen- and one-half inches. *Francis Historic Collections*

Yellowstone Park Transportation bus with park visitors at Liberty Cap, Mammoth Hot Springs. Original artwork by James Reed, painted for the 150th birthday of Yellowstone National Park, 24 x 12 inch. *Bob Reynolds Collection*

The "Thunder Rolled" by Kenneth Yarus, Yellowstone, 2018, original oil on board, Lower Falls, frame: 17 x 14-inch, painting: 12 x 9 inch. *Francis Historic Collections*

Yellowstone, three and seven sixteenth by two- and one-half inch original painting by Ray Dicken, 2021, park visitors with Lower Falls and Grand Canyon of the Yellowstone. *Francis Historic Collections*

Old Faithful Geyser original oil on canvas painting Anne Van Briggle Ritter circa 1924 twenty-two and three quarter by eighteen- and three-quarter inch frame Yellowstone Park. *Jack & Sue Davis Collection*

Old Faithful Inn, Yellowstone National Park, 36 x 24-inch heavy metal sign, no maker. *Bob Reynolds Collection*

Yellowstone, For the benefit and enjoyment of the people... Copyright Gary Carter, 1997, frame: forty-two and one half by thirty-inch, print: thirty-four and three quarter by twenty-two- and one-half inch poster. *Bob Reynolds Collection*

Forty Winks, bear cub in tree, Copyright Olive Fell (1896-1980), framed color print, frame: 12 x 10-inch, print: eight and one half by six inches. *Jay C. Lyndes Family Collection*

Yellowstone Falls & Us, Olive Fell (1896-1980), signed print, nine by seven- and one-half inch, hand printed by artist. *Jack & Sue Davis Collection*

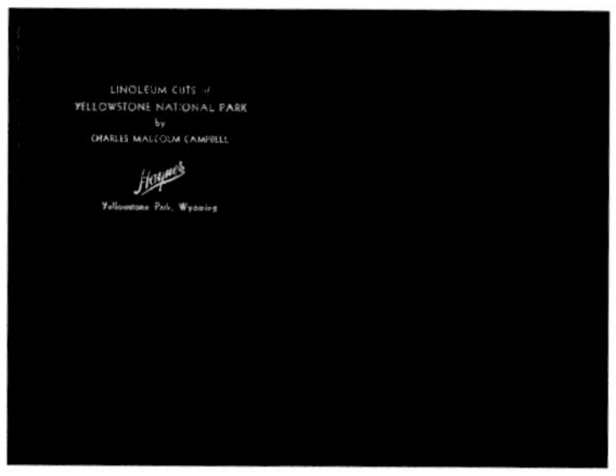

Linoleum Cuts of Yellowstone National Park by Charles Malcolm Campbell (1905-1985), Haynes, Yellowstone Park, Wyoming, fourteen and three quarter by eleven- and three-quarter inch folder for five art prints. *Francis Historic Collections*

Rotten Logging, Olive Fell (1896-1980), signed print, nine by seven- and one-half inch, hand printed by artist. *Jack & Sue Davis Collection*

"The Three Bears," Original Etching, C.E. Johnson (1866-1906), eight and one quarter by six-inch print. *Jack & Sue Davis Collection*

150 Feet, Original Etching, Yellowstone National Park, C.E. Johnson (1866-1906), eight and one quarter by six and two sixteenth inch. *Jack & Sue Davis Collection*

Greetings, Yellowstone Park, five and seven sixteenth by four and six sixteenth inch paper card. *Jack & Sue Davis Collections*

STANDING BEAR. Linoleum Cut by Charles Malcolm Campbell (1905-1985), Copyright Haynes Inc, Yellowstone Park, Wyoming, fourteen and one half by eleven- and one-half inch art print. *Francis Historic Collections*

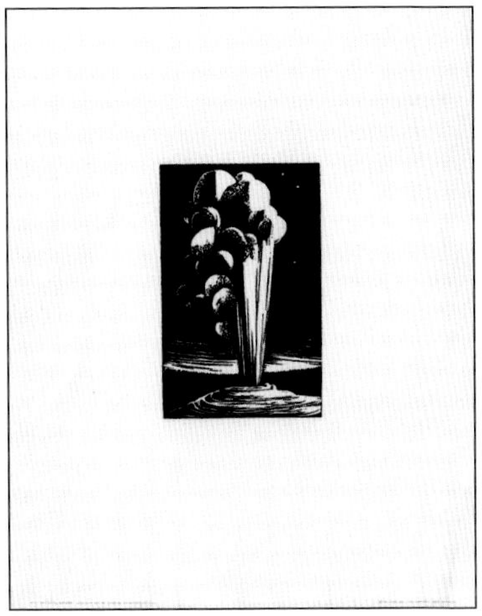

OLD FAITHFUL GEYSER. Linoleum Cut by Charles Malcolm Campbell (1905-1985), Copyright Haynes Inc, Yellowstone Park, Wyoming, fourteen and one half by eleven- and one-half inch art print. *Francis Historic Collections*

Old Faithful, original serigraph or silk screen print signed by Jack Beauchamp, (1906-1957), 10 x 8 inch, 1930s. *Francis Historic Collections*

Grand Canyon of the Yellowstone with Great Falls, by Thomas Moran (1837-1926), framed color print, frame: twenty-four and one quarter by twenty and one quarter inch, print: 16 x 20 inch. *Jay C. Lyndes Family Collection*

Terraces, Mammoth Hot Springs, Yellowstone Park, Copyright 1910, By M. Boettiger, Germany, raised card stock, framed under glass, print: twenty-three and one half by eleven- and one-half inch. *Bob Reynolds Collection*

Northern Pacific Railroad, The Dining Car Train between the East and Yellowstone National Park and Pacific Coast, Chas. S. Fee, Genl Pass Agt., St. Paul, Minn., Printed by Goes & Quansel, Chicago, circa 1879 to 1890, print: 21 x 13-inch, glass frame: twenty-three and one half by thirty-one- and one-half inch. *Jay C. Lyndes Family Collection*

December Evening, Old Faithful Inn, Limited Edition 186 / 275, Robert Spannering, Copyright 1989, framed color print, frame: 24 x 20-inch, art: fifteen and one quarter by eleven and one quarter inch. *Francis Historic Collections*

Old Faithful and Inn, Standard Oil Company of California, framed color print, frame: 10 x 8 inches. *Jay C. Lyndes Family Collection*

YELLOWSTONE - PARK, Ludwig Hohlwein, Munchen, Printed by G. Schuh & Co., Munich, Bavaria, sixty five and ten sixteenth by fifty-two inch frame and forty-seven and one third by thirty-six inch poster, 1910, Yellowstone Park. *Bob Reynolds Collection*

Books

Historic Yellowstone Park hardcover books. Jay C. Lyndes Family Collection, Bob Reynolds Collection, and Francis Historic Collections

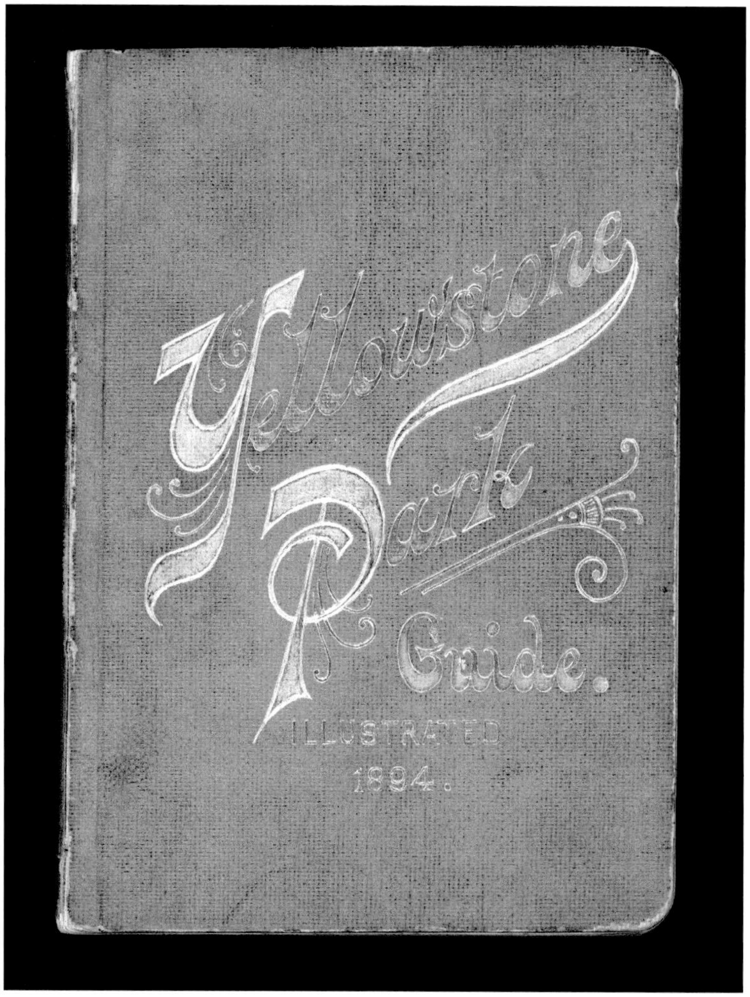

Yellowstone Park Guide, Illustrated, 1894, six and ten sixteenth by four and fourteen sixteenth inch book, 131 pages plus 4 blank pages for notes, By A.B. Guptill, Illustrated And Published By F.J. Haynes, Official Photographer N.P.R.R., 392 Jackson Street, St Paul, Minn., H.L. Collins Co., Printers, Binders, Engravers, St. Paul. *Bob Reynolds Collection*

Yellowstone Books

Leslie J. Quinn

While collecting Yellowstone memorabilia is an addiction that is safer for one's long-term health than some other addictions (heroin comes to mind), it too can prove detrimental to one's personal life, as well as just as expensive in the long run. Some of us have found that restricting ourselves to a subset of these collectibles can keep a marriage stable and the mortgage paid. For me, that subset is rare and antiquated Yellowstone books.

Books have a couple of things going for them as items for a Yellowstone collector. First, compared to many other collectibles, you can actually do things with books. Intellectual curiosity is rewarded by reading them, and if you would like to gain authority on the history of the Park, books are the best avenue towards this. Also, if you are (like many of us) on the clumsy side, you'll be happier picking up that copy of John H. Raftery's *The Story of the Yellowstone* (McKee Printing Company Press, Butte, MT, 1912) that fell on the kitchen floor rather than the remains of one of Andrew Wald's "sand bottles" suffering the same fate. (I personally do such delicate items a great favor by not collecting them.)

Getting Started

If you head to your local antiquarian bookseller (or to eBay, or to the better internet book sites like abe.com), you'll be able to find a book to get you started, namely the *Haynes Guide*. This famous guidebook was first published and illustrated by Frank J. Haynes in 1890 and revised editions were issued almost annually through 1966. Frank Jay Haynes (1853-1921) and his son Jack Ellis Haynes (1884-1962) were the Park's official photographers from 1883 to 1962.

Because the *Haynes Guide* was updated almost every year, the books chronicle changes to the Park's landscape that would otherwise be lost (from no one paying attention or writing about it). The text was authored by Albert Brewer Guptill 1890-1909, by Frank Jay Haynes 1910-1915, and by Jack Ellis Haynes 1916-1962.

Titles varied over the years from *Practical Guide to Yellowstone National Park* in 1890 to *All About Yellowstone Park* (1892-93) to *Haynes Guide Handbook of Yellowstone Park*. The guidebook was published annually, except that there were no editions in 1891, 1895, 1901, 1911, 1917-18, 1925, 1931-33, 1937-

38, 1941, 1943-45, 1950, 1960, 1963, and 1965--and two editions were published in 1946. *All About Yellowstone Park* was issued in 1892 and 1893, and apparently the only difference between the two is what date is stamped (not in ink, but drilled holes) on the lower front cover. While there was no edition published after the 1916 that contained a new date on the title page until 1919, there were in fact changes made to the 1916 text for publication in the two intervening years, each distinct, and these constitute de facto 1917 and 1918 variant editions (and a real rarity is the 1917 variant of the 1915 *Haynes Guide*). The same is true in 1937, which contained a new (and dated) map in the back that separates it from the first (true) 1936 edition. Haynes may have been caught short of books in 1946, as he issued a second printing, clearly marked as such.

The fun thing about collecting *Haynes Guides* is that the later ones (post World War II) may be had inexpensively, and just paging through the guide can pass enjoyable hours. The between-the-World-Wars copies run generally twice as much as the later ones (and hardbacks more than soft), early 20th century ones pricier still, and those of the 19th century may easily run many hundreds of dollars. But every one is a treasure and offers an unmatched look into the Park's early history. After Jack Ellis Haynes's death in 1962, a few more editions were published, and then the Haynes photo shops were sold to Hamilton Stores, Inc.

Others besides Haynes issued guidebooks to Yellowstone. The quality of the guide seems to be of less influence to its price nowadays than does its rarity (while lack of sales of the poor-quality guides would influence their rarity, and therefore price, today). Other quality guides include Philetus W. Norris's *The Calumet of the Coteau* (J. B. Lippincott, Philadelphia, 1883), William Wallace Wylie's *Yellowstone National Park; or the Great American Wonderland, a complete description of all the wonders of the park, together with distances, altitudes, and such other information as the tourist or general reader desires* (Ramsey, Millett, & Hudson, Kansas City, MO, 1882), Reau Campbell's *Campbell's New Revised Complete Guide and Descriptive Book of the Yellowstone Park* (published 1909, 1913, 1914, and 1923), and *Hamilton's Guide: Yellowstone National Park* (taking over for Haynes, these were published from the latter 1960s into the early 21st century, authored by Alan W. Crandall and/or Herbert T. Lystrup).

A very interesting item is Henry Winser's *The Yellowstone National Park: A Manual for Tourists* (G. P. Putnam's Sons, New York, 1883). Two years later someone named John Hyde republished it under a slightly different title but with virtually the same text. The title page declared the book to have been "edited by John Hyde," but neither there nor anywhere does he mention Winser!

Of course, there are other rare Yellowstone books that are great fun to add to one's collection. Here's a list of ten historic titles just to get you started:

About Leslie Quinn

Leslie J. Quinn, a native of Cape Cod, Massachusetts, arrived in Yellowstone National Park in 1980 for a summer as a tour bus driver. As it has done for so many others, the Park got in the way of a career in more settled locales, and Leslie has worked in Yellowstone ever since. As Interpretive Specialist for the hotel concessioner today, he trains and evaluates the Park's tour guides, and in his off time he collects Yellowstone memorabilia (chiefly books). He feels his Yellowstone career is just getting started.

Journal of a Trapper
Osborne Russell.
Syms-York Company, Boise, Idaho, 1921

Russell's actual, unedited journal resides in the Yale University Library. Originally published by Syms-York Company (and this one's a pricey option today!), the version edited by Aubrey L. Haines (Oregon Historical Society, 1955) is worthwhile as Haines generated a set of maps to accompany the text. The First Edition of this printing was a special edition of 750 copies, and some that survive today have yet to have their pages cut! A decade later a paperback was offered by Bison Books, and their first six printings have fold-out maps rather than maps sewn into the center, so grab one of these as your reading copy.

The Great Divide: Travels in the Upper Yellowstone in the Summer of 1874
The Earl of Dunraven
Chatto & Windus, London, 1876
Scribner, Welford, and Armstrong, New York, 1876

The Earl of Dunraven's glorious read was published in 1876 in both London and New York. The Chatto & Windus edition (London) came out first and is the true first edition, but the Scribner, Welford, and Armstrong edition (New York) includes two maps that the Chatto & Windus edition does not. Take care to ensure that the maps are still present in a copy you purchase (or that it's a cheap price if they're not). For sheer reading interest, pick up the paperback edition published by the University Press of Nebraska (Lincoln, 1967).

The Yellowstone National Park
Hiram Martin Chittenden
The Robert Clarke Company, Cincinnati, 1895

The first actual history of Yellowstone ever written is a rare find in first edition, but more than a dozen subsequent editions were issued, the last about 1964. Another one of Chittenden's works, *Verse* (Holly Press, Seattle, 1916, a single edition in glove leather that the author shared with friends), is among the rarest Park books to be found, with only a dozen copies in libraries around the world and an unknown few in private collections.

A Western Trip
Carl E. Schmidt
Published by the author, no location given, 1910

Like Verse, the publication of A Western Trip was paid for by its author. The images in the true first edition were tipped in, while those in the one subsequent printing were printed on text pages.

The Yellowstone Story
Aubrey L. Haines
Yellowstone Library and Museum Association, Yellowstone National Park, Wyoming, 1977, two volumes

The greatest history of the Park ever written, it's worth owning the original, dust-jacketed hardback. If you find the copyright date of 1977 and four ISBNs on the back of the title page, that's the second printing. Oddly, the first printing has no such clues.

The Discovery of Yellowstone Park 1870
Nathaniel Pitt Langford
Privately published, no location given, 1905

Alternately titled *Diary of the Washburn Expedition to the Yellowstone and Firehole Rivers in the Year 1870*, the true first edition does not include a rubber stamp on the title page that reads "Published only by J. E.

Haynes, Selby at Virginia, St. Paul, Minnesota." While identical to the first, these copies were apparently acquired by Haynes after the author's death, and they were issued with a dust jacket with a one-paragraph requiem of the author by Olin D. Wheeler. Haynes published another edition, deceptively like a *Haynes Guide* in appearance, in 1923. The University of Nebraska Press's Bison Books published a nice softback in 1972. This book is worthwhile for its subject matter, despite including the story, since proven as fantasy, that the members of this expedition created the national park idea at their campsite at Madison Junction in 1870.

Preliminary Report of the United States Geological Survey of Montana and Portions of Adjacent Territories; Being a Fifth Annual Report of Progress
Ferdinand Vandeveer Hayden
Government Printing Office, Washington, 1872

This is the First (and only) Edition of the report of the 1871 Hayden Survey into the Yellowstone region. Hayden would return with his survey in 1872 and 1878 and publish reports about those trips as well.

Souvenir: Yellowstone National Park
Frank Jay Haynes
Privately published, Fargo, Dakota Territory, 1889

This booklet is interesting in that it has a single page which is accordion-folded 23 times to provide 24 pages, all of which contain wood-cut images derived from Haynes's photographs. (At that time, it was not easy or economical to print photographs for large-scale inclusion in books, but wood-cut images could be printed using the same ink and on the same paper as the text.) There are another half-dozen or more similar works by various publishers from the same era, and most of them are much rarer than the Haynes booklet.

Through the Yellowstone Park on Horseback
George Wood Wingate
O. Judd Co., New York, 1886

The author came west in the hope, which proved successful, that the cold, clear air of the Rockies would cure his daughter's respiratory complaints. A delightful look at the Park of that era, it's also notable because the author was one of the founders of the National Rifle Association. Unless it's really inexpensive, make sure the copy you purchase has the map folded in the back pocket.

Yellowstone National Park: A Bibliography
Hazel Hunt Voth and Carl P. Russell
USDI National Park Service, no location given, 1940

I'll include this one here because, if you want to get started on a Yellowstone book collection, this is a great resource because it lists most of the publications concerning the Park up to its time.

A final word: It's way too easy in both real and online auctions to get caught up in it all and bid far beyond what you should. The discipline you must find is that of deciding what you believe an item is worth, and letting others take it if they're willing to pay more. While you may lose an item now and again, you'll end up with more in your collection in the long run because you have more means to keep bidding. Have fun!

The Discovery of Yellowstone Park, 1870, N.P. Langford, eight and one eighth by six-inch hardcover book, 127 pages, first edition signed by author, March 20 1907, Diary of the Washburn Expedition to the Yellowstone and Firehole Rivers, by Nathaniel Pitt Langford, Copyright 1905. *Francis Historic Collections*

Through the Yellowstone Park On Horseback, By George W. Wingate, New York, O. Judd Co., David W. Judd, Pres't., 751 Broadway. 1886, seven and ten sixteenth by five and six sixteenth inch hardcover book, 250 pages plus 6 pages of ads. *Jay C. Lyndes Family Collection*

Yellowstone National Park, By Hiram Martin Chittenden, New and Enlarged Edition, Entirely Revised, Printed from new plates, Cincinnati, Stewart & Kidd Company Publishers, Twelfth Impression, September 1920, 350 pages, eight by five- and one-half inch hardcover book. *Francis Historic Collections*

A Western Trip, Harold Press, Detroit, Carl E. Schmidt, circa 1904, privately printed from 1901 trip, signed by author in 1905, 91 pages, nine by six- and one-half inch tanned leather cover, 12 mounted full color Detroit photographs by W. H. Jackson plus 18 smaller black and white images tipped in from trip. *Jay C. Lyndes Family Collection*

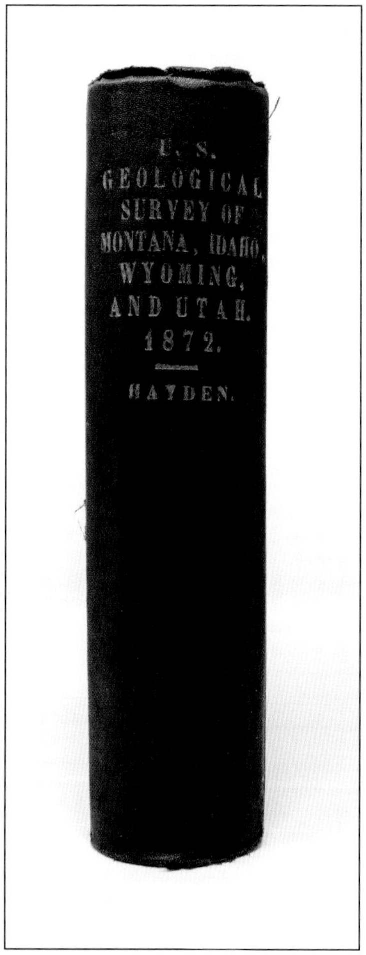

U.S. Geological Survey Of Montana, Idaho, Wyoming, And Utah, 1872, Hayden, Sixth Annual Report Of The United States Geological Survey Of The Territories, By F.V. Hayden, United States Geologist, Washington: Government Printing Office, 1873, nine and two sixteenth by six and one quarter inch hardcover book, 844 pages. *Jay C. Lyndes Family Collection*

The Discovery Of Yellowstone Park, 1870, Langford, Title Page: Diary Of The Washburn Expedition To The Yellowstone And Firehole Rivers, In The Year 1870, By Nathaniel Pitt Langford, Copyright 1905, eight and one quarter by five- and three-quarter inch hardcover in leather, 127 pages. *Jay C. Lyndes Family Collection*

Souvenir: Yellowstone National Park, Haynes, Published & Copyrighted 1889 by F Jay Haynes, Fargo Dakota, Branch Studio Yellowstone Park, seven- and one-half inch by five- and three-quarter inch book with a single page accordion-folded 23 times to provide 24 pages of wood cut images from Haynes photographs. *Francis Historic Collections*

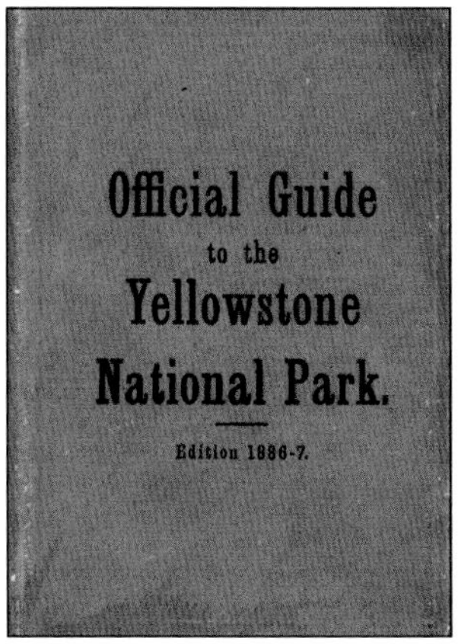

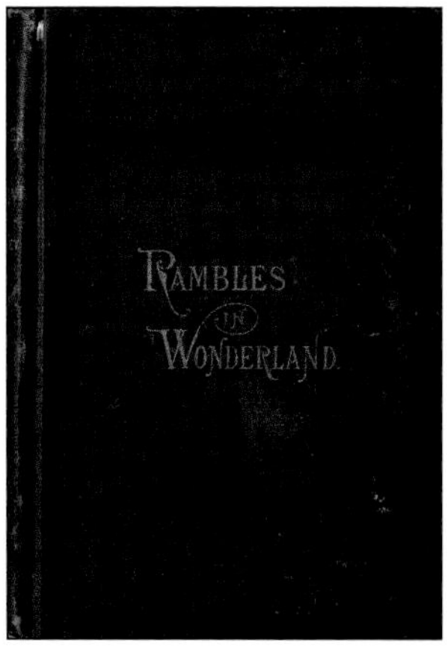

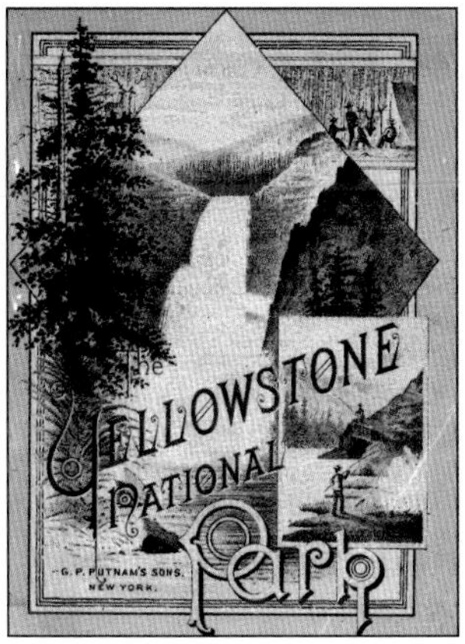

Figure 1. Official Guide to the Yellowstone National Park, Edition 1886 -7., Route of the Northern Pacific Railroad, AA Manual For Tourists, Revised By John Hyde, Riley Bros., St Paul, Minn., 1886, seven by five and one eighth inch hardcover book, 139 pages. *Bob Reynolds Collection.* **Figure 2.** A Ride Through Wonderland, Georgia M. Synge, London, Sampson Low, Marston & Company, Limited, St Dunstan's House, Fetter Lane, Fleet Street, E.C., 1892, 166 pages, seven and ten sixteenth by five and six sixteenth inch hardcover book. *Tom Murphy Collection.* **Figure 3.** Wonder Land Illustrated, Or Horseback Rides Through The Yellowstone National Park, By Harry J. Norton, Virginia City, Montana, 1873, 132 pages, seven and eleven sixteenth by four and fourteen sixteenth inch hardcover book, with map. *Jay C. Lyndes Family Collection.* **Figure 4.** Rambles In Wonderland, Or, A Trip Through The Great Yellowstone National Park, By Edward J. Stanley, Map And Twelve Illustrations. Fourth Edition, Southern Methodist Publishing House, Nashville, Tenn., 1885, eight by five- and three-quarter inch hardcover book, 218 pages plus map. *Francis Historic Collections.* **Figure 5.** The Yellowstone National Park: A Manual for Tourists, G. P. Putnam's Sons, New York, soft cover book, 97 pages, plus map, By Henry J. Winser, 1883, six and fourteen sixteenth by five inches. *Tom Murphy Collection.* **Figure 6.** Chaperoning Adrienne Through The Yellowstone, nine and one eighth by six-inch hardcover book with dust jacket, By Alice Harriman - Browne, with illustrations by Charles M. Russell, Metropolitan Press, Seattle, 92 pages. *Bob Reynolds Collection.* **Figure 7.** Im wilden Westen, von Rudolf Cronau, or In the Wild West, 1890, 383 pages, hardcover book. *Tom Murphy Collection*

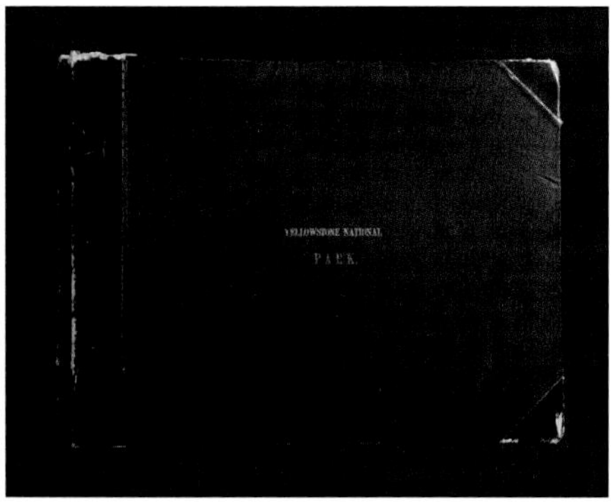

Yellowstone National Park, Published By F. Jay Haynes & Bro., hardcover book with 24 Mammoth Plate images, each twenty and one quarter by fifteen and six sixteenth inch, this book may be one of a kind. *Jay C. Lyndes Family Collection*

Views In The Yellowstone National Park, Vol. 1, fourteen and one quarter by twelve-inch leather hardcover book of Crissman photos, 15 black and white images nine and one quarter by seven- and one-half inch, Published by Wm. I. Marshall, Copyright 1876, Fitchburg, Mass., book may be one of a kind. *Jay C. Lyndes Family Collection*

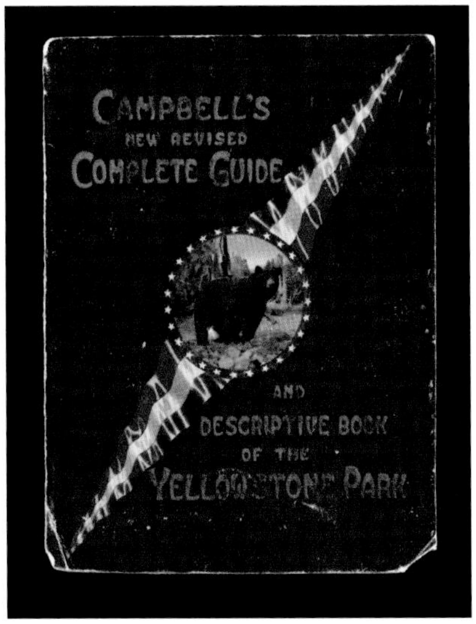

Campbell's New Revised Complete Guide And Descriptive Book Of The Yellowstone Park, By Reau Campbell, Chicago, 1909, Published and Sold by H. E. Klamer, Upper Basin, Yellowstone Park, Wyoming, Press and Binding, Rogers & Smith Co., Chicago, Engravings, J. Manz & Co., Chicago, Columbian Engraving Co. Chicago, seven by five and one quarter inch soft cover book, 173 pages with map, *Jay C. Lyndes Family Collection*

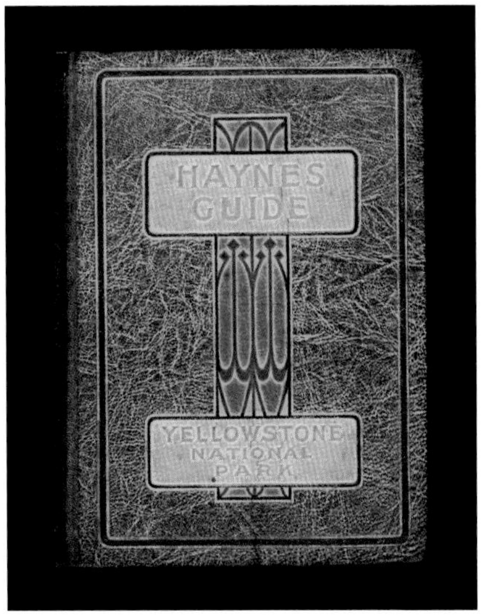

Haynes Guide, Yellowstone National Park, By J. E. Haynes, B.A., Thirty-Sixth Edition, J.E. Haynes Publisher, St. Paul, 1924, 192 pages with map, six and three quarter by five and one quarter inch hardcover book. *Jay C. Lyndes Family Collection*

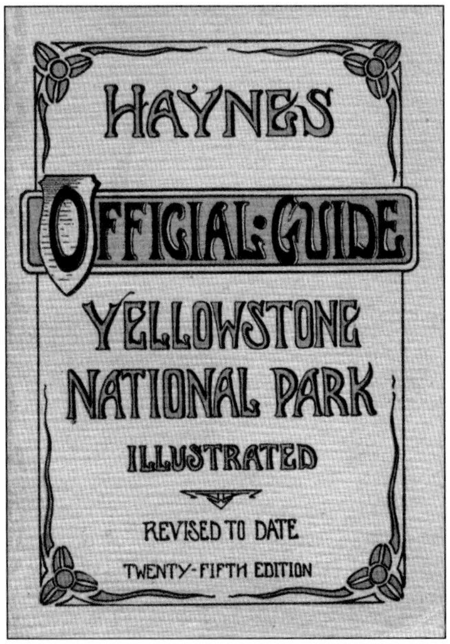

Haynes Official Guide, Yellowstone National Park, Illustrated, Revised To Date, Twenty - Fifth Edition, six and ten sixteenth by four- and three-quarter inch soft cover book, 142 pages plus map, Copyright, 1910, by F. J. Haynes. *Francis Historic Collections*

The Wonderland, View And Guide Book Of Yellowstone National Park, Containing 36 Superb Views By Wm F Hatfield, Mammoth Hot Springs, Yellowstone National Park, Wyo, ten and one half inch by six and three quarter inch booklet, Price $1.00, circa 1899. *Jay C. Lyndes Family Collection*

Animal Life Of Yellowstone National Park, By Vernon Bailey, Price $4.00, Charles C Thomas, Publisher, 1930, nine by six and one eighth inch hard-cover book with dust jacket, 241 pages. *Jay C. Lyndes Family Collection*

Book Of A Hundred Bears, A Tale Of Yellowstone Park, signed by author, By F. Dumont Smith, Second Edition, Rand McNally & Company, Chicago, Illinois, 1909, seven and three quarter by five and one half hardcover book, 235 pages. *Jay C. Lyndes Family Collection*

Bears in the Yellowstone, by M. P. Skinner, Publishers A. C. McClurg & Co., Chicago, eight by five- and one-half inch hardcover book with dust jacket, 158 pages. *Francis Historic Collections*

Yellowstone Migrations, Joe Riis, Braided River, $29.95, eleven by nine- and three-quarter inch hardcover book with dust jacket, 176 pages, 2017, ISBN 978-1-68051-089-8. *Francis Historic Collections*

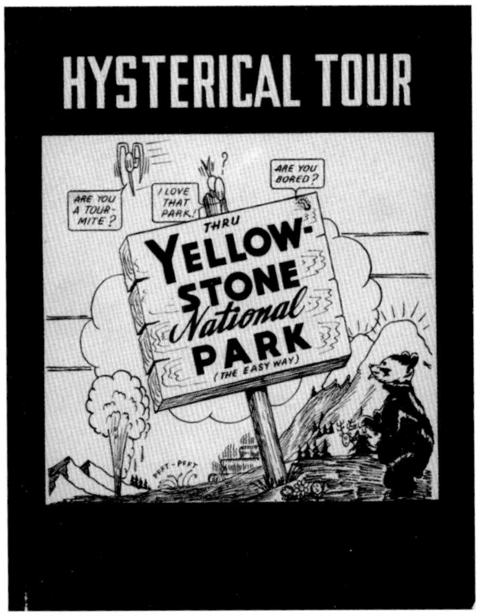

Hysterical Tour, Thru Yellow-Stone National Park, seven and one quarter by five and three quarter inch soft cover book, 126 pages, Words by Ted Turner, Jr., Cartoons By Jolly Lindgren, Copyright 1947, Lindgren Brothers - Spokane, Wash. *Jay C. Lyndes Family Collection*

Westy Martin In The Yellowstone, by Percy Keese Fitzhugh, Approved By The Boy Scouts Of America, seven and one half by five and one quarter inch hardcover book with dust jacket, 229 pages, Grosset & Dunlap Publishers, New York, Made in the United States of America, 1924. *Francis Historic Collections*

Grace Harlowe's Overland Riders In The Yellowstone National Park, Grace Harlow's Overland Riders Series, Jessie Graham Flower, hardcover book with dust jacket, The Saalfield Publishing Company, Akron Ohio, New York. Copyright MCMXXIII, 212 pages orig. *Francis Historic Collections*

Six Weeks On Horseback through Yellowstone Park, by L Louise Elliott, July 1913, The Rapid City Journal, Rapid City, SD, eight and three quarter by six inch soft cover book, 195 pages. *Jay C. Lyndes Family Collection*

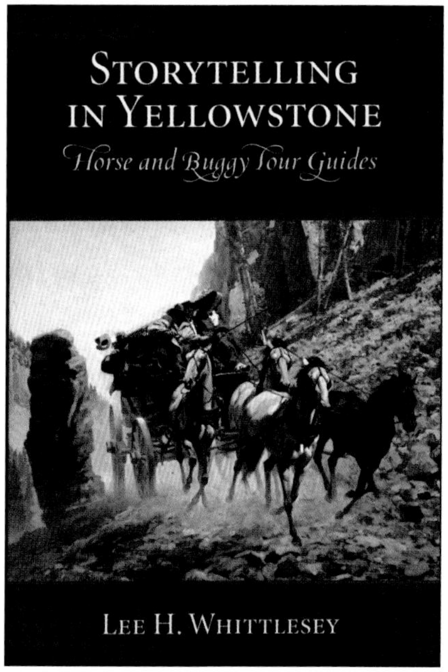

Storytelling In Yellowstone, Horse and Buggy Tour Guides, Lee H. Whittlesey, nine and one quarter by six and one half inch hardcover book with dust jacket, 377 pages, University of New Mexico Press, Albuquerque, 2007, ISBN 978-0-8263-4117-4. *Francis Historic Collections*

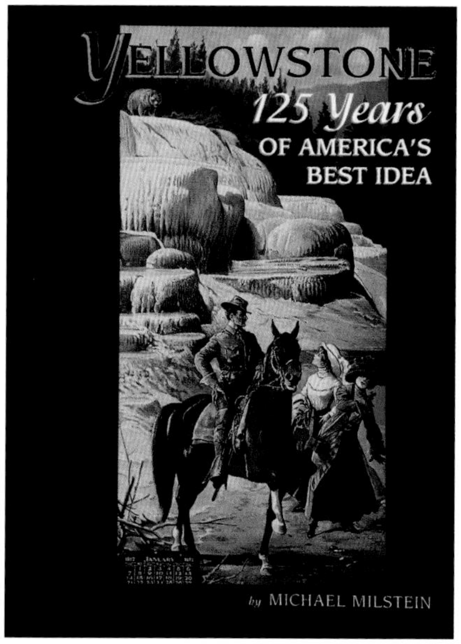

Yellowstone 125 Years Of America's Best Idea, By Michael Milstein, thirteen and one quarter by nine and three quarter inch soft cover book, 112 pages, Published by The Billings Gazette, 1996, ISBN 0-9627618-9-3. *Francis Historic Collections*

Photography

Color magic lantern glass slide in wood holder. View of the Lower Falls of the Grand Canyon of the Yellowstone. *Jay C. Lyndes Family Collection*

Yellowstone National Park, WY, An interview with Bruin (park visitors with beggar black bear), Pacific Stereopticon Co., Los Angeles, magic lantern glass slide, colorized. *Francis Historic Collections*

Photographs and Postcards

Michael H. Francis

Photographs

The collecting of photography from Yellowstone National Park began practically simultaneously with the 1871 expedition by the U.S. Geological Survey of the Territories led by F. V. Hayden, along with photographer W. H. Jackson. Jackson and his friend and fellow photographer Joshua Crissman from Bozeman, Montana Territory, were each quick to process and make available their images after this trip, especially Stereoviews, which were eagerly sought by the public.

From then on, people have been collecting various forms of photography from the Park, including "Magic Lantern Glass Slides," postcards, transparencies such as the Haynes Picture Shops' framed glass-window transparencies, more recent 35mm slides, large and medium-format black and white prints, and both private and professionally produced photo albums.

My personal favorites are the private albums of park visitors and park employees. These photographs are often one-of-a-kind items and show the park through their owners' individual eyes. In early years, wealthy travelers often set off on lengthy vacation-excursions across the country, including a visit to the Park. Instead of taking their own photographs, they would purchase prints of each place they visited, later putting them into large albums. Sometimes they paid to have a photographer accompany them on a tour. Haynes Picture Shops in the Park offered such a service.

Stereoviews and postcards are crucial to understanding the history of the park. In many cases these may be the only existing images available to researchers and collectors. Both were around almost from the very beginning of the Park, and thus they show early transportation, buildings (including hotels that may no longer exist), thermal features, guests' clothing, and Park employees at work.

Postcards

Deltiology is the official term for collecting (and studying) postcards. Collecting postcards is the largest hobby in the world after sports-cards, stamps, and money. There is no telling how many total postcards have been printed for Yellowstone National Park, but the number is certainly in the hundreds of thousands if not millions. The Yellowstone Postcard Checklist from 2006 by Francis/Burke/Bodell lists over 210 publishers/photographers.

The nice thing about collecting postcards is that many of the early historic images are still available at reasonable prices. You can expect to find cards priced from 50 cents to $3.50 each at antique shops, flea markets, estate sales, and on-line auction sites such as eBay. Rarer images do command premiums, and it is not unusual to see prices for uncommon postcards and especially the one-of-a-kind, real-photo cards topping $300 each.

A handful of publishers dominated the Yellowstone market. Most prolific was F. Jay Haynes and his son J. E. Haynes. No one produced more postcards than this family business, starting with "Private Mailing Cards" in 1900 and ending with linen cards in the late 1960s.

Another of the larger publishers was the Detroit Photographic Company, also known as Detroit Photochrome Company and Detroit Publishing Company. Their beautiful cards that were printed from 1898 to 1931 are highly sought after, especially the "Private Mailing Cards" that are overprinted with Northern Pacific Railroad and Wylie Permanent Camping Company advertising.

Albert Kayser of Oakland Journal Print published a very hard to find and early Gruss Aus-style mailing card, circa 1897, that is among the earliest known production cards of the Park. This card is continental-sized at four inches by six-and-three-sixteenth inches. Often when found, a card has been cut down to fit into a standard-size album.

A fun postcard illustrated by famous artist Charles M. Russell is called "The Bears in the park are awful Tame." Produced in 1907, its publisher was W. T. Ridgely Calendar Company, Great Falls, Montana, and this card was reprinted a number of times. One of the early printings was overprinted with the words, "Seen from Wylie Permanent Camp, Yellowstone Park."

Many of the postcard publishers issued boxed sets that were often found at curio stores outside the park. Others were sold in the various shops and stores within the park. Often you can date these boxes by who sold them, as stores changed hands through the years. The Haynes Picture Shops updated their sets almost yearly, and you can date their cards by using the five-digit number on them; the first two digits indicate the year the image was photographed.

Greetings from Yellowstone Park, various scenes including Great Falls, Liberty Cap, National Hotel and Valley, Giantess, Cascades, Old Faithful, Rainbow Falls, Old Faithful and Virginia Cascades, Copyright 1897 by Albert Kayser, Oakland Journal Print, Gruss Aus-style mailing card, continental size, four by six and three sixteenth inch pre-private mailing card, postmarked July 14, 1898, from Mammoth Hot Springs. *Francis Historic Collections*

"WHAT ALFALFA DOES FOR THE WILD GAME, No 44-S, Pronghorn Antelope and Elk feeding in field at park entrance with buildings of Gardiner MT in background including soldier station at far left black and white photo by W. S. Berry, 1902 to 1918. *Francis Historic Collections*

Death Gulch B&W - eight by ten inch black and white mounted photo, by T. A. Jagger, "Dead Bears - Due to Poison Gases emitted From The Earth", Death Gulch, YNP, July 1897, 7 dead bears were in the area, YNP. *Jay C. Lyndes Family Collection*

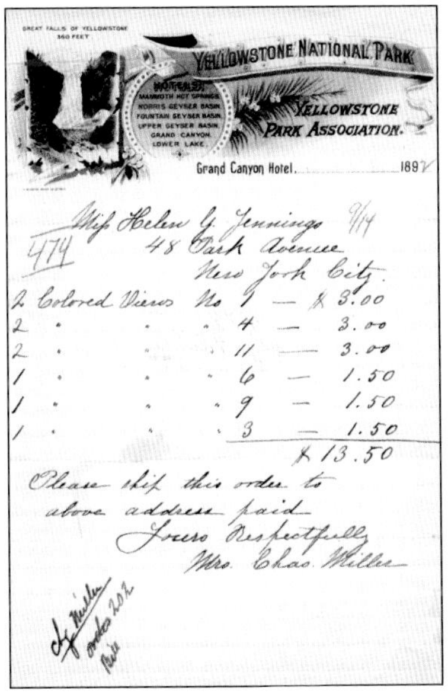

GREAT FALLS OF YELLOWSTONE 360 FEET

YELLOWSTONE NATIONAL PARK

HOTELS: MAMMOTH HOT SPRINGS, NORRIS GEYSER BASIN, FOUNTAIN GEYSER BASIN, UPPER GEYSER BASIN, GRAND CANYON, LOWER LAKE.

YELLOWSTONE PARK ASSOCIATION.

Grand Canyon Hotel, 1892

Miss Helen G. Jennings 9/14
474 48 Park Avenue
New York City.

2 Colored Views No 1 — $ 3.00
2 " " " 4 — 3.00
2 " " " 11 — 3.00
1 " " " 6 — 1.50
1 " " " 9 — 1.50
1 " " " 3 — 1.50
$ 13.50

Please ship this order to above address paid
Yours Respectfully
Mrs. Chas Miller

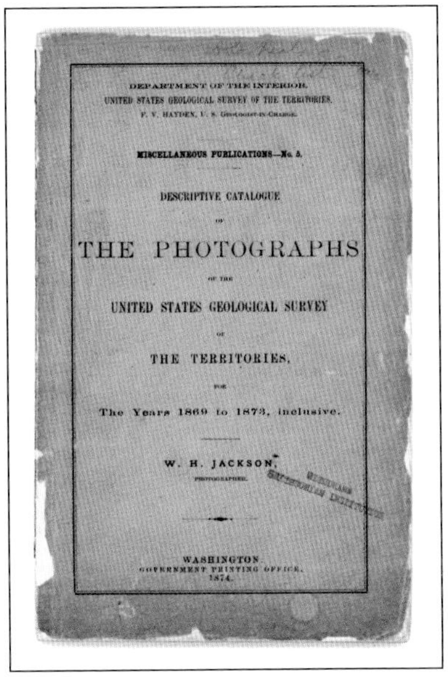

DEPARTMENT OF THE INTERIOR.
UNITED STATES GEOLOGICAL SURVEY OF THE TERRITORIES.
F. V. HAYDEN, U. S. GEOLOGIST-IN-CHARGE.

MISCELLANEOUS PUBLICATIONS—No. 5.

DESCRIPTIVE CATALOGUE
OF
THE PHOTOGRAPHS
OF THE
UNITED STATES GEOLOGICAL SURVEY
OF
THE TERRITORIES,
FOR
The Years 1869 to 1873, inclusive.

W. H. JACKSON,
PHOTOGRAPHER.

WASHINGTON:
GOVERNMENT PRINTING OFFICE.
1874.

Far left. Yellowstone Park Association, Grand Canyon Hotel, 1892, letterhead, order for colored views by Mrs. Chas Miller to Helen G Jennings, 48 Park Avenue New York City. *Francis Historic Collections*

Left. Miscellaneous Publications - No. 5, Descriptive Catalogue Of The Photographs Of The United States Geological Survey Of The Territories For The Years 1869 to 1873, inclusive., W. H. Jackson, Photographer, Department Of The Interior., United States Geological Survey Of The Territories, F. V. Hayden, U.S. Geologist-In-Charge, Washington, Government Printing Office, 1874, nine by five- and three-quarter soft cover booklet, 83 pages. *Jay C. Lyndes Family Collection*

Stereo-Travel Co., box set of 100 views, with viewer, seven and three quarter by three and three quarter by six- and one-half inch. *John Alley Collection*

Stereoview cards and viewer. *Francis Historic Collections*

Stereoviews

Paul Rubinstein and Bob Berry

The stereoview consists of two photographs taken simultaneously about four inches apart. Mounted side-by-side on a card, they can then be observed through a stereoviewer, providing a three-dimensional effect.

This complex process dates to 1832 and the invention of the stereoscope by Sir Charles Wheatstone; it predated the practical camera by seven years. More than a decade later, Sir David Brewster modified the invention and called it the refracting stereoscope.

Stereoviews were first exhibited to the public in 1851 at the London International Exhibition. Brewster exhibited his refracting stereoscope to an intrigued Queen Victoria. Within three months, more than 250,000 refracting stereoscopes were sold along with over a million stereoscopic prints. By the mid-1850s, companies were producing stereoviews around the world.

In 1859, Oliver Wendell Holmes designed a less expensive, hand-held stereoviewer. Now the enjoyment of stereography was affordable to everyone.

By 1860, large publishing firms had begun producing stereos. These companies offered images through mail order, door-to-door salesmen (canvassers), and in stores. They offered the images individually, in small groups, or in boxed sets.

The most popular subjects were tourist sites and exotic locales. News-related series that would cover local or regional tragedies were also popular. The Civil War propelled the stereoview to new heights.

A rich narrative of the stereoview in Yellowstone spans the years from 1871 until the early 1940s. The photographers ranged from ones involved with official, government-sponsored expeditions to regional professionals and even proficient amateurs. To date more than 150 photographers and publishers of Yellowstone stereoviews have been identified. Views of every kind, both in the "front country" and the backcountry of Yellowstone can be found.

Card stock varied in size from 3.5-by-7 inches to 4.5-by-7 inches. The smaller size became the standard size during the late nineteenth century. During the late 1870s, B.W. Kilburn introduced his curved mounts. A horizontal "warping" of the card stock (making the card curved in shape) increased its three-dimensional effect. By 1895, this technique had become the industry standard in all stereoview publishing.

It is believed that the first Yellowstone stereoviews were taken during the summer of 1871. The photographers were William Henry Jackson and Joshua Crissman, photographers for the Hayden Expedition (both men returned to the Park on a number of occasions); Thomas Hine, photographer for the Barlow/Heap Expedition; and Augustus F. Thrasher, a member of the Raymond/Clawson tourist party who visited the Park that same summer. These four men were the pioneer Yellowstone photographers.

Of the four, Jackson became the most prominent, mainly due to government backing. For the first time the world could see Yellowstone's remarkable natural features in all their three-dimensional glory without traveling. The others were not as fortunate. Joshua Crissman would return to Bozeman with limited success. Today, his images are rare and relatively unknown. Thomas Hine was the most ill-fated. He would go on to lose most of his work in the Great Chicago Fire of 1871. His surviving stereoviews of Yellowstone (labeled Copelin and Son, Chicago) are among the rarest in the world. Meanwhile, none of August Thrasher's work has been found to date.

Other notable 1870s photographers and publishers were John Fouch, L.A. Huffman, Thomas Rutter, Oliver Bundy, Edgar Train, and H.B. Calfee. Of these, Calfee's views stand out for their breadth of human-interest. No other photographer in the 1870s took so many photos of both people and backcountry locales within in the Park.

The next wave of photographers came during the mid to late 1880s. Most prominent were Benjamin Kilburn, Charles Savage, and Carleton Watkins.

The most dominant Park photographers of the 1880s were F. Jay Haynes and T.W. Ingersoll. Both published in St. Paul, Minnesota, and each produced an enormous amount of stereo material. Ingersoll became an extremely successful businessman in many ventures in St. Paul. His views were widely distributed, copied (pirated), and re-issued through many lesser publishers well into the 1900s. Haynes would become the "official" photographer of the Park and marketer of images of Yellowstone through his connection with the Northern Pacific Railroad. Living in the Park in the summers gave him a huge advantage, and there he established a large network of curio shops and a transportation business.

Mention should be made of vacationing photographers during this period who only distributed Yellowstone images in their own locales. The most important of this group were E. F. Everitt, William M. Myers, B. F. Hoyt, W. E. Hook, and D. Marsh.

Some of the photographers and companies of note from 1890 to 1910 were Norman Forsyth, O. W. Watson, Darius Kinsey, Solomon Butcher, Griffith & Griffith, H. C. White, and Underwood & Underwood.

Stereoview publishing gradually diminished until only one notable company remained: The Keystone View Company, which issued Yellowstone images as early as 1897 and continued to roughly 1940. The majority of this company's views were printed for use in primary schools and libraries and as boxed sets, and they generally remain quite common today.

By 1910, to boost sales, stereoviews were issued in color, usually hand tinted or in half tone lithographs. With the exception of select, high end, hand-tinted views, these common views were of inferior quality. Rare Yellowstone glass stereoviews were also produced at this time. They were generally made by amateurs in black and white, sepia, or color.

Lastly, we must address the subject of "pirated" images, or simply put, stolen stereoviews. These were created by "re-photographing" existing views. This practice occurred extensively during the 1880s and 1890s. With no copyright laws in place, this practice was not illegal, and not necessarily unethical. Almost all "pirated" views were of extremely low quality.

Comprehensive collecting of Yellowstone stereoviews began in the 1960s with the late "Tex" Treadwell and William C. Darrah, who pioneered the gathering of stereoviews in general. As the Park has grown in popularity, so has the interest in its many souvenirs. Stereoviews are a special and significant genre of that souvenir-collecting. These images are often one of a kind and make "Wonderland" come alive when viewed through this "Looking Glass."

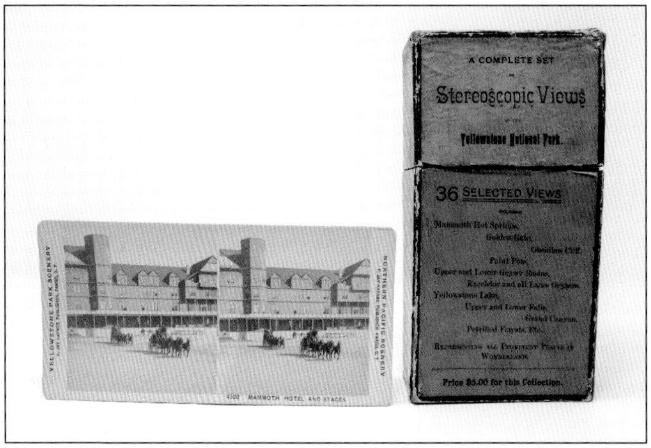

Thirty-Six Selected Haynes Stereoscopic Views Of The Yellowstone National Park, Price $5.00 for this collection, Cards have: Yellowstone Park Scenery / Northern Pacific Scenery, F. Jay Haynes, Publisher, Fargo, D.T., box - seven and one quarter by three and three quarter by two-inch, box colored red on sides. *Jay C. Lyndes Family Collection*

About Paul Rubinstein

Paul Rubinstein arrived in Yellowstone in 1989. He worked 12 seasons at Old Faithful Village for the park concessionaire, Hamilton Stores, Inc. During this time, he also photographed and videotaped extensively in the park's remote backcountry, logging more than 3,000 miles of hiking. In addition, along with Yellowstone National Park Historian, Lee Whittlesey, and seasoned Yellowstone tour guide, Mike Stevens, he co-authored the groundbreaking book, *The Guide to Yellowstone Waterfalls and their Discovery*. During his extensive research for the manuscript, he began studying and collecting Yellowstone stereoview images. This hobby led directly to the creation of a full-time business. Today, Paul is one of the principal stereoview dealers in the world.

About Bob Berry

Bob Berry is a native Texan whose love affair with Yellowstone began in 1974. He was mentored by stereoview master and close personal friend T.K. "Tex" Treadwell in the early 1980s. His one-of-a-kind collection of Yellowstone stereoviews has grown from a passing hobby to a nationally known resource for books, articles, and videos, including Ken Burns' National Park Series. It is featured in the book *Yellowstone Yesterday & Today*, which he co-authored with Paul Horsted. Berry's collection has often been publicly displayed, most notably in Yellowstone National Park.

Tower Falls - handwritten on front, Copelin & Son, Photographers, 131 Lake Street, Chicago, Views In The Yellow Stone Valley, Montana, Wyoming, Thomas J. Hine photographer (not shown on mount), 1871, from Barlow Military Expedition, one of 16 stereoview images known to exist. *John Weiler Collection*

H. B. Calfee black and white glass slide, with original wood shipping box and label: The Enchanted Land, Wonders Of The Yellowstone National Park, Illustrated, BY H. B. Calfee, Bozeman, Montana Territory. *Jay C. Lyndes Family Collection*

FALLS OF THE WEST GARDNER, 75 FT , Yellowstone National Park, Published By F. Jay Haynes., Fargo, D.T., plain verso, seven by three and fourteen sixteenth inch, orange mount with white title over photo, stereoview card. *Jay C. Lyndes Family Collection*

AMATEUR PHOTOGRAPHY 1269, .Yellowstone National Park Series, red letter, Photographed By T. W. Ingersoll, St. Paul, seven by four-inch stereoview card, 1885. *Jay C. Lyndes Family Collection*

Antler Peak from Swan Lake Flat with park visitor and vehicle, July 1922. Colorized magic lantern glass slide, photographer and publisher are unknown. *Francis Historic Collections*

H. B. Calfee magic lantern glass slide, circa 1875 to 1880. Fishing in the Park, two hours fishing and three hundred pounds of trout, Lake Abundance. *Francis Historic Collections*

Yellowstone Park, mule deer buck on hind legs being fed by man in snow, black and white real photo postcard, photographer, and publisher unknown, it may be a J. C. Haberstroh, Livingston, Montana. *Francis Historic Collections*

"WELCOME! To Cody Wyoming, The Home of "Buffalo Bill" And the Scenic Entrance to Yellowstone Park, artwork by Olive Fell, five and one half by three- and one-half inch color post card. *Francis Historic Collections*

No 276, "Am 2500 miles from home and enjoying my trip very much." Yellowstone Aug 31, 1904, postmarked from Yellowstone Park on Private Mailing Card. *Francis Historic Collections*

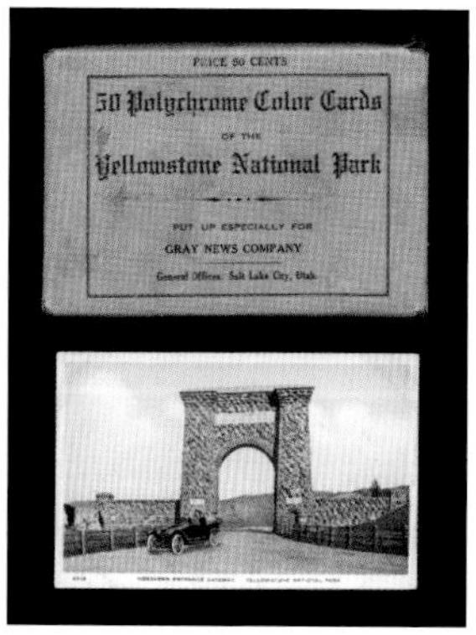

Figure 4. Coaching Party postcard glued to top of box, Yellowstone Park., five and ten sixteenth by three quarter inch cardboard postcard box, The Acmegraph Co, Chicago, circa 1910 to 1916. *Francis Historic Collections*

Figure 5. 50 Polychrome Color Cards Of the Yellowstone National Park, Put Up Especially For Gray News Company, General Offices, Salt Lake City, Utah, Price 50 Cents, H. H. Tammen Co., Denver, Colorado, circa 1917, five and fourteen sixteenth by four-inch grey postcard box. *Francis Historic Collections*

Haynes Photo Studios and Picture Shops

Elizabeth Watry

The photographs of Frank Jay and Jack Ellis Haynes most likely advanced public perceptions of Yellowstone National Park more than any other medium from 1881 to the end of the twentieth century. Considering the estimated fifty-five million postcards manufactured by the father and son photography enterprise, let alone the vast number of photographs they both produced, that impression could be easily imagined. Indeed, for more than eighty years, imagery of the park's astonishing landscape circulated around the world, a thousand times over, thanks to the enormous number of photographs and postcards produced by the House of Haynes.

"The Professor"

Frank Jay Haynes, affectionately known as the "Professor" because of his exceptional artistic talent with a camera, began his photographic career in 1874 when photography was still in its formative years. F. Jay advanced his knowledge in this relatively new field over the next two years working for various photographers in Wisconsin where he learned the fundamentals and basics of photography. By 1876, he had contracted with the Northern Pacific Railroad (NPRR) to take landscape photographs along the railroad's route that would promote its westward progress and also opened his first studio in Moorhead, Minnesota. F. Jay married Lily Snyder in 1878, who promptly became his lifelong partner in the photography business and with whom he had three children, Bessie, George, and Jack. He moved his studio to Fargo, North Dakota in 1879 and by 1881 had been appointed "Official Photographer" for the NPRR.

As the NPRR tracks advanced closer to Yellowstone National Park, Haynes made his first trip there in 1881. Enthralled with the park's amazing landscape he wrote to Lily, "It is simply wonderful to see [the geysers] spout up 300 feet with a column of hot water..." Viewing the geysers through the eyes of a creative photographer, which would later become his forte, he told Lily that, "each one can be seen in a hundred different ways." He returned the following year to complete a collection of stereoscopic and large-format views of park scenery.

By the end of 1883, F. Jay knew he had found his

photographic calling in Yellowstone and applied to the Department of Interior to lease a parcel of land for a studio and residence. In 1884, he obtained two leases, one for a four-acre site at Old Faithful and another for a four-acre site at Mammoth Hot Springs. Erecting a prefabricated structure located directly across from the Mammoth Hot Springs Hotel, F. Jay built his first Yellowstone studio in 1885.

He moved his studio from Fargo, North Dakota to St. Paul, Minnesota in 1889 and published the first *Haynes Guide to Yellowstone National Park* in 1890. F. Jay built his "Log Cabin Studio" at Old Faithful in 1897 on his leased site across from Klamer Curio Store, which was also constructed that same year. The studio would later be identified on a map in the 1910 *Haynes Guide* as the Haynes Picture Shop, a business name his son Jack would use for future Haynes stores.

In 1900, F. Jay started publishing his photographs on postcards, effectively launching a perpetual ephemera-market that continues today. However, not content to only sell his photographs as prints, enlargements, stereoscopic views, color photogravures, lantern slides, post cards, and souvenir albums, he resourcefully began putting his images on an assortment of curios as well. Souvenir spoons, collector plates, pin trays, trinket boxes, hand mirrors, paper weights, leather pillows, match safes, fashion pins, and playing cards represented just a few of the curios sporting a famous Haynes photograph in the early 1900s.

The close of Yellowstone's 1916 season signaled the end of an era as horses and stagecoaches were "put out to pasture" to be replaced in 1917 with motorized vehicles. And after photographing Yellowstone for thirty-five years, Frank Jay Haynes retired, bestowing his successful photography business to his son Jack. Symbolically, the "Professor" brought a personal close to the bygone pioneer era that had once lured him westward and to America's Wonderland. F. Jay continued to return to Yellowstone every summer, just as he had done since 1881, until he passed away in 1921.

In 1934, the United States Post office honored F. Jay with the publication of a 5-cent stamp bearing the image of Old Faithful geyser in eruption that he had photographed decades earlier. The Yellowstone stamp was one of ten stamps issued in 1934 as part of a National Park Series, which are frequently found on auction sites today.

"Mr. Yellowstone"

Born in 1884, Jack Ellis Haynes spent his first season in Yellowstone in 1888. As smitten by America's Wonderland as his father had been, Jack made learning and knowing everything possible about the park his lifetime passion. His commitment to chronicling the Park's history in addition to his generous assistance to the educational arm of the National Park Service earned him the nickname, "Mr. Yellowstone."

By the time he took over the Haynes photography enterprise in 1916, Jack was fully immersed in the business having worked with his father from a young age. He advanced to operating the photo stand in the Mammoth hotel lobby at age 20, managing postcard production at age 24, and taking over publication of the *Haynes Guide* at age 26. Upon his assignment of the lease by the Department of Interior, Jack began incrementally expanding the business.

In 1917, he converted a former Yellowstone-Western Stage Company office building at Tower Fall into a photo shop and general store. In 1936, Jack built a much larger store with an ice cream parlor and delicatessen, where visitors could find served meals, sandwiches, ice cream, a vast array of curios and supplies such as film, postcards, pictorial souvenirs, books, camping provisions, and a postal station. After twenty-three years of service, the store was razed in 1959 and replaced with a new Haynes Tower Fall store in 1960.

Jack erected a new photo shop in Mammoth in 1920, at the base of Capitol Hill, next door to his father's original studio that had been moved there in late 1902. However, within seven years, his photography business had outgrown the relatively new facility, which Jack refurbished into a residence. On the corner, at the far end of Capitol Hill, he had a larger, two-story shop constructed in 1928-1929. The building would later become known as the Christmas Store and the Hamilton Nature Store, and today serves as the administrative offices for Xanterra, the current hotel concessioner.

Between 1922 and 1928, Jack built new shops at Fishing Bridge and Canyon Junction (today's brink of Upper Falls parking area), as well as the Mammoth and Old Faithful Auto Camps. Adding to the existing photo stands in the Mammoth and Canyon Hotels, he set up stands in the Lake Hotel and Old Faithful Inn as well as the Lodges in Mammoth, Old Faithful, Lake, and Canyon. In an effort to keep up with visitors' desires, Haynes Picture Shops branched out in the mid-1920s to offer film developing at Mammoth and Old Faithful. By 1929, the company was broadly advertising overnight developing at all its locations except Tower Fall. Adding to his expanding collection of retail outlets, Jack opened a Haynes Picture Shop at West Thumb and a general store at Roosevelt Lodge in the 1930s.

As part of the Mission 66 project, a system-wide national park refurbishing plan that began in 1956, all visitor services in the area known as Canyon Junction as well as Canyon Lodge were relocated to the new, modern-styled Canyon Village. The newly constructed Canyon Lodge opened in 1957 as well as the Hamilton Store. From 1957 to 1959, Jack maintained a shop in the lobby of the new Canyon Lodge until his Picture Shop was completed and opened in 1960.

Jack's merchandising and marketing of Hayes postcards won him a second moniker, the "Postcard Man." Assuming responsibility of postcard production in 1908, Jack developed the 100 Series postcards, which were arranged and numbered in order of the popular sights that travelers would see on a tour around the park on the Grand Loop Road. The 100 Series proved to be a very successful strategy and postcard sales increased significantly. Perhaps one of the most noteworthy changes Jack made to the Haynes postcard production was the numbering format. Somewhere around 1920, he developed a five-digit identification system. With this five-digit arrangement, the first two numbers designated the year the photo was taken and the following three numbers referenced the sequence in which the image was taken that year. Jack's ingenious numbering system has proven to be invaluable to historians, libraries, museums, archival repositories, and collectors for many years.

The *Haynes Guide to Yellowstone* proved to be another enduring and long-lasting production, especially under Jack's meticulous eye. In 1910, he took over publication of the *Haynes Guide* and revamped it from being a descriptive travel narrative to a practical handbook. Featuring maps, mileages, sites to visit, and available services, his revised guide provided visitors with useful information for touring and navigating the park, especially when more and more travelers preferred roaming the park in their own automobiles after 1915. Jack faithfully updated and republished this indispensable guide nearly every year until his death in 1962. Under the direction of his wife, Isabel, the *Haynes Guide* remained in publication through 1966.

For over thirty years, Isabel Nauerth Haynes served as a valuable business partner to her photographer husband. When Jack passed away in 1962, she took over operation of the Haynes Picture Shops and kept the company running for the next six years. Sadly, the death of their daughter Lida, in a car accident in 1952, left the business without an heir. In 1968, Isabel sold the Haynes Shops to the Hamilton Stores. As the last living Haynes Picture Shop family member, Isabel requested the retirement of the Haynes name as part of the agreement with the Hamilton Stores. Even though the Haynes name is scarcely observable in the park today, the legacy of Frank Jay and Jack Ellis lives on in the thousands of Haynes photographs, postcards, guide books, postage stamps, and other collectibles still in existence.

About Elizabeth Watry

Elizabeth "Betsy" Watry holds a Master's Degree in History from Montana State University and is an independent scholar specializing in nineteenth and early-twentieth century cultural history of the American West. A published author with several books on Yellowstone National Park, her book *Women in Wonderland: Lives, Legends, and Legacies of Yellowstone National Park* won the 2013 WILLA Literary Award for Scholarly Non-fiction.

Sketch Artist - Norris, 5 x 8 inch black and white, photo by F. Jay Haynes, 1887, unmounted Boudoir View, Yellowstone Park Scenery, Published By F. Jay Haynes, Fargo D/T. *Bob Reynolds Collection*

Haynes Studios, Selby Ave, St Paul, Minn, USA, black and white converted from color magic lantern glass slide, label missing, Cleopatra Terrace, Mammoth Hot Springs. *Jay C. Lyndes Family Collection*

Haynes Souvenir Playing Cards, Yellowstone Park, Published By F. Jay Haynes, Official Photographer, St. Paul, Minn. USA, light blue box, three and ten sixteenth by two- and three-quarter inch, Copyright 1904, by The U.S. Playing Card Co., flower reverse. *Jay C. Lyndes Family Collection*

Yellowstone Park Buffalo., Haynes - Photo, postmarked Aug 22, 1904, five and five sixteenth by three and five sixteenth inch black and white post card, 1904 to 1905. *Francis Historic Collections*

Collection Of 36 Stereoscopic Views Yellowstone Park, Haynes - Photo, Cards have: Yellowstone Park Scenery / Northern Pacific Scenery, F. Jay Haynes, Publisher, St. Paul, box - seven and one quarter by three and three quarter by two and one quarter inch, box color mint green, cards have: one quarter inch long arrow and cross, hand written title on verso. *Jay C. Lyndes Family Collection*

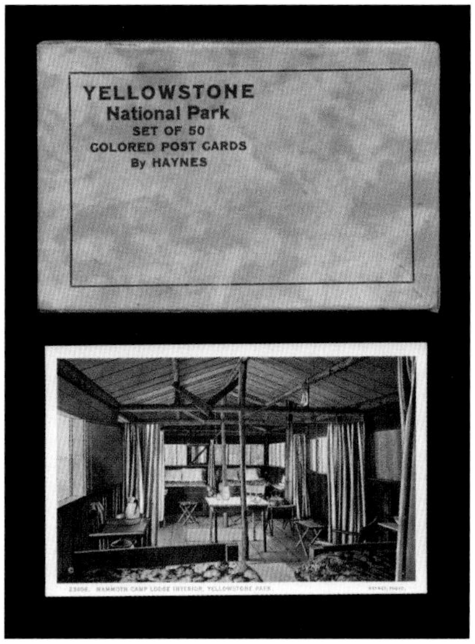

Yellowstone National Park, Set of 50 Colored Post Cards by Haynes, five and thirteen sixteenth by three and thirteen sixteenth inch marbled brown postcard box, circa 1925. *Francis Historic Collections*

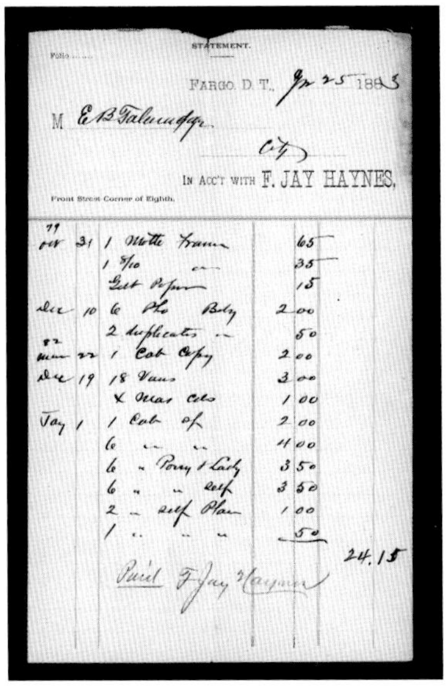

Statement, Fargo D. T., 1885, In Acct. With F. Jay Haynes, Front Street Corner of Eighth, eight and one quarter by five and three sixteenth inch. *Bob Reynolds Collection*

The Picture Shop, F.Jay Haynes, Upper Basin, Yellowstone Park, Wyo., Photographs, Souvenir Spoons, Guide Books, Albums, Postcards, one- and one-half inch gummed advertising stamp or sticker. *Bob Reynolds Collection*

Larry Mathews, Norris, July 29 1897, Yellowstone National Park. Mathews managed establishments in the park from 1888 to 1904 which included Lunch Stations and the first manager of the Old Faithful Inn. Photo by Haynes. *Francis Historic Collections*

Haynes Yellowstone Park, Series "B," Souvenir Folder, Copyrighted 1921 and sold only by J. E. Haynes, Official Photographer of Yellowstone Park, St. Paul, Minn., six and one quarter by four and one quarter inch accordion style photo display. *Francis Historic Collections*

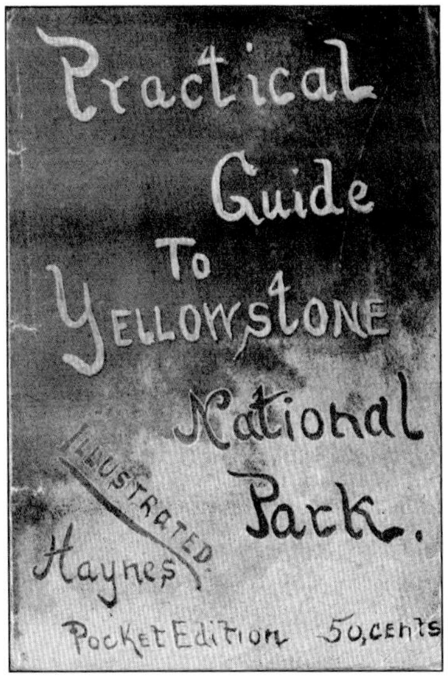

Guide to Yellowstone Park., By A. B. Guptill, Illustrated And Published By F. Jay Haynes & Bro., Official Photographer Of The Northern Pacific Railroad, No. 392 Jackson Street, St. Paul, Minn., 1890, Pioneer Press Company, seven and six sixteenth by four- and three-quarter inch hardcover book, 124 pages plus map. *Jay C. Lyndes Family Collection*

Lower Falls from Artist Point, Grand Canyon of the Yellowstone, Haynes, glass window transparency, metal chain and frame seven and four sixteenth by five and four sixteenth inch, 5 x 7-inch image. *Jay C. Lyndes Family Collection*

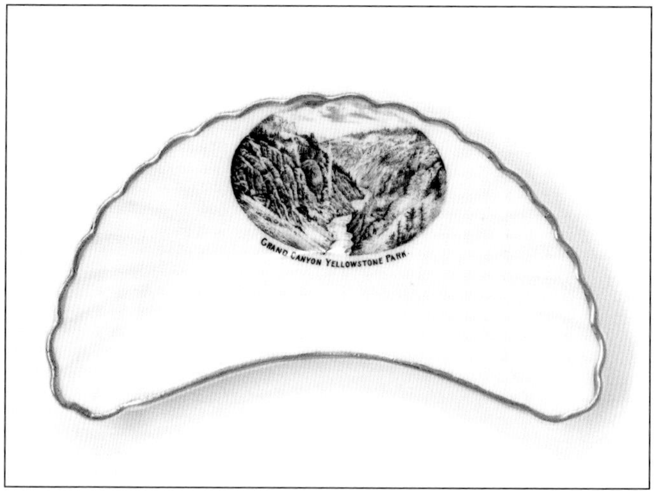

Grand Canyon Yellowstone Park, six and three quarter by four-inch Bone Dish, Made in Germany for F. Jay Haynes, St. Paul. *Jay C. Lyndes Family Collection*

"Fisherman's Luck Is Nothing But Correct Technique" Haynes, Dry Fly Oil, Jack E. Haynes - Yellowstone Park - Wyoming, USA, printing block, five and three quarter by four and one quarter inch. *Bob Reynolds Collection*

Haynes Dry Fly Oil, For Water-Proofing Artificial Flies, 25 Cents, box of 12 bottles, box - nine and one quarter by five- and three-quarter inch, each glass bottle -two- and one-half inch, Jack E. Haynes - Yellowstone Park, Wyoming, USA, Date of Manufacture 1934, discontinued 1943, *Jay C. Lyndes Family Collection*

Store Memorabilia

Yellowstone National Park, Souvenir Pin and Guard, Made in USA, on original card, one and three quarter by one and six sixteenth inch, no maker. *Bob Reynolds Collection*

Souvenir of Yellowstone National Park, three and three quarter by two- and one-half inch box of playing cards, no maker, Old Faithful Geyser on card reverse. *Jay C. Lyndes Family Collection*

Yellowstone Park, chalk bear thermometer, no maker, three by two- and three-quarter inch. *Bob Reynolds Collection*

Marketing Memorabilia in Yellowstone

Elizabeth Watry

Established in 1872, Yellowstone National Park, nestled deep within the confines of the Rocky Mountains, was slow to develop into a viable tourist-destination. Completion of the Northern Pacific Railroad's spur line to Cinnabar, Montana in 1883, a mere five miles from the north entrance of America's Wonderland, hastened the pace of development, but it would be another decade, the mid-1890s, before permanent curio shops and general stores would appear in the park. Unlike the major hotel concessions, none of the park's retail endeavors were backed with funding from the railroad. Thus, Yellowstone's mercantile establishments began with the investments of a few steadfast park residents and evolved into a substantial collection of family-owned and operated stores that would serve park travelers for more than a century. Evidenced by the vast array of Yellowstone memorabilia extant today, these merchants clearly strove to keep pace with travelers' ubiquitous desire for curios and keepsakes. Moreover, Yellowstone's storekeepers recognized that they were selling more than mere souvenirs; they were dealing in memories.

Jennie Henderson-Ash - George Whittaker

Jennie Henderson Ash, daughter of former assistant superintendent George L. Henderson, pioneered the park's first large general store in 1895. Following his appointment to the park in 1882, her father George arrived in Yellowstone with his five children, Helen, age 29; Barbara, 21; Walter, 20; Jennie, 18; and Mary, 11, all of whom would prove to be significant contributors to the development of Yellowstone's tourist-service industry. Shortly after the family arrived in Yellowstone, Barbara was appointed Postmaster. Jennie would follow in her sister's footsteps taking over as Postmaster in 1884, a position she would drift in and out of for the next ten years.

Early in 1885, Walter and Helen received a ten-year lease to build and operate the Cottage Hotel, at Mammoth Hot Springs. In addition to providing lodging for visitors, the family established the Cottage Hotel Museum with Jennie as proprietor. The museum offered a variety of items for sale such as park guidebooks by G.L Henderson, Henry Winser, Philetus Norris, and William W. Wylie as well as tourist supplies, cigars, tobacco, Haynes Park Views, coated specimens, and taxidermist-prepared wild game heads.

Resuming her position as postmaster in 1888, Jennie continued to learn about the increasing needs and desires of the traveling public. She requested permission from the Department of Interior (DOI) to continue the privilege of selling tourist-items as had the previous postmaster and to increase the line of goods to include stationery, writing utensils, toiletry items, colored glasses, sewing items, key rings, matches, scarves, park views, gum, lemons, oranges, and coated specimens. By 1889, the Post Office Store, as it had come to be known, proved to be the foundation for Yellowstone's first general store.

Following a previous marriage and divorce from John Dewing, Jennie married George Ash, former superintendent of the Yellowstone Park Association Stage Line, in 1893. Later that year, they filed an application to lease a small plot of land in Mammoth and build a new post office, store, and residence. In 1895, the DOI approved the application and issued a ten-year lease. The Ash & Henderson store opened in 1896. With a larger store, Jennie could also stock dry goods, clothing, shoes, and boots as well as park souvenirs. Additions built in 1897 and 1902 further enlarged the store and allowed space for larger items such as game heads and fur rugs. By 1902, the store advertised as the Yellowstone Park Tourist Supply Company and carried a wide assortment of Indian curios, with Indian baskets and Navajo blankets becoming a specialty.

After George's death in 1900, Jennie's family assisted with operating the store, which the DOI mandated be open seven days a week from 6 a.m. to 11 p.m. Brother-in-law Alexander Lyall, husband of Barbara, was appointed Postmaster in 1906 and became a partner in the business. After suffering with chronic health issues for several years, Jennie decided the Southern California climate better suited her, and sold the store in 1908 to Lyall and her brother, Walter. Jennie, as it turned out, made a wise choice for she lived a full life until passing away at the age of 83 in 1947. Following Jennie's formative lead, Lyall and Henderson continued to step up to visitors' expectations through 1912.

In 1913, George Whittaker purchased the Lyall & Henderson store. As an army soldier assigned to Fort Yellowstone in 1891 and a park Scout as of 1896, Whittaker had spent more than twenty years in the park and well-understood the opportunities of serving the growing tourism industry in Yellowstone. Along with the DOI approving his ten-year lease to own and operate the renamed Yellowstone Park Store, Whittaker was appointed postmaster. He expanded the store with additions in 1914 and 1921-22, resulting in the architectural profile that exists today.

Whittaker advertised a complete line of provisions such as souvenirs, notions, novelties, postcards, groceries, hardware, sporting goods, fishing tackle, tobacco, cigars, clothing, boots, and Kodak supplies. In the early years, the DOI issued and controlled concessioner contracts to manage competition amongst the various enterprises. Each contract stipulated what services and supplies a specific business could furnish as well as regulating the prices. The DOI also protected concessioners from incursion such as denying Whittaker permission to install a soda fountain in 1915 because Pryor and Trischman held that privilege at the Park Curio Store.

However, the DOI allowed Whittaker to sell gasoline in 1915 and in 1919 he built a gas station next to his store. As park visitation swiftly rose, so did the need for additional tourist services and Whittaker seized the opportunity to expand his operation. In 1918, he established a store and gas station at Canyon, which would grow substantially through the 1920s. By 1924, he also had a general store and delicatessen at the Mammoth auto camp. After spending nearly 40 years in Yellowstone, Whittaker sold all his businesses to Anna Pryor and Elizabeth Trischman in 1932.

Anna Pryor & Elizabeth Trischman

Anna and Elizabeth Trischman began their lifelong connection with Yellowstone in 1899, when their father, George, took a position as post carpenter for the army at Fort Yellowstone. Anna married George Pryor in June 1907, and in the spring of the following year the couple purchased the Ole Anderson Specimen House. Not content to merely sell coated specimens and bottles of colored sands from the Grand Canyon of Yellowstone, George requested permission to install a bakery and Yellowstone's first soda fountain in their newly acquired business, which they called the Park Curio Store. In 1909, they were granted authorization to double the size of their store and residence as well as to increase their product lines to include Indian moccasins, Navajo goods, Mexican serapes and rugs, and burnt-leather novelties. The marriage was not long lasting and in 1912, George signed over his share in the store to Anna's sister Elizabeth.

The Park Curio Store flourished under the new partnership of Pryor and Trischman. Their lease for 1916 added materially to their store offerings as they were permitted to sell newspapers, hats, veils, gloves, toiletries, cigars, tobacco, colored glasses, and boxed lunches. The two sisters responded to the needs of automobile travelers by joining forces with George Whittaker in 1924 to open a delicatessen at the Lower Mammoth auto camp, which they would convert into a full-service cafeteria the following year. The "Devil's Kitchenette," a refreshment stand located on Mammoth's Upper Terrace near the famous Devil's Kitchen cavern, which operated from 1924 until the late 1930s, proved to be one of the most unique of Pryor and Trischman enterprises.

Anna and Elizabeth purchased all of George Whittaker's operations at Mammoth and Canyon in 1932, which put them in control of all the general stores and gas stations in the northern half of the park. By 1933, Anna and Elizabeth were advertising their collection of three general stores, two gas stations, a cafeteria, curio shop, coffee shop, and the Devil's Kitchenette as "The Pryor Stores." With considerable holdings at stake, the two aging sisters incorporated in 1947. After forty-five years of attending to tourists' needs, Anna and Elizabeth decided to retire and sold all their operations to Charles Hamilton in 1953.

Henry Klamer – Charles Hamilton

In 1897, Henry Klamer established the second general store in Yellowstone at Old Faithful. Klamer first arrived in Yellowstone in 1881 as a government road worker. After a few years, he entered the hotel business, which included owning a share of the Firehole Hotel, working as a driver and guide for the Cottage Hotel, and supplying beef for the park hotels. In 1892, he married G.L. Henderson's youngest daughter, Mary. After observing Yellowstone tourism develop for almost fifteen years, Klamer decided to "toss his hat into the ring." In 1896, he requested a lease from the DOI to build a store and residence on a two-acre parcel at Old Faithful. Construction on his simple, two-story frame building began in spring 1897, and the H.E Klamer store opened in late June. As the only place within fifty miles where tourists could acquire provisions, Klamer stocked a wide range of merchandise such as groceries, canned goods, camping equipment, toiletries, stationary, tobaccos, periodicals, books, tobaccos, agates and precious stones, and curios.

Adjacent to Klamer's store, the Old Faithful Inn, with its knotty, gnarled-pine appearance was constructed over the winter of 1903 and opened in 1904.

Klamer's plain-looking building evidently paled in comparison and prompted him to engage Inn architect, Robert Reamer in 1903 to remodel the exterior of his entire store to mirror the rustic charm of the Old Faithful Inn as well as to build a 25-by-40-foot wing facing the Inn. Reamer, known for his ornamental accoutrements, even designed a sign made from twisted lodgepole pine branches that read "H.E. Klamer Curio Store" to grace the doorway.

By 1909, Klamer carried a wide array of Indian wares such as baskets ranging in origin from Alaska to the Southwest, moccasins, buckskin gloves, shirts, vests, and leggings, cedar flutes, Navajo blankets and jewelry, as well as various Mexican carved leather goods. His Yellowstone souvenirs ran the gamut from gold and silver spoons embossed with "Yellowstone Park to ___" to the "Game of Yellowstone," with fifty-two different views of the park, to guide-books such as Hatfield's Geyserland & Wonderland and Campbell's Complete Guide and Descriptive Book of the Yellowstone Park, which Klamer began publishing in 1909. Shortly after finishing an addition to his store in 1913-14, Henry Klamer suffered a fatal heart attack and died on August 14, 1914. With assistance from her brother Walter, Mary managed the store for the remainder of the 1914 season, and the following year she sold the business to Charles Hamilton.

Charles Ashworth Hamilton

Charles Ashworth Hamilton founded the chain of Hamilton Stores that operated in Yellowstone from 1915 to 2002. Hailing from his boyhood home of St. Paul, Minnesota, headquarters for the Northern Pacific Railroad, Hamilton began his lifelong Yellowstone career in 1905. With funding from his employer, Harry Child, Hamilton purchased the Klamer store in June 1915. From that point forward, Hamilton steadily advanced his concession domain across the southern half of the park. In 1919, he opened his second store in an abandoned E.C. Waters building at Lake, where years earlier, Waters's wife, Martha, had special-ordered hand-painted plates bearing the inscription "Made in Germany for M.B. Waters," that portrayed E.C.'s boat, the Zillah, and Yellowstone Lake scenery. Hamilton also opened a store at West Thumb in 1919.

By the mid-1920s, Hamilton had established stores at Fishing Bridge and at all the auto camps from Old Faithful to West Thumb to Lake. In 1933, he purchased the Henry Brothers Bathhouse & Plunge that sat directly across from his first store at Old Faithful. Within the next ten years, he would completely rebuild the structure that sported an indoor "geyser water" pool with log beams, a high-peaked roof, and outdoor "sand porches" for sunbathing. Throughout the 1930s and 1940s, Hamilton remained in constant motion, adding additions to existing buildings or building newer, bigger stores at all his locations, including a second store at Old Faithful, called the Upper Hamilton Store.

As expected, Hamilton Stores' merchandise changed with the times, eventually carrying Yellowstone pennants, popular in the 1920s-30s, in addition to perennial souvenir favorites like collector spoons, figurines, jewelry, pins, belt buckles, and plush bears. For many years, Hamilton and his wife May traveled the world in search of unique souvenirs and curios to sell in the Hamilton Stores. Some of the most beautiful items Hamilton imported were Staffordshire plates and mugs decorated with various iconic Yellowstone scenes such as an eruption of Old Faithful. Some of this impressive china was made in England exclusively for the Hamilton Stores. An astute businessman, Hamilton strove to suit any sized wallet by selling everything from one-of-a-kind objects to Hamilton Stores' signature items to kitschy knickknacks.

Purchasing Anna Pryor and Elizabeth Trischman's businesses in 1953 effectively put Hamilton at the helm of every general store throughout the Park. At the apex of his concession empire, Charles Hamilton died suddenly from a heart attack in his office on the second floor of the former Klamer store on May 28, 1957. His daughter Eleanor "Ellie" and her husband Trevor Povah, who had already been managing much of the day-to-day operations, took over the entire company. In 1967, Isabel Haynes, widow of the late photographer Jack Haynes, who had passed away in 1962, sold all thirteen of the Haynes Picture Shops to Hamilton Stores. By the early 1970s, Hamilton Stores was considered the largest, privately held park concession in the country. The Hamilton Stores, last of Yellowstone's family-owned and operated businesses, passed into history in 2002, when a change in park policy eliminated their preferential right of renewal and they were unable to compete with a major corporate competitor for a new contract.

Sitting bear, Yellowstone National Park, K&O shield, metal Indian head bank, three and three quarter by two- and three-quarter inch, Kronheimer & Oldenbusch Co., Brooklyn, NY, in business 1895 to 1935. *Bob Reynolds Collection*

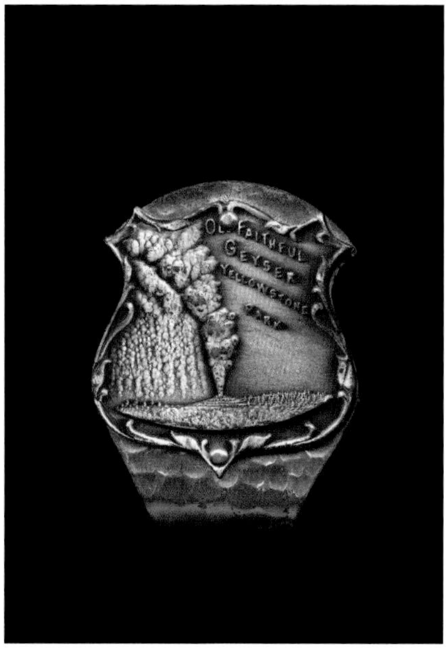

Old Faithful Geyser, Yellowstone Park, K&O shield, one- and three-quarter inch money clip, Kronheimer & Oldenbusch Co., New York. *Francis Historic Collection*

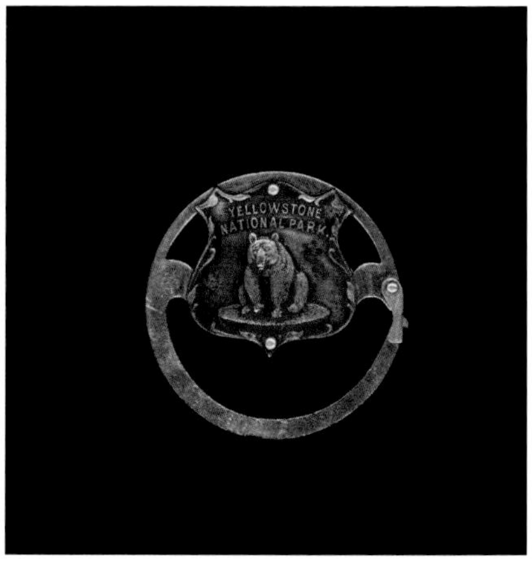

Yellowstone National Park with sitting bear K&O shield, 2-inch metal ring, Kronheimer & Oldenbusch Co., NY. Jay C. *Lyndes Family Collection*

Yellowstone Park, K&O metal banner, Kronheimer & Oldenbusch Co., New York, 3x3x2 inch metal bear calendar. *Bob Reynolds Collection*

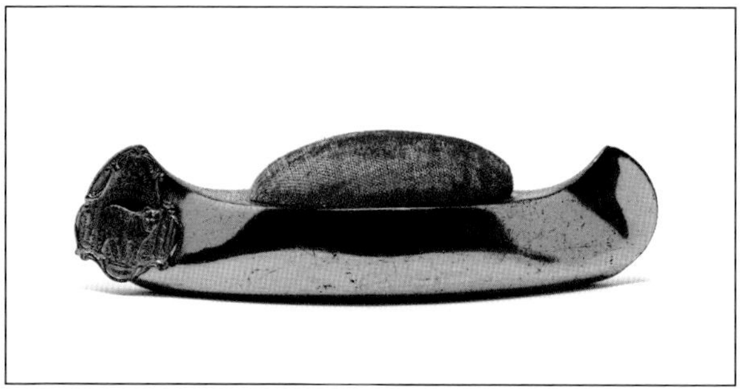

A Park Bear, Yellowstone National Park, K&O shield, metal pin cushion canoe, Kronheimer & Oldenbusch Co., New York, six and one half by one- and three-quarter inch. *Bob Reynolds Collection*

Kronheimer & Oldenbusch Company

Michael H. Francis

Few companies managed to stock shelves in park gift shops with as many souvenir items as the Kronheimer & Oldenbusch Company, also known as K&O. The company was incorporated on February 28, 1900, in New York, and the main purpose was to manufacture novelties of hollowware and fancy metal goods. Not only did the company produce tourist items for Yellowstone, but you will find the same items for most of the other popular tourist attractions of the day, such as Niagara Falls. The only real difference was a custom "Souvenir Shield" for each area that was applied to the products. The company specialized in metal items and figurines.

In addition to its own manufacturing, it appears that K&O purchased surplus stock from other manufactures and applied K&O shields to those items, so not everything with a K&O shield was manufactured by K&O. The company used shields until roughly 1940.

Old Faithful Geyser, Yellowstone Park, K&O shield, 6 inch pounded brass paperweight with bear, Kronheimer & Oldenbusch Co., New York. *Francis Historic Collections*

Entrance Arch, Yellowstone Park, K&O shield, Kronheimer & Oldenbusch Co, New York, metal jewelry box with hinged lid, three and one quarter by one- and three-quarter inch. *Bob Reynolds Collection*

Great Falls and Old Faithful Geyser, K&O shields on same metal bear casting, different colors, three and one quarter by two inch, Kronheimer & Oldenbusch Co, New York. *Bob Reynolds Collection*

A Park Bear, Yellowstone National Park, metal women's high heel shoe, K&O shield, Kronheimer & Oldenbusch Co., New York, JB 515, three and one half by one- and one-half inch. *Bob Reynolds Collection*

Metal pelican, K&0 shield with Yellowstone National Park, Kronheimer & Oldenbusch Co., New York, two by one- and three-quarter inch. *Jack & Sue Davis Collection*

Yellowstone Park, bear on shield, K&O, Kronheimer & Oldenbusch, Brooklyn, NY, five by two- and one-half inch metal mirror compact. *Jay C. Lyndes Family Collection*

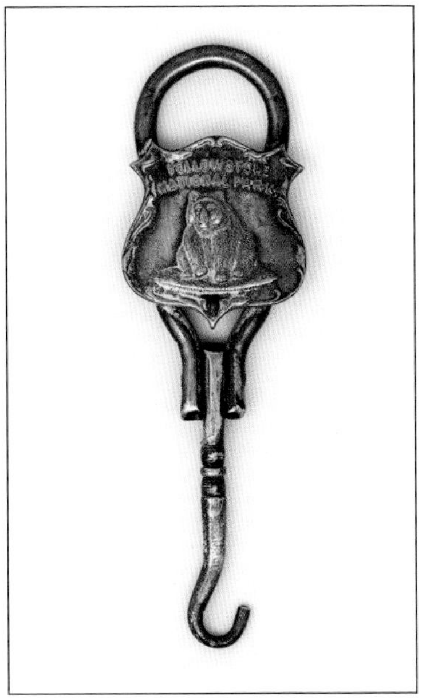

Yellowstone National Park, K & O Co. shield with bear, Kronheimer & Oldenbusch Co., Brooklyn, NY, four and one quarter inch metal shoe lace hook. *Bob Reynolds Collection*

Great Falls Yellowstone Park and Yellowstone National Park with sitting bear K&O shield, two and one quarter inch pair of candle holders, Kronheimer & Oldenbusch Co., New York. *Francis Historic Collections*

Entrance Arch, Yellowstone Park, K&O shield, 4-inch metal bank, Kronheimer & Oldenbusch Co., New York. *Francis Historic Collections*

Yellowstone National Park, bear K&O shield, one- and three-quarter inch metal trophy shaped three handled cup, Kronheimer & Oldenbusch Co., New York. *Francis Historic Collections*

Yellowstone Park, bear button, 3 x 2 inches metal lidded compact case with 3 compartments and chain, S. Blecher & Son, Philadelphia or Robbins Co., Attleboro, Mass. *Bob Reynolds Collection*

Yellowstone National Park, Old Faithful, three and one half by one- and one-half inch four-legged metal hinged jewelry box, Made in Japan. *Jay C Lyndes Family Collection*

Jewelry

Bobby Reynolds

While there is no formal term for people who collect jewelry, several names do come to mind, such as Blingoholic and Jewel-Junkie. Having a rather large collection of Yellowstone jewelry, I feel either name could be applied.

There is a wide variety of jewelry one can collect. Rings, bracelets, necklaces, perfume holders, etc., come in a multitude of variations and makers. As such, it is much like collecting spoons. The fun is finding the unique and rare item. Whether you collect vintage or modern jewelry, both can bring pleasure and add value to your collection.

Yellowstone Park, two and one quarter inch metal stick pin, Sterling Top, no maker. *Francis Historic Collections*

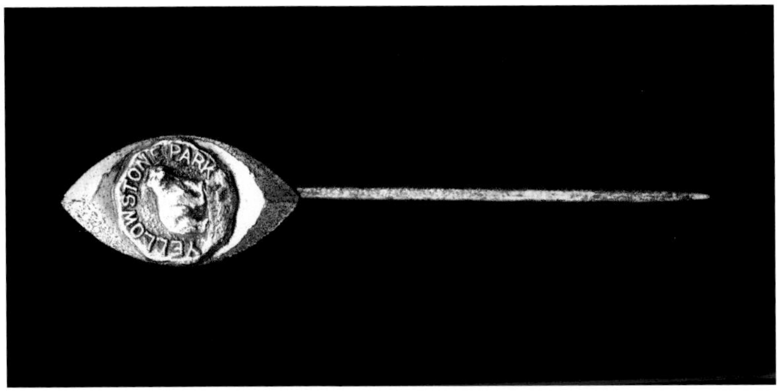

Yellowstone Park, two and one eighth inch hat or hair pin with bear button, Robbins Co Attelboro. *Kate Spangler Collection*

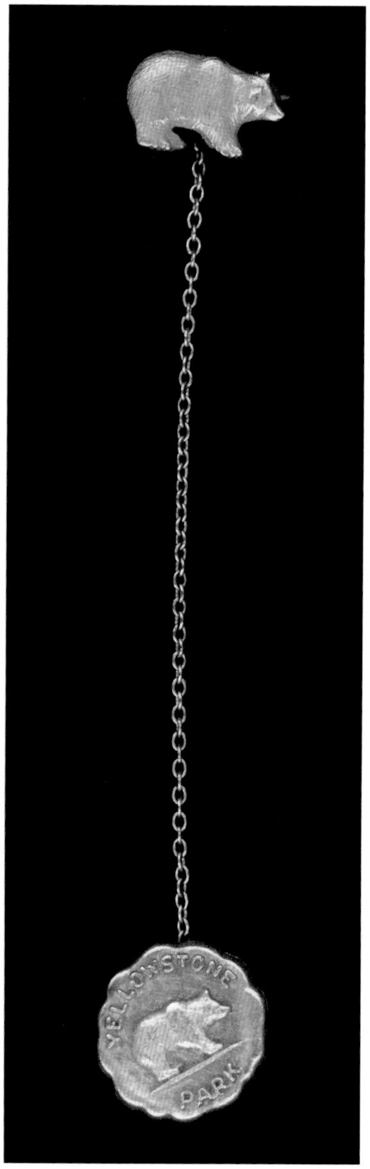

Yellowstone Park, chain brooch pin with bear on each end, gold colored, two and ten sixteenth inch in total length, no maker, possible Bates & Klinke Inc., Attleboro. *Bob Reynolds Collection*

Yellowstone Nat'l Park, four leaf clover and bear brooch pin, three and one quarter inch, no maker, may be Robbins Co. *Bob Reynolds Collection*

Yellowstone Park, broach pin with bear, one- and one-half inches on original card, Robbins, Co., Attleboro. *Bob Reynolds Collection*

Upper Geyser Basin, Yellowstone Park, enamel brooch pin one and one quarter inch, Made In Czecko Slovakia. *Bob Reynolds Collection*

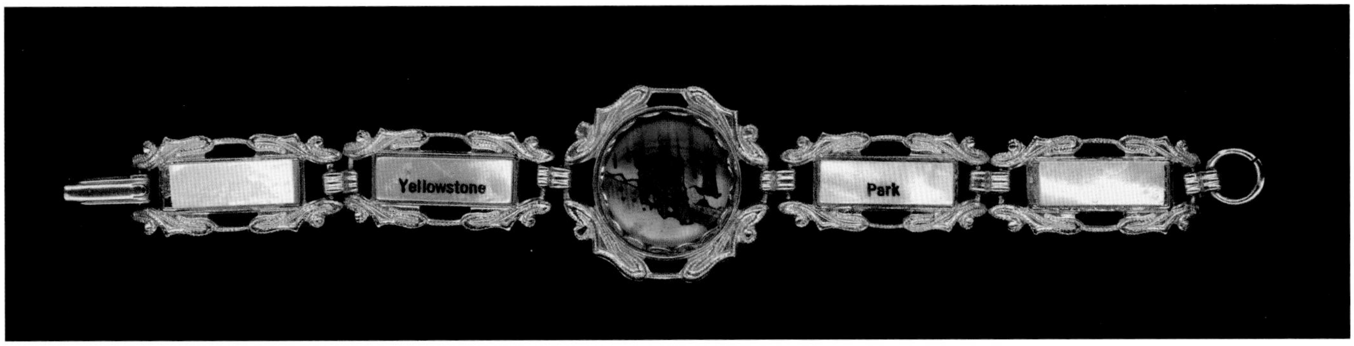

Yellowstone Park with bear, six-inch-long bracelet, no maker. *Bob Reynolds Collection*

Yellowstone Park, bear, two and one half by one and one quarter inch metal bracelet, no maker. *Bob Reynolds Collection*

Yellowstone Park, bear button, two and one eighth inch metal bracelet with cats and dogs, Robbins Co., Attleboro, MA. *Bob Reynolds Collection*

COMPACTS

No Hugging Allowed, Yellowstone Park, bear chained to tree, two and one eighth inch lid to compact, Made In USA, no maker. *Bob Reynolds Collection*

Yellowstone Park, bear button, one- and one-half inch silver nickel compact with chain, Robbins Co., Attleboro, MA. *Bob Reynolds Collection*

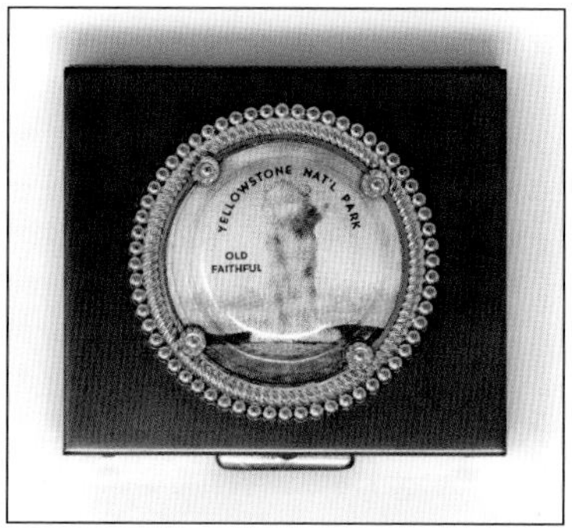

Yellowstone Nat'l Park, Old Faithful, metal compact with hinged lid and mirror inside, no maker, two and three quarter by two- and one-half inch. *Francis Historic Collections*

PERFUME

Left: Yellowstone Park, one and one half by one inch metal perfume container with bear, either S. Blecher & Son, Philadelphia or Robbins Co., Attleboro. *Bob Reynolds Collection*

Right: Yellowstone Park 2 x 1 inch metal perfume container with bear, either S. Blecher Son, Philadelphia, or Robbins Co., Attleboro. *Bob Reynolds Collection*

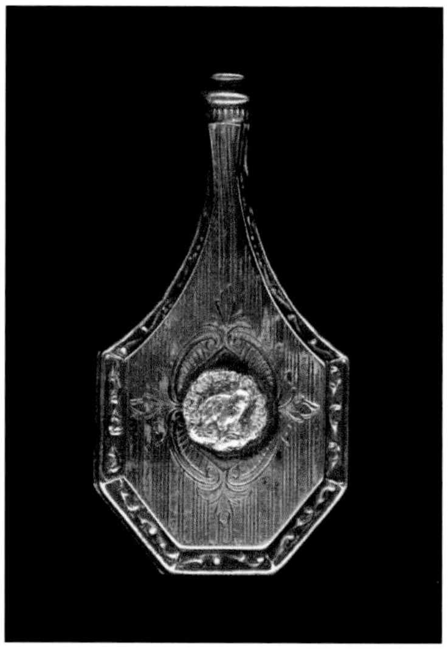

TINS & BOXES

Yellowstone National Park, metal hinged lid jewelry box, Japan, powder blue, three and one quarter by two and six sixteenth inch. *Bob Reynolds Collection*

Great Falls, Yellowstone Park, 3 x 4-inch tin three-legged storage unit or powder puff, Helvetic Importer and Manufacturers Corp, New York. *Bob Reynolds Collection*

THIMBLES

Yellowstone Park, bear, three quarter inch metal thimble, Sunburst, Made in USA, Copyright 1999. *Bob Reynolds Collection*

Yellowstone Park, bear button, three quarter inch sterling silver thimble, Robbins Co., Attleboro, Mass. *Bob Reynolds Collection*

Key Carrying Device, Patented Dec 1, 1908, A. H. Merrilll, Inventor, four and one eighth inch steel key ring, Robbins Co., Attleboro, Mass., Yellowstone Park. *Bob Reynolds Collection*

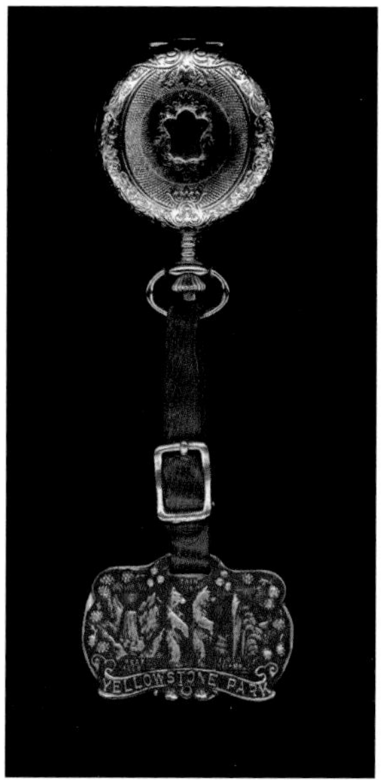

Yellowstone Park, metal twin cubs fob with leather strap and Arenix quartz pocket watch, owned by Luis B Ortega, PO Box 1251, Walnut Creek, Calif., fob is two by one and one quarter inch, total with watch and strap is 6 inches, no maker on fob, most likely Robbins Co. *Bob Reynolds Collection*

Yellowstone Park, one and ten sixteenth by one and one eighth inch metal suitcase shaped fob with bear, Robbins Co., Attleboro. *Bob Reynolds Collection*

Yellowstone Pocket Watch with bear on reverse, Waltham pocket watch, nickel silver circa 1890's, both sides scanned. *Jay C. Lyndes Family Collection*

CUFF LINKS

Yellowstone Park, metal bear cuff link pair, 1 inch combined, Robbins Co., Attleboro. *Bob Reynolds Collection*

TIE CLASPS

Yellowstone Park, metal bear tie clasp, fourteen sixteenths of an inch, Robbins Co., Attleboro. *Bob Reynolds Collection*

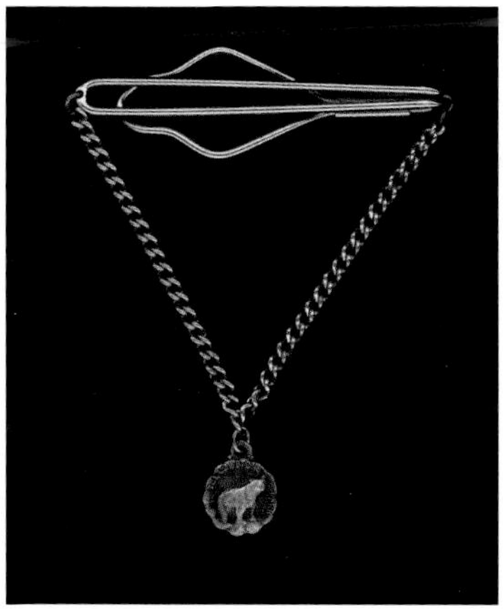

Yellowstone Park, metal bear chain charm on tie clasp, may have been used by park bus driver, two and one half by three-inch, Robbins Co., Attleboro. *Bob Reynolds Collection*

RINGS

Yellowstone Park, bear and eagles, no maker, one by three quarter inch metal ring. *Bob Reynolds Collection*

Yellowstone Park, Old Faithful, gold color, three quarter by ten sixteenth inch metal ring, no maker. *Bob Reynolds Collection*

MONEY CLIP & BELT BUCKLES

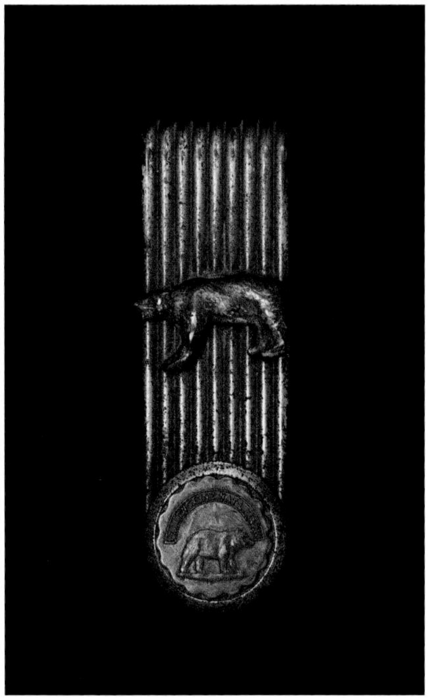

Figure 1. Yellowstone Park, bear button, metal money clip, maker unknown, two and one half by thirteen sixteenth inch. *Bob Reynolds Collection*

Figure 2. Yellowstone Park, bear button on sterling belt buckle with leather belt, Robbins Co., Attleboro, Mass, one and one half by three quarter inches. *Bob Reynolds Collection*

Figure 3. Yellowstone, metal buckle on leather belt, may be a hat band, Yellowstone Park. *Tom Murphy Collection*

GRAND CANYON FROM GRAND VIEW, YELLOWSTONE NATIONAL PARK, five and fourteen sixteenth inch plate, Made in Germany for Hefferlin Mercantile Co., Tourist Outfitters, Livingston and Cinnabar, Mont. *Jay C. Lyndes Family Collection*

Lower Falls, Yellowstone Park, Hand - painted, The Jonroth Studios, Germany, Painted and Imported for Alex Stuart, West Yellowstone, Mont., two and three quarter by four and one eighth inch handled pitcher. *Jay C. Lyndes Family Collection*

Steamer Zillah, Yellowstone Lake, Viola, Germany, Wheelock, Made In Germany for the Yellowstone Lake Boat Co., Yellowstone National Park, USA, Dresden. *Jay C. Lyndes Family Collection*

Old Faithful Geyser, Yellowstone Park, Wheelock Dresden Germany, three and one half by four-inch cobalt blue pitcher with handle. *Jay C. Lyndes Family Collection*

Punch Bowl, Yellowstone Park, Wyo., 6-inch plate, Wheelock, Made in Austria for H. E. Klamer, Upper Geyser Basin, Yellowstone Park, Wyo., Vienna. *Tom Murphy Collection*

Old Faithful Geyser, 10-inch plate, Souvenir of Picturesque Yellowstone Park, Old English Staffordshire Ware, Made in England, Imported for Frost Curio Shop Cody Wyoming. *Francis Historic Collections*

Fine Staffordshire Ware set, Designed Exclusively For Hamilton Stores, West Yellowstone, Montana, Made In England. *Bob Reynolds Collection*

Old Faithful Geyser, Yellowstone Park, Jonroth England, Royal Winton, three-inch creamer. *Francis Historic Collections*

Souvenir Of "Yellowstone Park", no maker, handled pitcher, three by one- and one-half inch. *Bob Reynolds Collection*

Indian Paint Brush, Imported For Yellowstone Park Co., Yellowstone Park, Wyoming, Fine Bone China, Made In England, 3379 N, cup: four and one half by two- and three-quarter inch, saucer: five- and three-quarter inch, hand painted. *Francis Historic Collections*

Entrance To Yellowstone Park, Monida, Mont., no maker, two and five sixteenth by two-inch custard glass container. *Tom Murphy Collection*

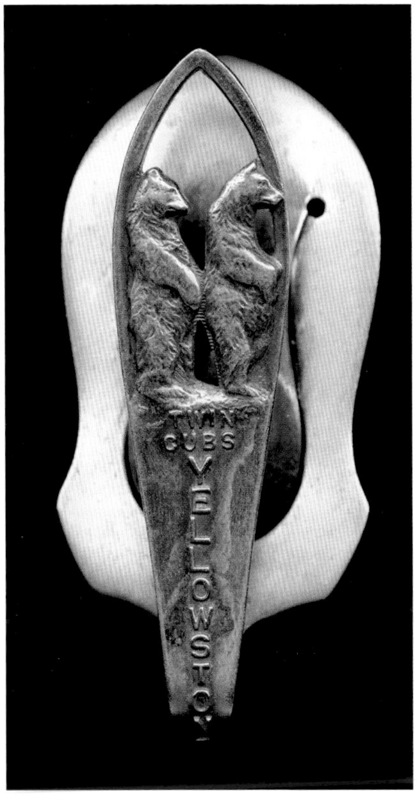

Figure 1. Yellowstone National Park, Robbins Co, Attleboro, Mass, bear shield, hammered copper metal napkin holder, gold colored, two and three quarter by one- and one-half inch. *Bob Reynolds Collection*

Figure 2. Twin Cubs, Yellowstone Park on folded cutout handle two and one quarter inch metal folded bill or napkin clip, silver colored, Robbins Co., Attleboro, Mass. *Francis Historical Collection*

Yellowstone Park, two sterling metal napkin holders, 2 x 1 inch, 33, Robbins Co., Attleboro, MA. *Bob Reynolds Collection*

SALT & PEPPER SHAKERS

Old Faithful Inn and Old Faithful Geyser at Sunrise, Yellowstone Park, metal and celluloid salt and pepper shakers, no maker, two and one quarter inch. *Bob Reynolds Collection*

"Yellowstone Park", salt and pepper shaker set shaped like a television, three and six sixteenth by one and ten sixteenth by two and fourteen sixteenth inch, no maker. *Francis Historic Collections*

BOTTLE OPENERS

Yellowstone Park, five and nine sixteenth by one- and one-half inch metal bottle opener, Colonial Prov., USA. *Bob Reynolds Collection*

Yellowstone Park, four and five sixteenth by one- and one-half inch metal bottle top opener, no maker. *Bob Reynolds Collection*

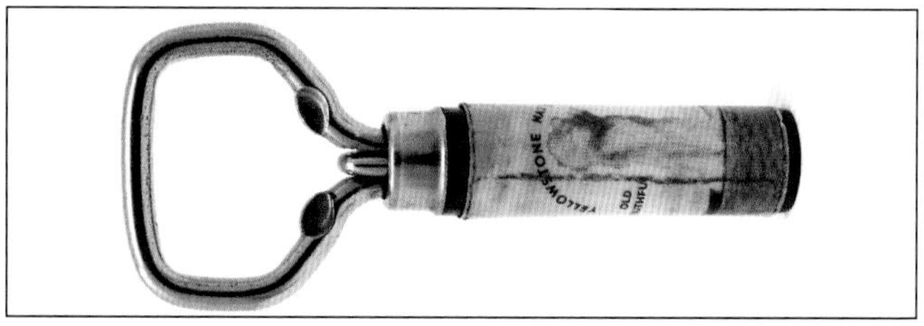

Left: Yellowstone Nat'l Park, Old Faithful, three- and three-quarter inch metal bottle opener, no maker. *Francis Historic Collections*

MUGS

Yellowstone Ceramics, P.O. Box 551, West Yellowstone, Mont., Wallace China, Los Angeles, Calif., three and one half by four-inch coffee mug, Yellowstone Park, Flowers, 4-U, 1954. *Bob Reynolds Collection*

Handled stein with metal top lid, Old Faithful Geyser, twin bear cubs, Liberty Cap, made in Germany, eight and one half by five- and one-half inch. *Francis Historic Collections*

Yellowstone Park, Treasure Craft founded by Alfred A. Levine in 1945, Gardena, California, Made in USA, four and one eighth by five and one eighth inch ceramic mug. *Francis Historic Collections*

SHOT GLASSES

Yellowstone Nat'l Park, bear button, Only A Thimble Full, metal shot glass, may be Robbins Co., Attleboro, Mass., one and three quarter by one and ten sixteenth inch. *Bob Reynolds Collection*

Yellowstone National Park, two- and one-half inch genuine pewter shot glass, no maker. *Francis Historic Collections*

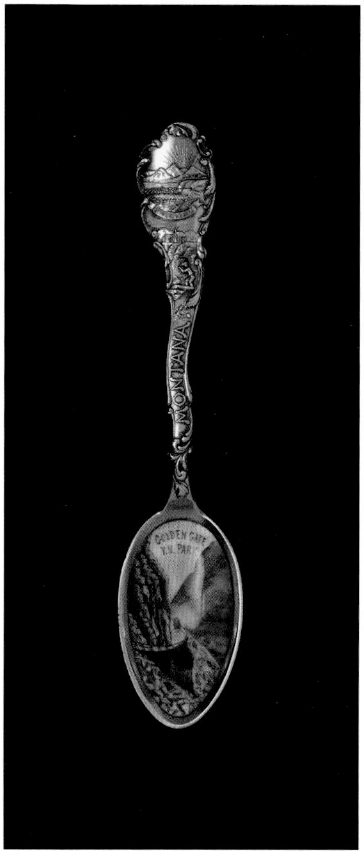

Golden Gate Y.N.Park enamel bowl, Montana handle, five and ten sixteenth inch sterling spoon, Shepard Mfg. Co., Melrose Highlands, MA. , in business from 1893 to 1923. *Bob Reynolds Collection*

Shepard Mfg. Co, Melrose Highlands, MA, in business 1893 to 1923, enamel Geyser erupting on handle, five and seven eighth inch sterling gold wash spoon, Yellowstone Park engraved on bowl. *Jay C. Lyndes Family Collection*

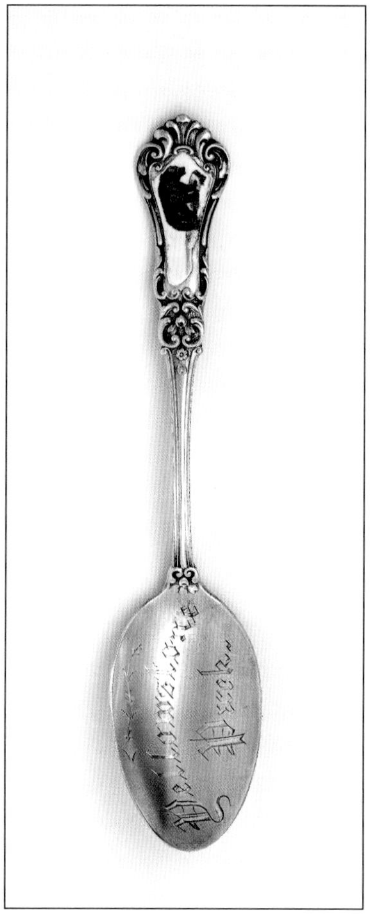

Enamel bear on handle, Yellowstone Park engraved on bowl, five and one quarter inch sterling spoon, Shepard Mfg Co., Melrose Highlands, MA. *Jay C. Lyndes Family Collection*

Collecting Spoons

Bobby Reynolds

Even though there is no term for spoon collecting, it is a hobby that many people enjoy. Very easy to display, spoons trigger fond memories of places traveled. Spoons also create exciting treasure hunts as collectors look for rare hallmarks and uniquely engraved spoons.

Spoon collecting dates back to the 1890s and flourished until World War I. Today spoons are making a comeback because they are a great way to start a collection at a reasonable cost. There are many variations, such as length, shape, scenes, wording, material such as silver or copper, as well as enameled or plain. We have ornate forks that fall into this category as well.

Paye & Baker Manufacturing Co., North Attleboro, Mass., in business 1901 to 1960, stag with cutout lattice on handle, five-inch sterling spoon, engraved Yellowstone Park on bowl. *Bob Reynolds Collection*

H. H. Tammen Curio Co., three- and three-quarter inch sterling spoon, makers hallmarks on reverse, Bear handle, with engraved Yellowstone Park bowl. *Bob Reynolds Collection*

A Family Group, cutout deer on handle with Yellowstone Park, Robbins Co., Attleboro, Mass., five and one eighth inch sterling sugar spoon. *Bob Reynolds Collection*

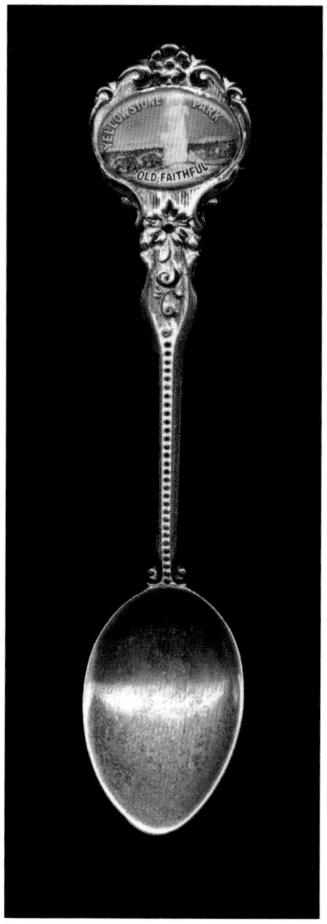

Yellowstone Park, Old Faithful, four- and three-quarter inch silverplated spoon, Celest, Perfection Plate PTY LTD Australia. *Francis Historic Collections*

Watson Company, Attleboro, Mass., running buffalo on twisted handle, 4-inch sterling spoon, Yellowstone Park engraved on bowl. *Bob Reynolds Collection*

Yellowstone, metal bear bell, no maker, three and one quarter by two and seven sixteenth inch. *Bob Reynolds Collection*

A Family Group, Yellowstone Nat'l Park, hammered copper clip, Robbins Co., Attleboro, Mass, three and one half by two- and one-half inch. *Bob Reynolds Collection*

Yellowstone Park, four and three quarter inch standing bear figurine, Lawrence Stevens Tenney sculptor, 1934. *Francis Historic Collections*

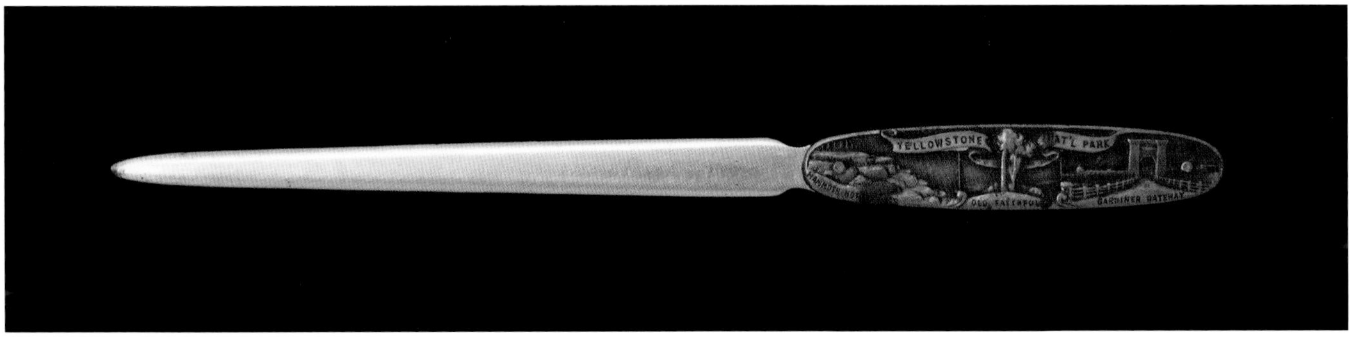

Souvenir of Yellowstone Nat'l Park, no maker, seven and four sixteenth inch copper coloration letter opener with park scenes. *Bob Reynolds Collection*

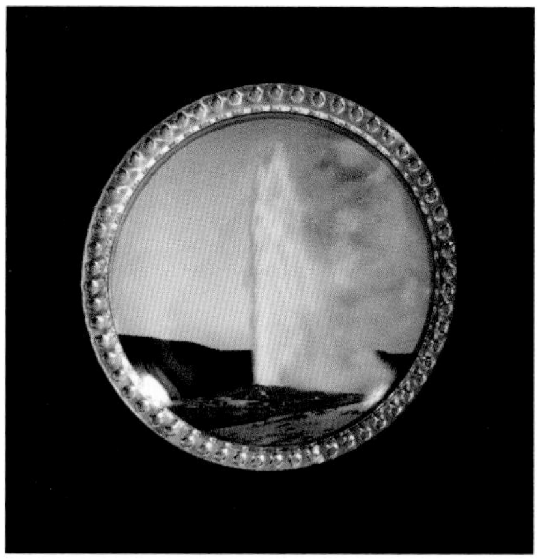

Old Faithful Geyser erupting, glass domed paperweight, 4 inch with embossed glass plate by Haynes Photo on verso. *Jay C. Lyndes Family Collection*

Yellowstone Park, Old Faithful and bear, metal pencil holder, no maker, three by two- and one-half inch. *Bob Reynolds Collection*

Yellowstone Park with bear, metal pad and pencil set, unknown maker. *Jay C. Lyndes Family Collection*

Three and one quarter by three inch metal cowboy on rearing horse toy, Made in USA, HNP, Souvenir of Yellowstone Park. *Jay C. Lyndes Family Collection*

Yellowstone, moose family in winter snow on hanging metal ornament, no maker, three and one quarter by two and one eighth inch. *Francis Historic Collections*

Yellowstone Park, MOTHER, 11 inch leather pillow with fringe, no maker. *Francis Historic Collections*

Yellowstone National Park including scenes of Old Faithful, Jupiter Terrace, Golden Gate, Old Faithful Inn, Fort Yellowstone, NPR Station Entrance Gate, 8 x 4-inch mirror, no maker, circa 1907. *Bob Reynolds Collection*

Bison casserole pottery with lid, made at Old Faithful Lodge by Carl Sheehan, 2002, Price $285, 10 x 9 inch. *Francis Historic Collections*

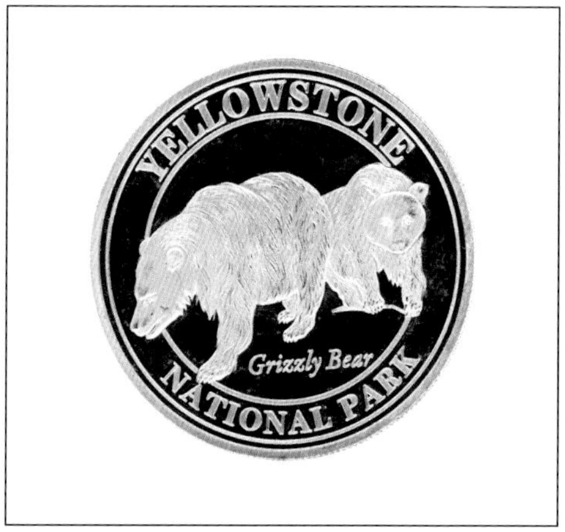

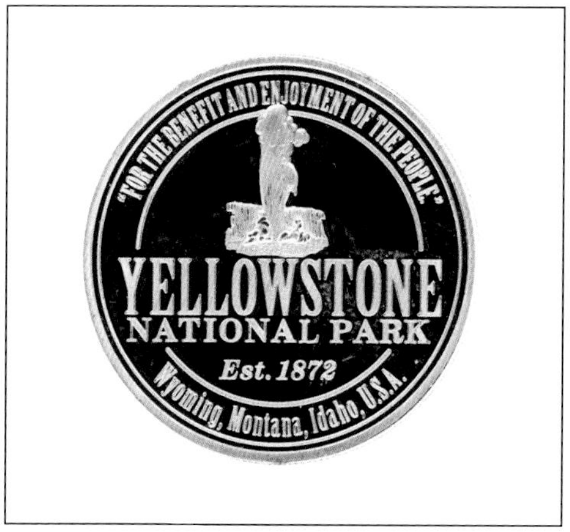

Yellowstone National Park, Grizzly Bear, Est. 1872-, one- and one-half inch coin or medallion, Old Faithful geyser on reverse. *Bob Reynolds Collection*

Yellowstone National Park, Old Faithful, Souvenir Paperweight, large metal coin, no maker, two- and three-quarter inches. *Bob Reynolds Collection*

Bus driver shaped hat with owners name '"Sheldon" on top, made of leather and metal with hinged door on bottom for coin storage, no maker, two and three quarter by two and twelve sixteenth inch. *Bob Reynolds Collection*

Yellowstone Park, Indian in headdress, four- and one-half inch bank, Made in Japan. *Francis Historic Collections*

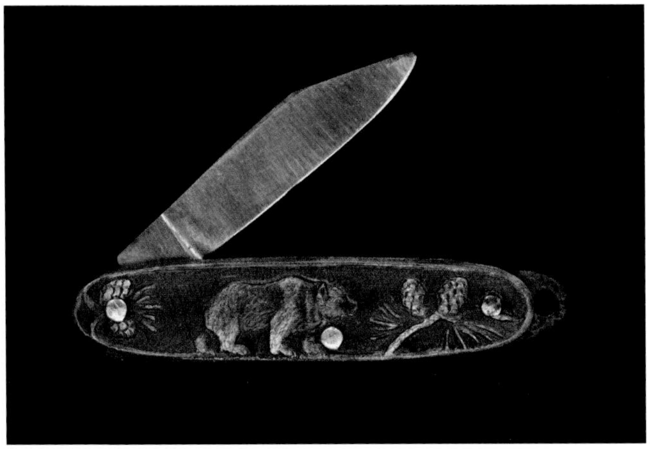

Yellowstone Park, bear, and pinecones, one- and one-half inch metal pocketknife, Tammen Germany. *Bob Reynolds Collection*

Yellowstone Park, two and six sixteenth inch metal two blade pocketknife, possibly S. Blecher & Son, Philadelphia or Robbins Co., Attleboro. *Bob Reynolds Collection*

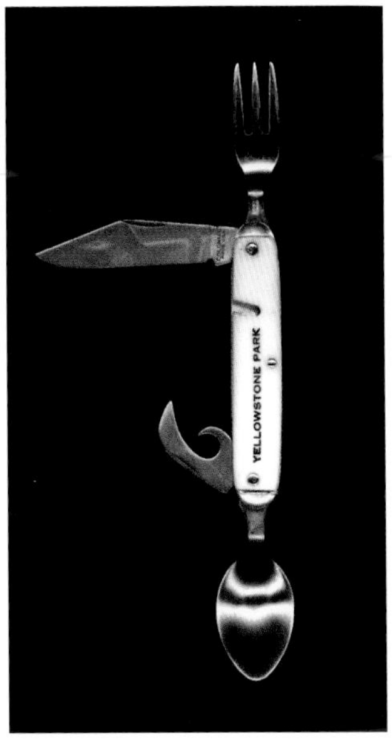

Paye & Baker Manufacturing Co., North Attleboro, Mass., in business 1901 to 1960, stag with cutout lattice on handle, five-inch sterling spoon, engraved Yellowstone Park on bowl. *Bob Reynolds Collection*

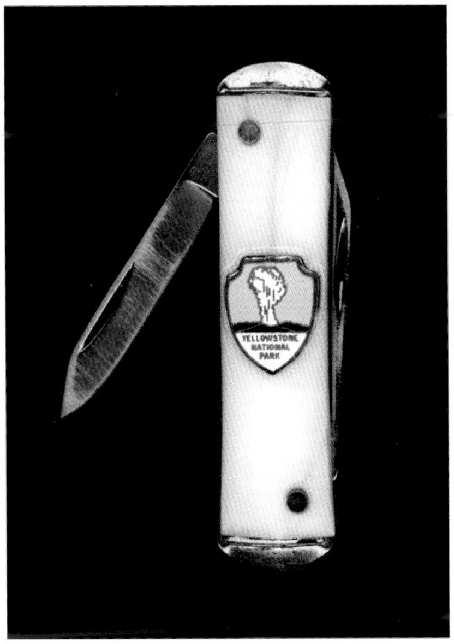

Yellowstone National Park, two and nine sixteenth inch two bladed pocketknife with plastic handle and geyser in shield, maker unknown, USA. *Bob Reynolds Collection*

1925, Coming From Yellowstone Park, navy and orange color, thirty-five and one quarter by thirteen inch felt pennant, no maker. *Jay C. Lyndes Family Collection*

1926, Yellowstone Park, thirty-four and three quarters by thirteen and one quarter inch felt banner, purple and pastel yellow color, bear, Manufactured by Bloom Bros Co., The Quality Line, Minneapolis. *Jay C. Lyndes Family Collection*

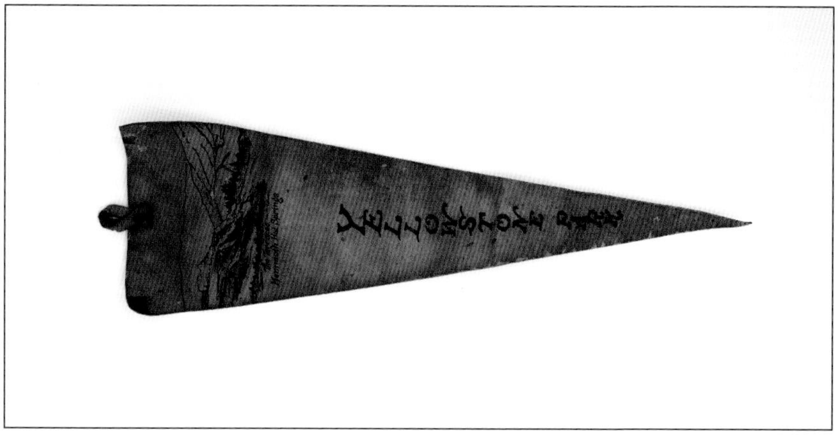

Yellowstone Park, The Terraces, Mammoth Hot Springs, no maker, fifteen- and one-half inch leather pennant. *Bob Reynolds Collections*

GAMES

Game of Yellowstone, No 1122., H. E. Klamer, Upper Geyser Basin, Yellowstone Park, Wyo., 3-6-Y, dark red box, three and three quarter by two and thirteen sixteenth inch, The Cincinnati Game Co., Cincinnati, USA, bison and Lower Falls card reverse, 52 game cards. *Jay C. Lyndes Family Collection*

Yellowstone Park Souvenir Playing Cards, Published By Yellowstone Park Tourist Supply, three and ten sixteenth by two and ten sixteenth inch playing card box and sample card. *Tom Murphy Collection*

HATS

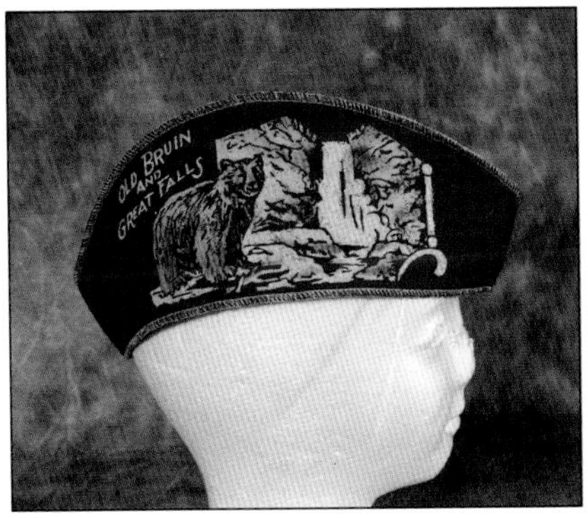

Yellowstone National Park, eleven and one quarter by three- and three-quarter inch red felt envelope hat, Old Bruin And Great Falls. *Bob Reynolds Collection*

Yellowstone Park, ten- and one-half inch checkerboard design touring hat, no maker. *Jay C. Lyndes Family Collection*

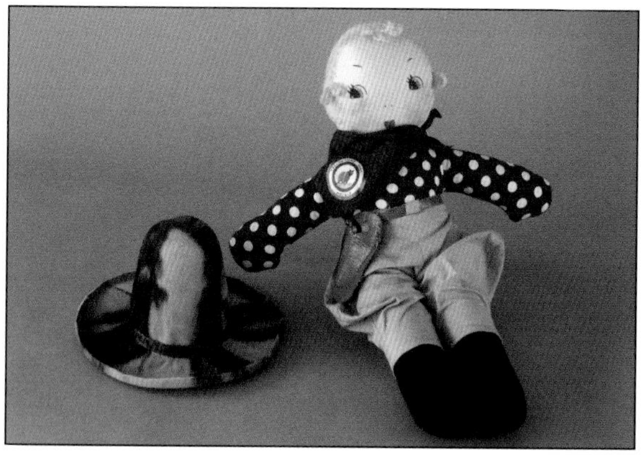

Cloth cowgirl doll with hat and Yellowstone Park Hotels sticker, Photo by Tom Murphy. *Jack & Sue Davis Collection*

YNP wooden park bus, four and one half by two-inch, D and Me, LLP. Stevensville, MT 59870, Made in Montana. *Kate Spangler Collection*

Yellowstone, bison or buffalo snow globe, Tom Murphy's Wilderness Collection, Limited Edition, five and one half inch by *four inch, $17.09, Made in China. Tom Murphy Collection*

A Real Souvenir Of Yellowstone, Bark Dolls, Made from the bark of trees, includes packaging card, doll nine- and one-half inch, California Redwood Doll, Patent #109402, P. D. Wilson Company, 2510 Durant Avenue, Berkeley, California, circa 1930s. *Bob Reynolds Collection*

Yellowstone Park, Indian Motifs, American Indian Made, heavy cardboard with rubber top and bottom, six and three quarter by six- and one-half inch toy drum. *Bob Reynolds Collection*

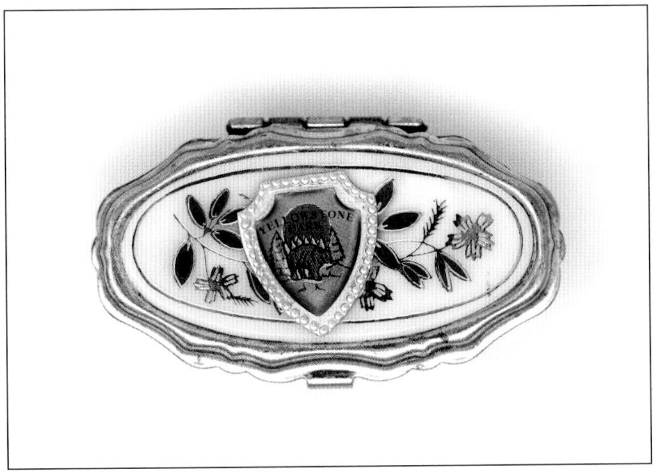

Yellowstone Park, metal pocket or purse ashtray, Made in China, two and one quarter by one and one quarter inch. *Bob Reynolds Collection*

Yellowstone Park, metal bear ashtray, Robbins Co., Attleboro, MA, three and ten sixteenth by three and ten sixteenth inch. *Bob Reynolds Collection*

Yellowstone Park, two by one and one quarter inch metal lighter with bear, Robbins Co., Attleboro, Mass., Gem. Jay C. *Lyndes Family Collection*

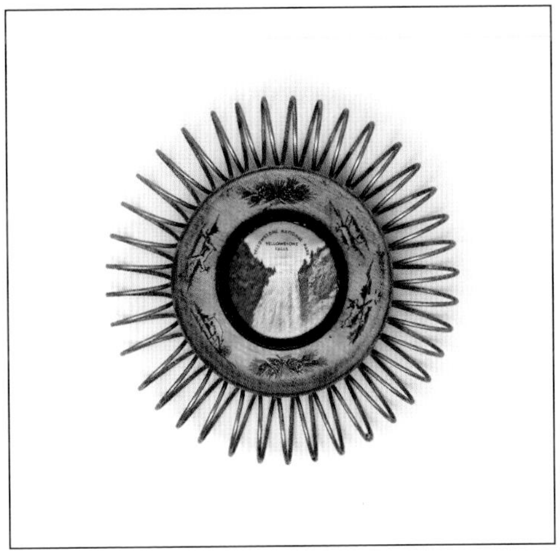

Yellowstone National Park, Yellowstone Falls, five and one quarter inch metal ash tray, no maker. *Francis Historic Collections*

Yellowstone Park, metal cowboy hat, no maker, two and one eighth inch. *Francis Historic Collections*

A Good Luck Bear from Yellowstone Park, sent from Gardiner, Mont. for 3 cents, three and six sixteenth by two and one quarter inch. *Francis Historic Collections*

Yellowstone National Park, JB 1423, three and one half by two inch metal women's shoe with bow, unknown maker. *Bob Reynolds Collection*

Yellowstone Park, metal electric miniature iron with cord, four by two and one quarter inch. *Jay C. Lyndes Family Collection*

Yellowstone National Park, 1910, six and three quarter inch wood hand carved bear brush, no maker. *Jay C. Lyndes Family Collection*

Yellowstone Park special "one of a kind" spurs with park wildlife, eight by three and three quarter inch, made by L&M, Denny Lytle & Jim Mower, Bountiful, Utah with Gordon Andrus Sage Creek Saddlery, Coalville, Utah doing the carved leather straps, David Hewitt Collection

Yellowstone Park, bear with fish, figurine tape measure, no maker, two and one half by one and six sixteenth inch. *Bob Reynolds Collection*

Twin Cubs, Yellowstone Park, K&O shield, metal matchbox cover, Kronheimer & Oldenbusch Co., New York, two and six sixteenth by one and nine sixteenth inch. *Bob Reynolds Collection*

Yellowstone National Park, four- and three-quarter inch plant spray mister bottle with nozzle, Made in Taiwan. *Francis Historic Collections*

Yellowstone National Park, four- and three-quarter inch jar container with lid, Copyright DESMOND. *Francis Historic Collections*

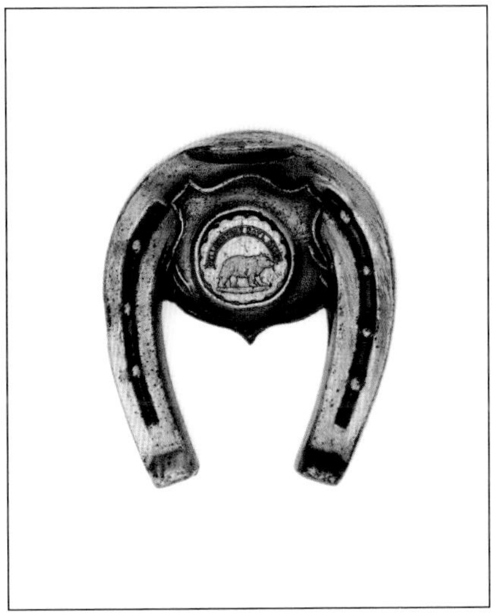

Yellowstone Park, bear button, metal horseshoe, maker unknown, two and one quarter by two and one eighth inch. *Bob Reynolds Collection*

Four-inch metal painted figurine with Yellowstone Park signpost, no maker. *Jay C. Lyndes Family Collection*

Yellowstone Park, two- and three-quarter inch by one- and three-quarter inch metal note pad and pencil, no maker. *Francis Historic Collections*

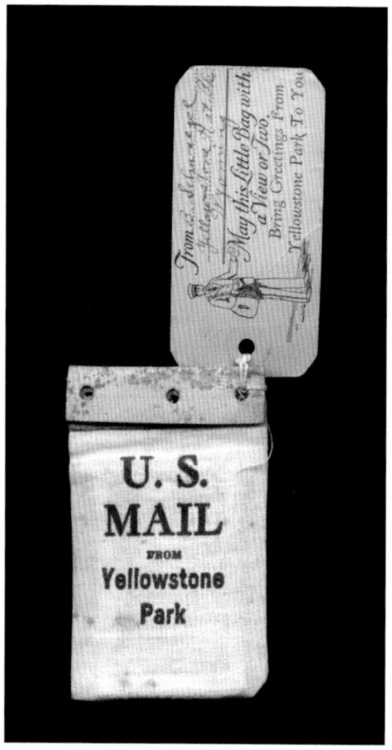

U.S. Mail From Yellowstone Park, four by two- and one-half inch cloth bag with bear and photos attached to address mailing card. *Francis Historic Collections*

Yellowstone Nat'l Park metal book mark with bear, two- and one-half inches, no maker. *Bob Reynolds Collection*

Yellowstone Park, metal bear medallion and thermometer key, eight and one quarter inch, no maker. *Francis Historic Collections*

Yellowstone, five- and three-quarter inch bear chalk book-ends, no maker. *Francis Historic Collections*

Anniversaries and Celebrations

Yellowstone Diamond Jubilee Anniversary 1872 - 1947, Northern Pacific Railway, Yellowstone Park Line, two and one half by one- and three-quarter inch gummed stamp. *Bob Reynolds Collection*

National Park Service, 50th Anniversary, 1916 to 1966, two- and one-half inch button pin. *Bob Reynolds Collection*

Fiftieth Anniversary, Yellowstone Park, one and six sixteenth inch metal fob, both sides scanned, W. &. H. Co, N.J., Created By Act of Congress, March 1, 1872, "For the Benefit and Enjoyment of the People." *Bob Reynolds Collection*

Old Faithful, Yellowstone National Park, 1872 - 1947, Diamond 75th Anniversary, one and one quarter inch coin or token. *Bob Reynolds Collection*

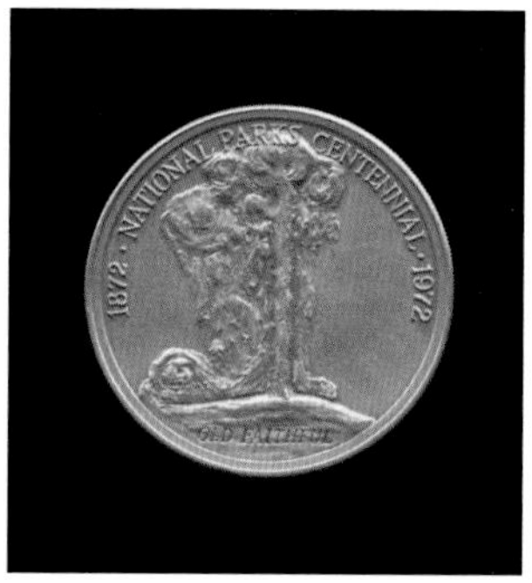

1872 National Parks Centennial 1972, Old Faithful, one- and one-half inch metal token. *Francis Historic Collections*

Yellowstone "Old Faithful" 1872 - 1972, Commemorating The 100th Anniversary Of Yellowstone National Park, 90 Proof Bourbon Whiskey, 1 Dozen Fifths, case is:15 x 11 x 10 inch, each bottle is individually numbered on a card, Hamilton General Stores, this box Serial No. M683377, Date Filled May 19, 1972. *Bob Reynolds Collection*

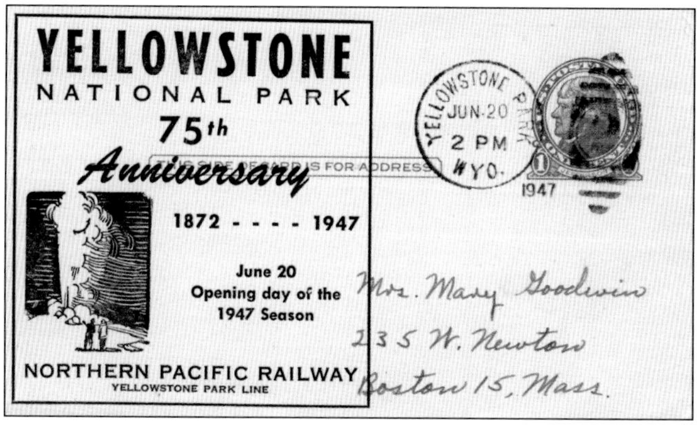

Yellowstone National Park, 75th Anniversary, 1872 - 1947, June 20 Opening day of the 1947 Season, Northern Pacific Railway, Yellowstone Park Line, June 20, 1947 postmark, five and one half by three and four sixteenth inch postcard. *Francis Historic Collectibles*

100th Anniversary, 1904 to 2004, Old Faithful Inn, Yellowstone National Park, four and one quarter by three-inch metal and glass paperweight, $19.99, Made in USA. *Francis Historic Collectibles*

Old Faithful Inn, Yellowstone National Park, 100th Anniversary 1904 to 2004, Genuine 24k Gold Flashed Brass, Made in China, $8.99, four and one sixteenth by four and one sixteenth inch hanging ornament in case. *Francis Historic Collectibles*

Old Faithful Inn, Centennial 1904 to 2004, Extra Strength Peppermints, Yellowstone National Park, Limited Edition Collector Tin, , Manufactured by Brown & Haley, three- and three-quarter inch unopened container. *Francis Historic Collectibles*

100th Anniversary 1904 to 2004, Old Faithful Inn, Yellowstone National Park, 7 x 5-inch postcard, Published by Impact Photo Graphics #26540. *Francis Historic Collectibles*

Old Faithful Inn, 100th Anniversary 1904 to 2004, Yellowstone National Park, nine and one quarter inch champagne glass. *Francis Historic Collectibles*

Old Faithful, Visitor Education Center, 2010, one and one half by one inch metal button pin. *Mary Heller Collection*

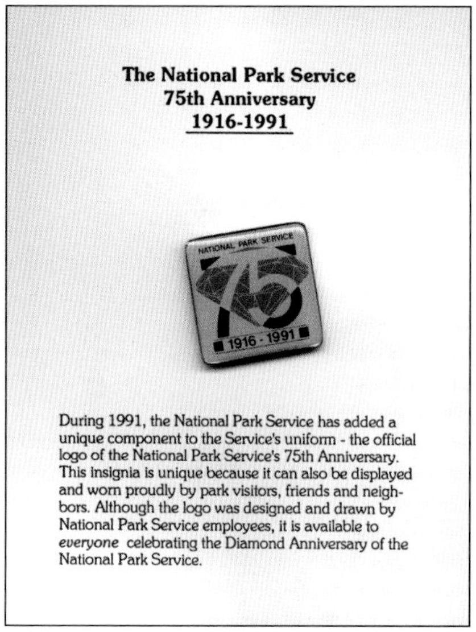

The National Park 75th Anniversary, 1916 - 1991, lapel button on original card, pin is one and one eighth by one and one eighth inch, Adeline Moulton estate. *Francis Historic Collections*

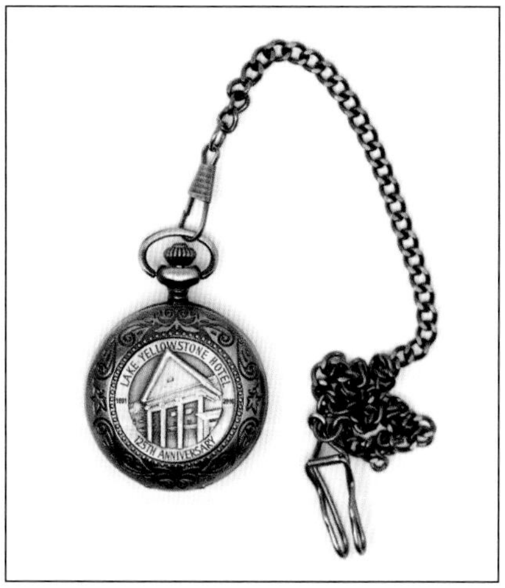

Lake Yellowstone Hotel, 125th Anniversary, 1891 to 2016, one- and three-quarter inch metal pocket watch and chain, Xanterra. *Rick & Karen Hoeninghausen Collection*

The Roosevelt Arch Centennial, 1903 to 2003, Yellowstone National Park, Yellowstone Park Foundation, Price 6 dollars, one and one eighth inch lapel pin. *Francis Historic Collections*

Park Employees

Savage Mug, Yellowstone Ceramics, PO Box 551, West Yellowstone, Mont., hand painted by Wallace Magner for park employees, Indian on front with Savage Daze, five and one half by five- and one-half inches reverse has Barb Bus Boy Food Slopper. *Bob Reynolds Collection*

Savage Mug, Yellowstone Ceramics, PO Box 551, West Yellowstone, Mont., hand painted by Wallace Magner for park employees, Indian on front, five and one half by five- and one-half inches, reverse has Byron Bus Boy UP Dining Lodge West Yellowstone. *Bob Reynolds Collection*

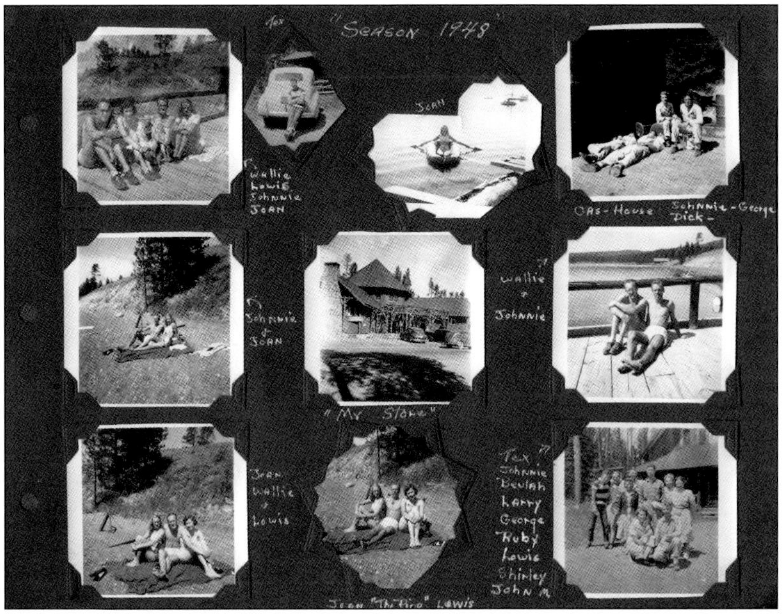

1948, Park Employee Album page, Lake Hamilton's General Store, black and white photos. *Francis Historic Collections*

Album page with group photo of Canyon Lodge staff. Park employee Helen Jacobs Canyon Hamilton's Store Photo Album, Canyon Lodge, 1952. This image shows both Yellowstone Park Company and Hamilton Store employees. *Francis Historic Collections*

Cabin boy and girl at guest cabin, 1933, Magic Lantern Glass Slide by J. E. Haynes. *Francis Historic Collections*

Park employees

Michael H. Francis

Working in Yellowstone is a prized summer job for thousands of people, including many young men and women, and undoubtedly most think those summers are the best of their lives—making new friends, being on their own, and enjoying the great Wonderland while they work. So, it is little wonder that collecting employee memorabilia is a favorite pursuit not only for former park employees but for the public as well.

For example, employee scrapbooks and photo albums allow a peek into the lives of seasonal workers, aka "savages," when they are not waiting on tourists or "dudes." These terms go back to the stagecoach days and were still in use when I started working in the park in 1974. Other nicknames included "pearl diver" for dishwashers, "pillow punchers" for room attendants, and "heavers" for waitresses.

Employee ephemera would include newspapers, contracts, pay stubs, certificates, and letters to and from home.

Bus driver hats, belt buckles, and tie clasps are also in demand for the avid collector.

Finally, and growing in collector popularity, are the so-called "Savage-Mugs."

Yellowstone National Park, 2-year employee pin, one half by seven sixteenth inch. *Bob Reynolds Collection*

Hamilton Stores, Yellowstone Park, 2-year employee pin. *Jack & Sue Davis Collection*

ASK ME ABOUT CANYON, two- and one-half inch round pin back, Yellowstone National Park, worn by front of house employees to promote Canyon Village, M L Schuman Co, Billings, MT. *Francis Historic Collections*

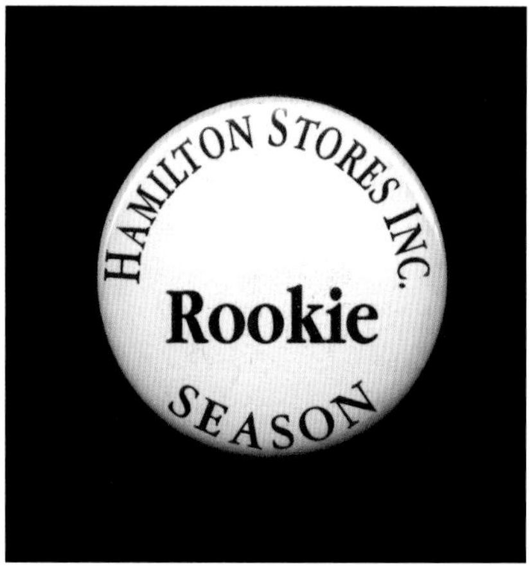

Hamilton Stores Inc, Employee Rookie Season, one- and one-half inch button pin. *Francis Historic Collections*

Hamilton Stores Inc, Employee 13-seasons pin, one half inch button pin. *Francis Historic Collections*

BUS DRIVERS

DICK, Yellowstone Park Company, metal bus driver belt buckle, circa 1954, Richard "Dick" Fullerton, Made by Hook-Fast, Red. U.S. Pat. Office, bus with long nose. *Francis Historic Collections*

Yellowstone Park Co., Transportation Division, bus driver hat with badge, star and two park bear buttons, Chet Herbert - driver, The Fechheimer Bros. Co., Uniforms, Cincinnati, Ohio, FBC, eleven and one half by ten by six-inch summer hat. *Bob Reynolds Collection*

EMPLOYEE PAPER DOCUMENTS

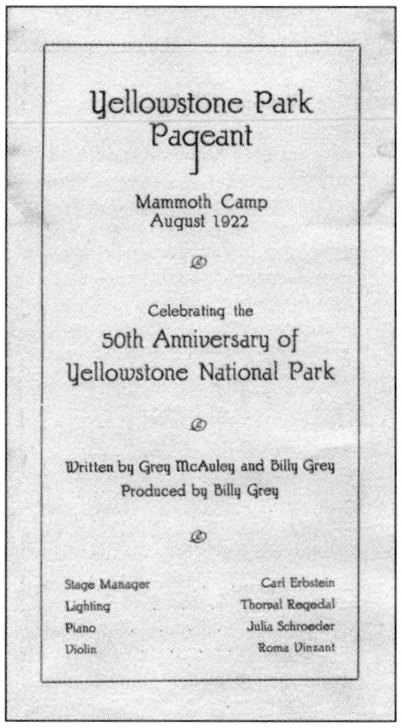

Yellowstone Park Pageant

Mammoth Camp
August 1922

Celebrating the
50th Anniversary of
Yellowstone National Park

Written by Grey McAuley and Billy Grey
Produced by Billy Grey

Stage Manager	Carl Erbstein
Lighting	Thorval Regedal
Piano	Julia Schroeder
Violin	Roma Vinzant

Yellowstone Park Pageant program, Mammoth Camp, Celebrating the 50th Anniversary of the Park, from Matte Kincaid Park Employee Album, Mammoth Hot Springs, August 1922. *Francis Historic Collections*

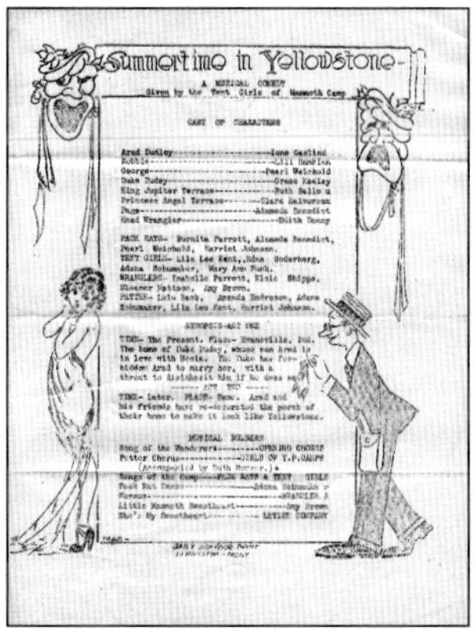

Mammoth Camp employee musical comedy entertainment flyer, Park employee Garnet Alder Mammoth Camp album, 1927. *Francis Historic Collections*

THE YELLOWSTONE CUB

Miss Yellowstone 1971

The Yellowstone Cub, Published by Yellowstone Park Concessioners' Recreation Program, August 28, 1971, 25 cents, fifteen and three quarter by eleven and six sixteenth inch newspaper cover. Printed by The Gallatin County Tribune, Bozeman, Editor - Sally Petersen, Lee Whittlesey –OF. *Jack and Sue Davis Collection*

MAMMOTH HOTEL, 8:15 P. M. Sept. 11, 1913.

On wit the Dance, Kid—
Let joy be unrefined!

EVERYTHING BARRED BUT THE

Turkey Trot	Grizzly Bear	Bunny Hug
Tango	Hook-Worm Wiggle	Camel Hump
Formation Glide	Half-Nelson	Hoochy-Mootchy
Trolley Twirl	Glad-Eye	Yiddisher Gavotte

N. B. The orchestra recently fell into Alum Creek and shrunk to two (2) members.

On wit the Dance, Kid - Let joy be unrefined! Mammoth Hotel, 8:15 P.M. Sept. 11, 1913. Five and five sixteenth by three and six sixteenth inch post card employee dance invitation. *John Alley Collection*

Savage Daze, three mugs decorated for the same park employee during her three-year span of 1965 to 1967, Patti from Missouri, five- and one-half inches tall, Old Faithful Inn and Lodge, Yellowstone Ceramics PO Box 551, West Yellowstone, Mont., hand painted by Wallace Magner for park employees only. *Bob Reynolds Collection*

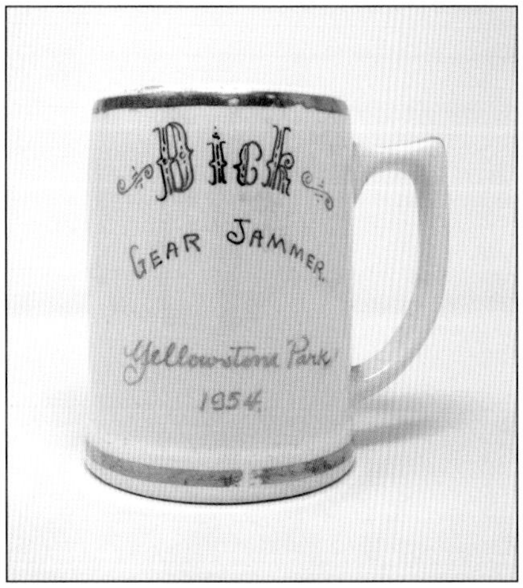

Savage Mug, Yellowstone Ceramics, P.O. Box 551, West Yellowstone, Mont., hand painted by Wallace Magner for park employees, front with bear, verso with: Dick, Gear Jammer, Yellowstone Park, 1954, five and one quarter by five- and one-half inch ceramic mug, Dick is Richard Fullerton who drove busses in the park during the mid-1950s. *Francis Historic Collections*

Indian caricature on front, on reverse: Jeannine, Hash Slinger, Fishing Bridge, Yellowstone Park, 1957, Wahpeton, H. S. Savage Mug made by Yellowstone Ceramics P.O. Box 551, West Yellowstone, Mont., hand painted by Wallace Magner for park employees, five and ten sixteenth by five- and one-half inch ceramic mug. *Bob Reynolds Collection*

Yellowstone Employee Savage-Mugs

Bobby Reynolds

Wallace B. Magner, Sr (1893-1972) was a well-known Western artist who painted famous Indians using oils on velvet. Because it became very time consuming to paint on velvet, Wallace turned to painting "savage-mugs" in West Yellowstone for the employees of the Park to fit the name they gave themselves, "Savages." These individualized mugs with hand-painted, roly-poly Indians or cute bears on them were inscribed in gold with the Savages' personal names and slogans, and were then heated in his kiln at Wallace's studio to make the gold inscriptions and finish on the porcelain mugs permanent.

If you worked in Yellowstone Park in the early 1950s through 1968 (the earliest we have record of is 1953 and the latest 1968 with one known mug having "1969" painted on after it was fired), chances are that you came in contact with the Yellowstone Ceramics Shop in West Yellowstone where Wallace Magner would create a one-of-a-kind mug for you with either a cartoon-style image of a Native American or a bear on one side and your name, summer job, and location in the park where you worked as well as possibly your home town, college, and the current year of employment in the Park.

I don't believe anyone knows for sure who started the tradition of getting a savage mug for each year of employment in Yellowstone Park, but we are only aware of Wallace Magner producing them for Park employees. We believe it was by word of mouth that you learned of the mugs and then went to the Yellowstone Ceramics Shop at 38 N. Canyon Street, West Yellowstone, Montana, to make the order for your personalized mug, because these one-of-a-kind mugs were not on sale to the general public.

When the infamous Yellowstone earthquake of 1959 hit, hundreds of Wallace Magner's Savage mugs that he had painstakingly created went crashing to the floor, breaking them into pieces and making unbroken ones all the more rare.

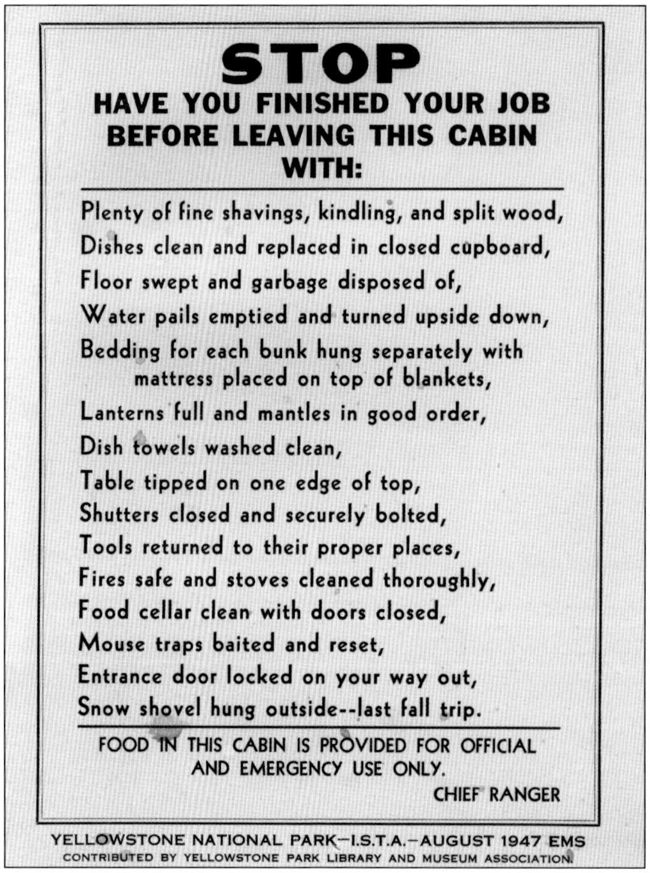

STOP

HAVE YOU FINISHED YOUR JOB BEFORE LEAVING THIS CABIN WITH:

Plenty of fine shavings, kindling, and split wood,
Dishes clean and replaced in closed cupboard,
Floor swept and garbage disposed of,
Water pails emptied and turned upside down,
Bedding for each bunk hung separately with
mattress placed on top of blankets,
Lanterns full and mantles in good order,
Dish towels washed clean,
Table tipped on one edge of top,
Shutters closed and securely bolted,
Tools returned to their proper places,
Fires safe and stoves cleaned thoroughly,
Food cellar clean with doors closed,
Mouse traps baited and reset,
Entrance door locked on your way out,
Snow shovel hung outside--last fall trip.

FOOD IN THIS CABIN IS PROVIDED FOR OFFICIAL AND EMERGENCY USE ONLY.

CHIEF RANGER

YELLOWSTONE NATIONAL PARK—I.S.T.A.—AUGUST 1947 EMS
CONTRIBUTED BY YELLOWSTONE PARK LIBRARY AND MUSEUM ASSOCIATION

STOP, Have You Finished Your Job Before Leaving This Cabin With: Food In This Cabin Is Provided For Official And Emergency Use Only. Chief Ranger, Yellowstone National Park - I.S.T.A. - August 1947 EMS, Contributed by Yellowstone Park Library and Museum Association, ten and one half by eight inch card stock for NPS backcountry cabin. *Francis Historic Collections*

National Park Service Collectibles

Ranger Naturalist Service, Yellowstone National Park, US Department of the Interior, Old Faithful Geyser, color poster, nineteen and three quarter by fifteen inches. *Bob Reynolds Collection*

Trailside Notes, For The Motorist and Hiker, Number Two, Fishing Bridge Museum To Mammoth Hot Springs, Yellowstone National Park, US Department Of The Interior, National Park Service, 1936, eight and fifteen sixteenth by five and thirteen sixteenth inch soft cover booklet, 24 pages. *Francis Historic Collection*

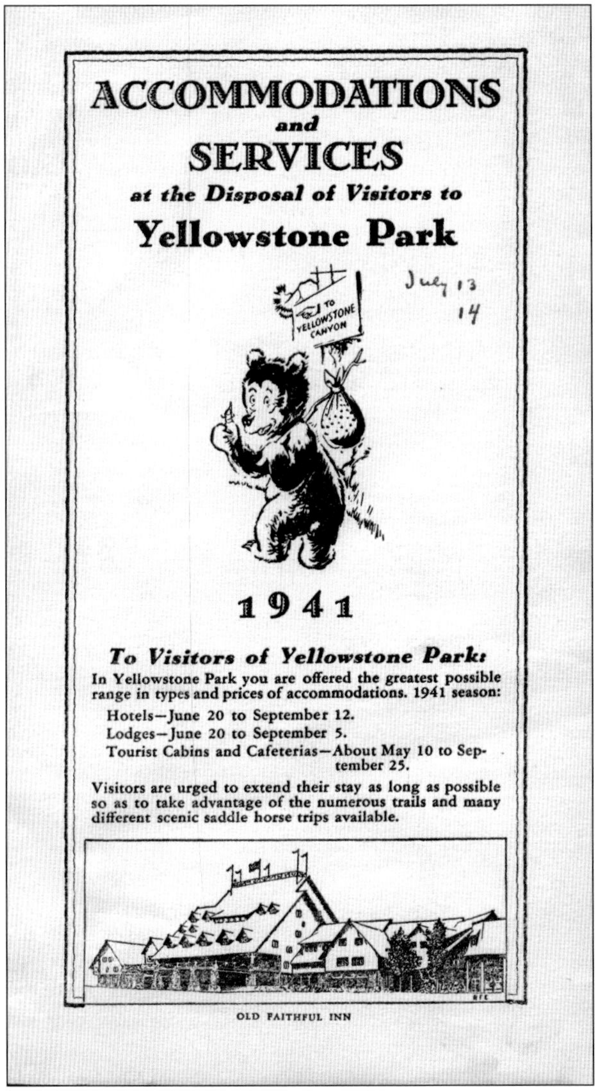

Accommodations and Services at the Disposal of Visitors to Yellowstone Park, 1941, 1 page folded eight and one quarter by four and eleven sixteenth inch brochure. *Francis Historic Collection*

Park Bears Are Dangerous, Park Bears and other animals are WILD! WATCH THEM FROM A SAFE DISTANCE, National Park Service, United States Department Of The Interior, Copyright Hanna-Barbera Prod., eight and fourteen sixteenth by three and nine sixteenth inch card. *Francis Historic Collection*

DANGEROUS, Park Bears and other animals are WILD, National Park Service, United States Department of the Interior, Form 10-108, (June 1957), U.S. Government Printing Office: 1957 O - 428004, six by three- and three-quarter inch flyer. *Francis Historic Collection*

WARNING, Many Visitors Have Been Gored By Buffalo, DO Not Approach Buffalo, Speed Kills, Slow Down, eight and one half by five- and one-half inch insert in Yellowstone Today, National Park Service, US Department of the Interior, Official Newspaper of Yellowstone National Park, Summer 2011. *Francis Historic Collection*

Canyon Area Trail Guide, Including North Rim Drive and South Rim Drive, Yellowstone National Park, 50 cents donation, April 2004, Yellowstone Association in cooperation with the National Park Service. *Francis Historic Collection*

Guide to the Canyon Area, 15 cents, 1 page folded, six and one quarter by three and three quarter inch, April 1978, Yellowstone Library and Museum Association in cooperation with the National Park Service, US Department of the Interior. *Francis Historic Collection*

Fort Yellowstone Historic District Tour Guide, National Park Service, 50 cent donation, eight and one half by five and one half inch booklet, Yellowstone Park Foundation, Published by Yellowstone Association in cooperation with the National Park Service, March 2010. *Francis Historic Collection*

West Thumb Geyser Basin Trail Guide, Including Fishing Cone and Thumb Paint Pots, National Park Service, Yellowstone National Park, 50 cent donation, eight and one half by five and one half inch booklet, Published by Yellowstone Association in cooperation with the National Park Service, April 2003. *Francis Historic Collection*

West Thumb Geyser Basin, 25 cents donation, 1 page folded, eight and one half by five and one half inch brochure, Published by The Yellowstone Association in cooperation with the National Park Service, Printed on recycled paper March, 1997. *Francis Historic Collection*

Yellowstone Yesterday

Celebrating 75 years of National Park Service history in Yellowstone National Park

Yellowstone, 1916: A Crossroads in History

Yellowstone Explorer

Campground and Lodging Information

The Bear Facts

Yellowstone Fishing

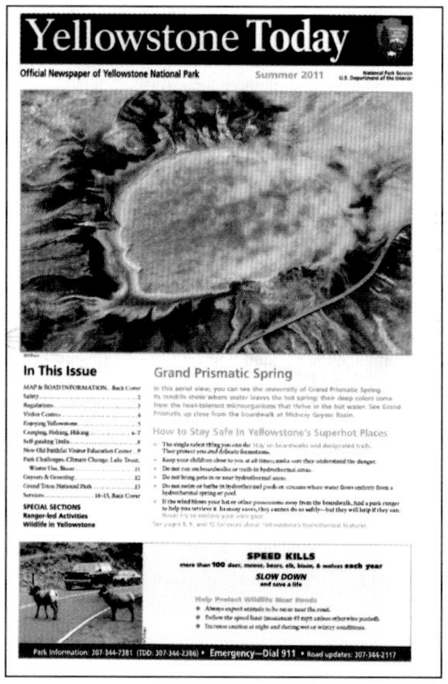

Yellowstone Today

Official Newspaper of Yellowstone National Park

Summer 2011

In This Issue

Grand Prismatic Spring

How to Stay Safe in Yellowstone's Superhot Places

SPEED KILLS

SLOW DOWN

Yellowstone Yesterday, Celebrating 75 years of National Park Service history in Yellowstone National Park, The Yellowstone Association, 4-page newspaper, 1991, NPS 75th Anniversary, seventeen by eleven- and one-half inch, *Mary Heller Collection*

Yellowstone Explorer, Featuring Activities with the National Park Service - July 1978, seventeen by eleven- and one-half inch newspaper, 8 pages, Printed by Livingston Enterprise. *Francis Historic Collection*

Yellowstone Today, National Park Service, US Department of the Interior, Official Newspaper of Yellowstone National Park, Summer 2011, 26 pages plus WARNING buffalo and bear flyer, seventeen and one half by eleven and one quarter inch newspaper. *Francis Historic Collection*

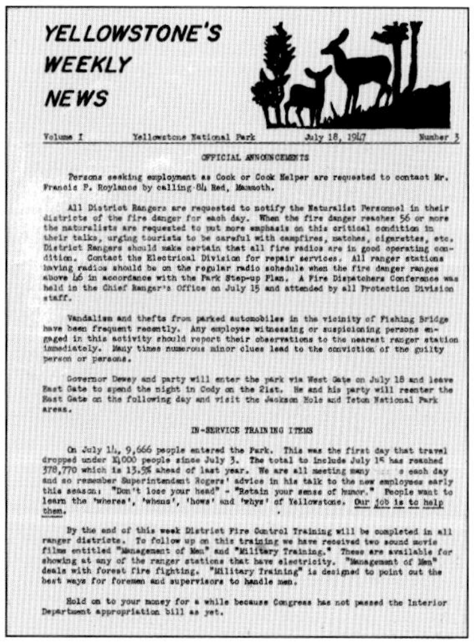

YELLOWSTONE'S WEEKLY NEWS

Volume I — Yellowstone National Park — July 18, 1947 — Number 3

OFFICIAL ANNOUNCEMENTS

Persons seeking employment as Cook or Cook Helper are requested to contact Mr. Francis P. Roylance by calling 84 Red, Mammoth.

All District Rangers are requested to notify the Naturalist Personnel in their districts of the fire danger for each day. When the fire danger reaches 56 or more the naturalists are requested to put more emphasis on this critical condition in their talks, urging tourists to be careful with campfires, matches, cigarettes, etc. District Rangers should make certain that all fire radios are in good operating condition. Contact the Electrical Division for repair services. All ranger stations having radios should be on the regular radio schedule when the fire danger ranges above 46 in accordance with the Park Step-up Plan. A Fire Dispatchers Conference was held in the Chief Ranger's Office on July 15 and attended by all Protection Division staff.

Vandalism and thefts from parked automobiles in the vicinity of Fishing Bridge have been frequent recently. Any employee witnessing or suspicioning persons engaged in this activity should report their observations to the nearest ranger station immediately. Many times numerous minor clues lead to the conviction of the guilty person or persons.

Governor Dewey and party will enter the park via West Gate on July 18 and leave East Gate to spend the night in Cody on the 21st. He and his party will reenter the East Gate on the following day and visit the Jackson Hole and Teton National Park areas.

IN-SERVICE TRAINING ITEMS

On July 14, 9,666 people entered the Park. This was the first day that travel dropped under 10,000 people since July 3. The total to include July 15 has reached 378,770 which is 13.9% ahead of last year. We are all meeting many [illegible]s each day and so remember Superintendent Rogers' advice in his talk to the new employees early this season: "Don't lose your head" - "Retain your sense of humor." People want to learn the 'wheres', 'whens', 'hows' and 'whys' of Yellowstone. Our job is to help them.

By the end of this week District Fire Control Training will be completed in all ranger districts. To follow up on this training we have received two sound movie films entitled "Management of Men" and "Military Training." These are available for showing at any of the ranger stations that have electricity. "Management of Men" deals with forest fire fighting. "Military Training" is designed to point out the best ways for foremen and supervisors to handle men.

Hold on to your money for a while because Congress has not passed the Interior Department appropriation bill as yet.

Yellowstone's Weekly News Volume I, Number 3, July 18, 1947, Yellowstone National Park, Official Announcements, 1 page flyer. *Francis Historic Collection*

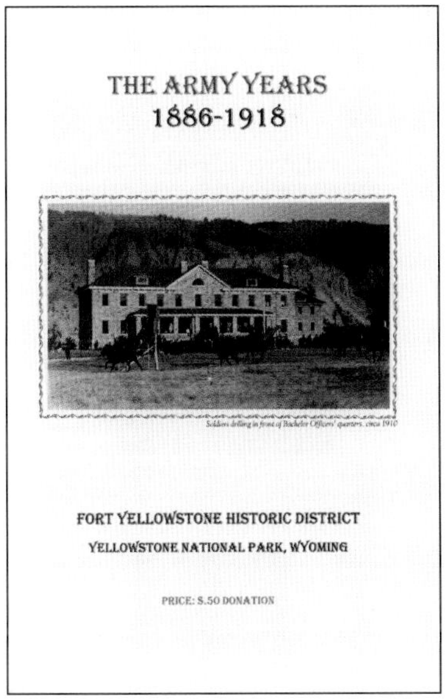

The Army Years 1886 - 1918, Fort Yellowstone Historic District, Yellowstone National Park Wyoming, Price: $.50 Donation, booklet. *Francis Historic Collection*

Yellowstone National Park, United States Department of the Interior, Harold L. Ickes, Secretary, United States Government Printing Office, 1933, 67-page booklet. *Francis Historic Collection*

Fossil Forests Of The Yellowstone National Park, United States Department of the Interior, Hubert Work, Secretary, National Park Service, Stephen T. Mather, Director, United States Government Printing Office, Washington, 1928, nine and one eighth by five and thirteen sixteenths inch booklet, 30 pages. *Francis Historic Collection*

Yellowstone National Park Nature Notes, Vol. VIII, August - 1931, No. 8., Grizzly And Cub- From Photo By Wm Rush, ten and one half by seven and fourteen sixteenth inch stapled newsletter, 9 pages. *Francis Historic Collection*

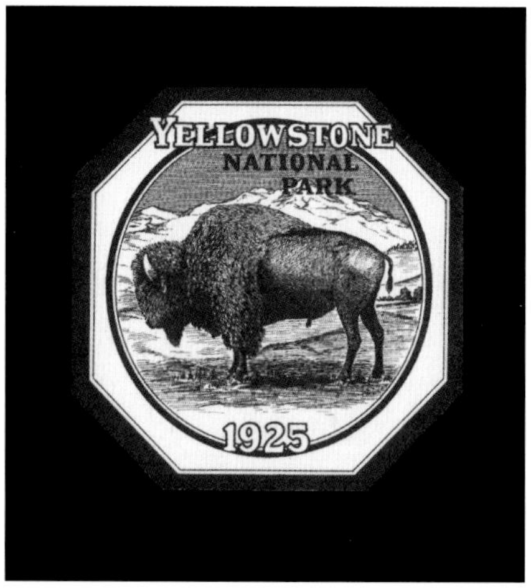

Yellowstone National Park, 1925, 3 x 3-inch entrance automobile two-sided window sticker or decal, Department of the Interior, National Park Service. *Bob Reynolds Collection*

Yellowstone National Park entrance fee receipt, June 28, 2021, $35.00, stapled to Yellowstone map, eight and one quarter by four inch, GPO:2021-416-165/82650. *Francis Historic Collections*

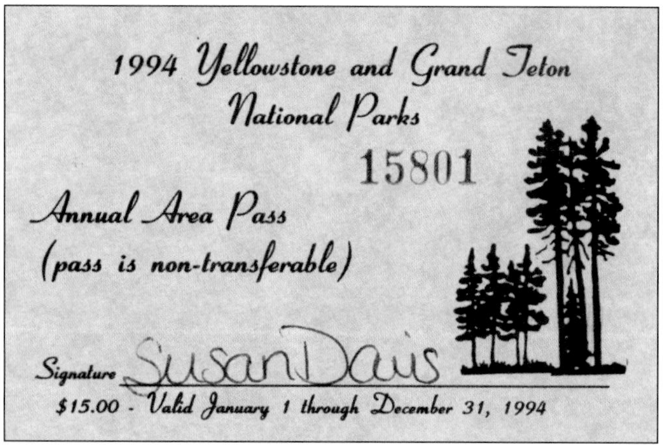

1994 Yellowstone and Grand Teton National Parks, 15801, Annual Area Pass (pass is non-transferable), Susan Davis, $15.00, Valid January 1 through December 31, 1994, three and one half by two- and one-half inch paper card. *Jack and Sue Davis Collection*

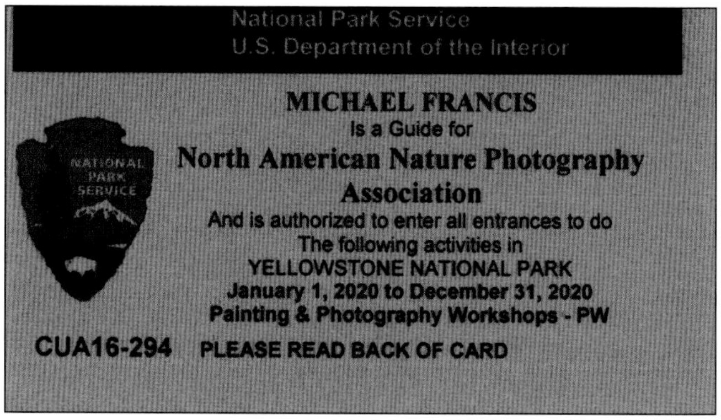

National Park Service US Department of the Interior CUA16294 2020 guide card for Michael Francis Yellowstone Park. *Francis Historic Collections*

Paper Collectibles

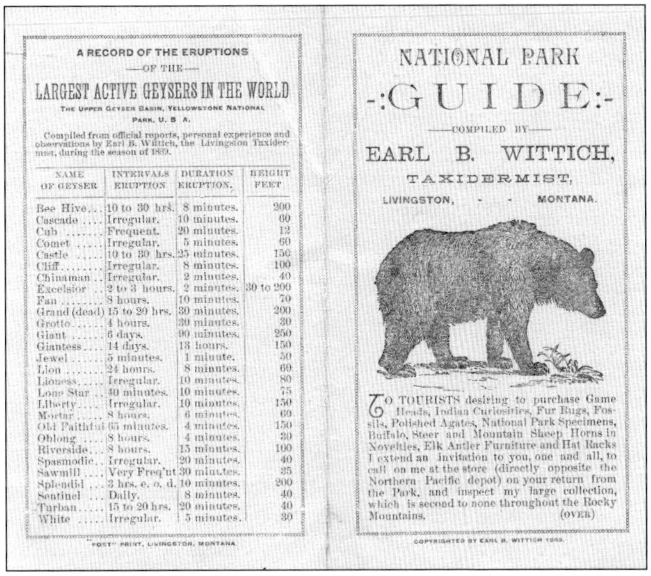

A RECORD OF THE ERUPTIONS

—OF THE—

LARGEST ACTIVE GEYSERS IN THE WORLD

THE UPPER GEYSER BASIN, YELLOWSTONE NATIONAL PARK, U. S A.

Compiled from official reports, personal experience and observations by Earl B. Wittich, the Livingston Taxidermist, during the season of 1889.

NAME OF GEYSER	INTERVALS ERUPTION	DURATION ERUPTION.	HEIGHT FEET
Bee Hive...	10 to 30 hrs.	8 minutes.	200
Cascade	Irregular.	10 minutes.	60
Cub	Frequent.	20 minutes.	12
Comet	Irregular.	5 minutes.	60
Castle	10 to 30 hrs.	25 minutes.	150
Cliff........	Irregular.	8 minutes.	100
Chinaman ..	Irregular.	2 minutes.	40
Excelsior ..	2 to 3 hours.	2 minutes.	30 to 200
Fan	8 hours.	10 minutes.	70
Grand (dead)	15 to 20 hrs.	30 minutes.	200
Grotto......	4 hours.	30 minutes.	30
Giant	6 days.	90 minutes.	250
Giantess....	14 days.	13 hours.	150
Jewel	5 minutes.	1 minute.	50
Lion	24 hours.	8 minutes.	60
Lioness.....	Irregular.	10 minutes.	80
Lone Star ..	40 minutes.	10 minutes.	75
Liberty....	Irregular.	10 minutes.	150
Mortar	8 hours.	6 minutes.	60
Old Faithful	65 minutes.	4 minutes.	150
Oblong	8 hours.	4 minutes.	30
Riverside...	8 hours.	15 minutes.	100
Spasmodic..	Irregular.	20 minutes.	40
Sawmill	Very Freq'nt	30 minutes.	35
Splendid ...	3 hrs. e. o. d.	10 minutes.	200
Sentinel ...	Daily.	8 minutes.	40
Turban.....	15 to 20 hrs.	20 minutes.	40
White	Irregular.	5 minutes.	30

"POST" PRINT, LIVINGSTON, MONTANA.

NATIONAL PARK

-:GUIDE:-

—COMPILED BY—

EARL B. WITTICH,

TAXIDERMIST,

LIVINGSTON, - - MONTANA.

TO TOURISTS desiring to purchase Game Heads, Indian Curiosities, Fur Rugs, Fossils, Polished Agates, National Park Specimens, Buffalo, Steer and Mountain Sheep Horns in Novelties, Elk Antler Furniture and Hat Racks I extend an invitation to you, one and all, to call on me at the store (directly opposite the Northern Pacific depot) on your return from the Park, and inspect my large collection, which is second to none throughout the Rocky Mountains. (OVER)

COPYRIGHTED BY EARL B. WITTICH 1899.

National Park Guide, Compiled By Earl B. Wittich, Taxidermist, Livingston, Montana, Copyrighted By Earl B. Wittich, 1899, "Post" Print, Livingston, Montana, 1 page folded, five and one half by three and one quarter inch. *Tom Murphy Collection*

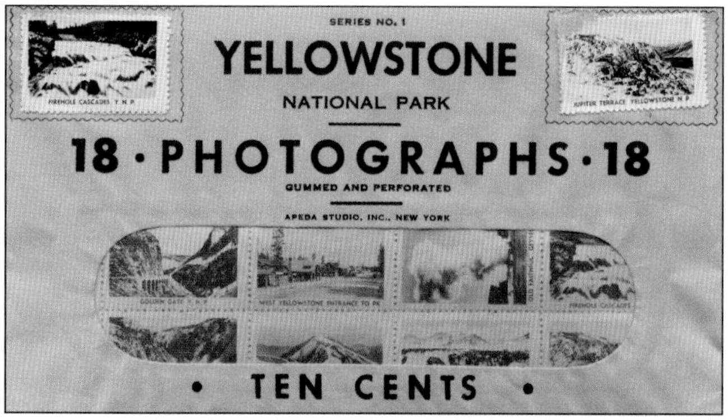

Yellowstone National Park, Series No. 1, 18 Photographs Gummed and Perforated, Ten Cents, APEDA Studio, Inc., New York, six and one half by three- and three-quarter inch envelope with stamps. *Francis Historic Collections*

National Parks Issue, Yellowstone, first day of issue, Jul 30, 1934, six and one half by three and ten sixteenth inch envelope. *Francis Historic Collections*

Wonderland Series No 3 stamps, Northern Pacific RY, ten in album. Jay C. *Lyndes Family Collection*

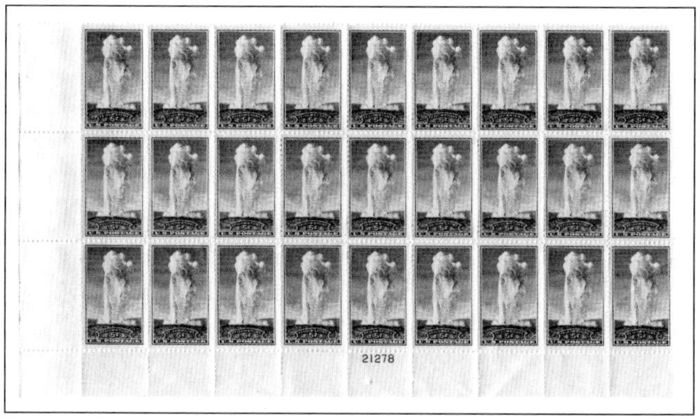

Plate block of 27 Old Faithful Geyser, 5 cent Yellowstone, US Postage stamps, 21278, 1934, nine and ten sixteenth by five and five sixteenth inch. *Jack & Sue Davis Collection*

Yellowstone Park, silhouette of park bus, M.C.W., five and ten sixteenth by three and fourteen sixteenth inch gummed sticker. *Bob Reynolds Collection*

Yellowstone Park, Old Faithful, four- and one-half inch window decal, Goldfarb Novelty Co., NYC, USA. *Jay C. Lyndes Family Collection*

Yellowstone Park, bear and geyser, four by three-inch window decal, Bloom Bros. Co., 25 N. 2nd St., Minneapolis 1, Minn., 151 -173. *Francis Historic Collections*

Yellowstone, Love And Kisses, This Paper Manufactured By Kodak, three and three quarter by two- and three-quarter inch sticker. *Francis Historic Collections*

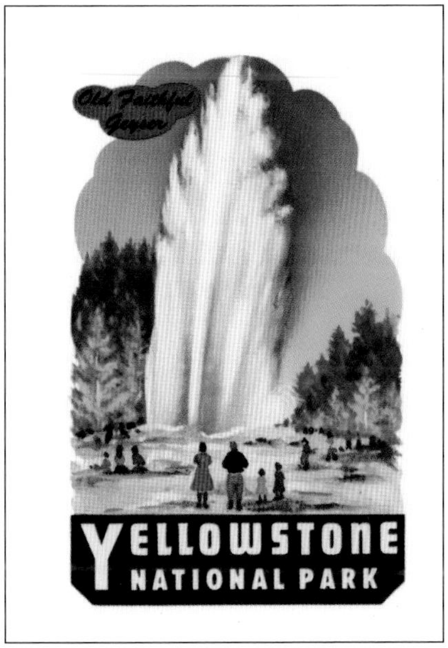

Old Faithful Geyser, Yellowstone National Park, Code 49 -A, 66081, 103-12-51, The Meyercord Co., Chicago 44, Ill., Made in USA, four and fourteen sixteenth by three- and one-half inch window decal. *Bob Reynolds Collection*

Yellowstone National Park, two and one quarter by one- and three-quarter inch gummed stamp, Haynes. *Francis Historic Collections*

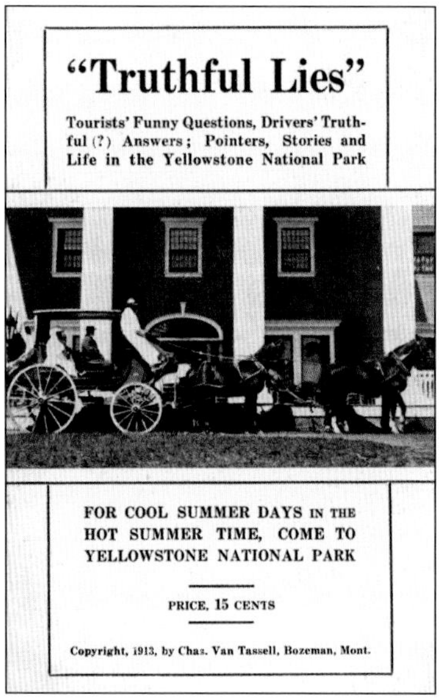

The Yellowstone News.

SOMETHING NEW IN YELLOWSTONE

FOUR TOURS THIS SUMMER

YELLOWSTONE'S 50TH ANNIVERSARY

PRES. HARDING INVITED

BOYS' SUMMER CAMP A SUCCESS

Figure 1. Sunset in the Yellowstone, Reverie, By Henry S. Sawyer, No 1786, McKinley Music Co. Chicago, New York, thirteen and one half by ten and one eighth inch sheet music, 1918. *Francis Historic Collections.* **Figure 2.** A Trip Through Yellowstone Park, Interesting Events Portrayed in Music, by Dr and Mrs. N W Christiansen, Price one dollar, Published by Belwin Inc., Rockville Centre LI New York, Copyright 1953, 32-page booklet, 12 x 9 inch. *Francis Historic Collections.* **Figure 3.** "Truthful Lies", Tourists' Funny Questions, Drivers' Truthful (?) Answers; Pointers, Stories and Life in the Yellowstone National Park, Price, 15 Cents, Copyright, 1913, by Chas. Van Tassell, Bozeman, Mont., five and ten sixteenth by three- and one-half inch booklet with postcard verso, Second Edition, 24 pages. *Bob Reynolds Collection.* **Figure 4.** The Yellowstone News, Volume V-No.5, May, 1922, Price: Your Good Will, 16 x 11-inch newspaper, 4 pages, Yellowstone Park Camps Co., Publisher, Howard H. Hays, President, E. H. Moorman, Sec. – Treas. *Francis Historic Collections*

Yellowstone Branded Products

The Jell-O Girl in Yellowstone, No. 11, two and fourteen sixteenth by two and seven sixteenth inch 1 page foldout, The Jell-O Co., Inc., Le Roy, NY. Tom Murphy Photography. *Jack and Sue Davis Collection*

Yellowstone national Artesian Water, Yellowstone Beverage Co., One Quart, 10-inch, D. I. Presler, Mgr, 808 Park St, Salt Lake City, Utah. *Jay C. Lyndes Family Collection*

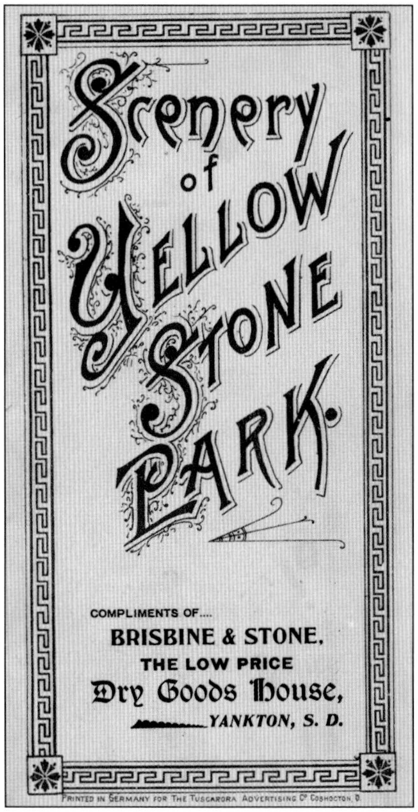

Scenery of Yellowstone Park, Compliments of ... Brisbane & Stone, The Low Price Dry Goods House, Yankton, S.D., Printed in Germany for the Tuscarora Advertising Co., Coshocton, six and three quarter by three and five eighths inch booklet. *Jay C. Lyndes Family Collection*

Branded Collectibles

Bobby Reynolds

As a person starts to collect Yellowstone memorabilia, the quest can take many twists and turns. Some people concentrate on paperweights, or bears, or spoons, or any number of other specific categories. If the item fits into their category, it fits into their collections. For other collectors, if an item simply shows a Yellowstone name or image, it will fill a niche in their collections.

Such is the case with any merchandise that advertises Yellowstone as part of its marketing strategy or is branded with a Yellowstone name or image. For example, there was a whiskey named Yellowstone, an Ohio spice company that gave away Yellowstone images with its coffee, and even a German maker of beef bouillon that used Yellowstone scenes in its advertising. As we feel these branded items enhance a Yellowstone collection, we are presenting a few pieces to pique the interest of those who may not have thought about adding such items to their collections.

Yellowstone Kentucky Straight Bourbon Whiskey, 90 Proof, Mellow Mash, Distilled & Bottled By Yellowstone Distillery Co., Louisville, KY, The Greatest American Whiskey, 6 Years Old, 15 inches with metal "Yellowstone" handle, One half gallon, D - 8, 5466. *Bob Reynolds Collection*

Old Faithful, Choice Pre-War Kentucky Whiskey Produced In 1916, One Pint, eight and one quarter by three and one half inch glass bottle with screw top metal lid, Produced By John Cochran & Co., Distillery No. 37 7th Dist. of Ky, Bottled In Bond at US General Bonded Warehouse No. 3 1st Dist of Illinois, Permit Illinois F10, WHISKEY, One Pint 100 Proof, Made Spring 1916, For Medicinal Purposes Only, Sale or use for other purposes will cause heavy penalties to be inflicted. *Jay C. Lyndes Family Collection*

Yellowstone, Taylor & Williams Incorporated, Distillers, Louisville, Kentucky, Lower Falls with Bourbon Whiskey Bottle on metal beverage tray, thirteen and one quarter by ten- and one-half inch. *Bob Reynolds Collection*

To him who, in the love of Nature, holds
Communion with her visible forms, she speaks
A various language: For his gayer hours
She has a voice of gladness and a smile
And eloquence of beauty; and she glides
Into his darker musings with a mild
And gentle sympathy, that steals away
Their sharpness, ere he is aware.

32 BRYANT.

HANDSOME, HISTORICAL, INSTRUCTIVE!

The Jersey Coffee

Series of Photo-Lithographic View Cards, consisting of

100 BEAUTIFUL VIEWS,

Is the most valuable collection of Picture Cards ever given to the Public. This Card belongs to the Series. One Card of this Series in each Package of JERSEY COFFEE. No two cards of same design in any single Case of Coffee.

USE JERSEY COFFEE!

And secure this valuable collection of American and Foreign Views.

Large Premium Picture

Mailed free to any address, on return of twenty-five trade-marks cut from the face of JERSEY COFFEE Wrappers. Write name and address in plain letters.

JERSEY COFFEE

Is Pure, Clean, Strong and Fine Flavored,

And is the Best Package Coffee on the Market. Sold only in One-Pound Packages.

THE DAYTON SPICE MILLS CO.,

Sole Manufacturers. DAYTON, OHIO, U. S. A.

Grand Geyser, Yellowstone National Park, both sides scanned, four and nine sixteenth by three and one sixteenth inch trade card, Ward Bros., Ph V. Columbus, O. #14, The Jersey Coffee, The Dayton Spice Mills, Co., Sole manufacturers, Dayton, Ohio, USA. *Francis Historic Collections*

Yellowstone National Park, First Boat On Lake, Yellowstone Lake, on verso: The Jersey Coffee, Series of Photo-Lithographic View Cards, consisting of 100 Beautiful Views, Jersey Coffee, The Dayton Spice Mills Co., Sole Manufacturers, Dayton, Ohio, USA, four and ten sixteenth by three and one eighth inch card. *Francis Historic Collections*

The First The Original Beer, 12 Fluid Ounces, Brewed & Bottled By Kessler Brewing Company, Helena, Montana, three and ten sixteenth by three and one quarter inch label. *Bob Reynolds Collection*

Old Faithful, Pale Beer, Gallatin Brewing Co., Montana Owned And Operated Bozeman, Mont., four and three quarter by three and one quarter inch label. *Bob Reynolds Collection*

Walt Disney presents Yellowstone Cubs. These Pranksters Turn A 2-Million Acre Playground Into Pandemonium! Narrator; Rex Allen, Technicolor, 40 x 30-inch poster. *Bob Reynolds Collection*

Yellowstone Brand Pie Sliced Apples, Paxton and Gallagher Co., Omaha, eleven by four and one quarter inch paper can label. *Jay C. Lyndes Family Collectiona*

Die heissen Mammuthsprudel von Yellowstone (Wyoming, Ver. St.), Liebig Company's Fleisch - Extract u-Pepton, Heisse Mammuth - Sprudel, four and six sixteenth by two and three quarter inch card, Yellowstone Park. *Francis Historic Collections*

Yellowstone Park, Smith's Pocatello, The National Chocolate, 2 boxes. Tom Murphy Photography. *Jack and Sue Davis Collection*

ICE CREAM, Yellowstone Falls, Yellowstone Park, 256, Box Patented Oct. 11, 1887, three and three quarter by three and one half by two and six sixteenth inch paper box with lid. *Jay C. Lyndes Family Collection*

Fort Yellowstone Brand, Roasted Coffee, Roasted and Packed By Keil Grocery Co., Billings, Mont. Tom Murphy Photography. *Jack and Sue Davis Collection*

Yellowstone Brand, Pure Lard, Yellowstone Packing Co., Billings, Montana, Net Weight 8 LBS. 10 Oz, metal handled bucket. Tom Murphy Photography. *Jack and Sue Davis Collection*

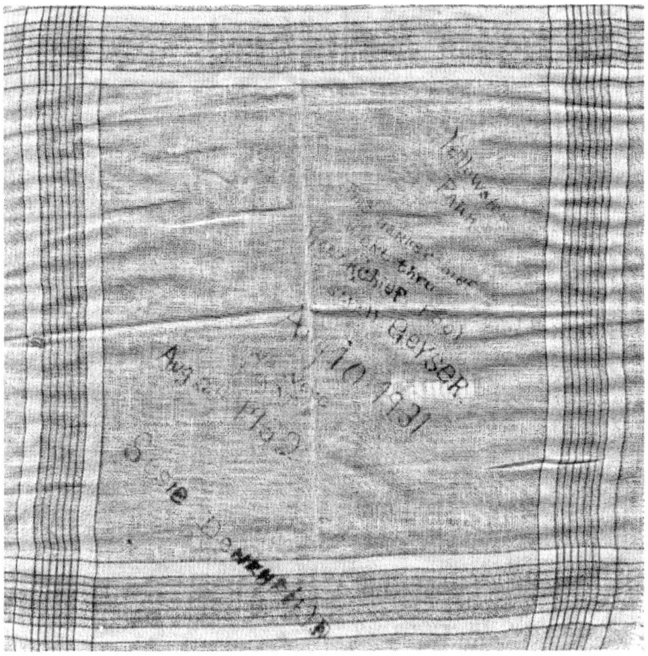

One Yellowstone collectible never to be repeated is the handkerchief on this page. It was placed in the Handkerchief Pool (above), a thermal spring in Black Sand Basin west of Old Faithful village. In its day, the pool was as popular as Old Faithful Geyser. When visitors placed a handkerchief or small piece of cloth in the pool, they watched it float for a moment before it was sucked into the water, disappearing into the depth of the spring. Usually within a few minutes, the cloth miraculously reappeared, completely clean. The iconic thermal spring ceased to function in 1926 after a visitor shoved a log into the vent. When the thermal feature was cleaned three years later, pieces of cloth, coins, hairpins, and a horseshoe, among other debris, were removed, yet the plumbing system was never the same. Soon it became illegal to throw anything into a thermal feature. *Photo from Francis Historic Collections*

Yellowstone Park, This Handkerchief Went thru Handkerchief Pool a small Geyser, Aug.10, 1931, we were back again Aug. 24, 1932, Susie Denehfield, 9 x 9 inch cloth. *Francis Historic Collections*